Agricultural Communication

Opportunities for Sustainable Agriculture and Rural Development

Agricultural Communication

Opportunities for Sustainable Agriculture and Rural Development

Editors
Vir Singh
Shivendra Kumar Kashyap
Gaurav Papnai

BIOTECH
2013
BIOTECH BOOKS®

ISBN 978-81-7622-277-8

Published by: **BIOTECH BOOKS®**
4762-63/23, Ansari Road, Darya Ganj,
New Delhi - 110 002
Phone: +91-011-23262132
E-mail: biotechbooks@yahoo.co.in

Printed at: **Chawla Offset Printers**
Delhi - 110 052

PRINTED IN INDIA

Preface

Communication is a critical input in any development process. The extension approaches have changed with time but communication has always remained as an important input since time-immemorial and will remain indispensable for ever. Right from intrapersonal to interpersonal to group to mass communication, it is eminent in every form and types.

Development Communication is a planned process of information sharing among stakeholders of the developmental process about development issues and strategies. The farmers, opinion leaders, change agents, development managers, scientists, extension functionaries, planners, policy makers, administrators, financial sources, and market forces link to each other in the broader perspective of development communication. It supports the development managers in understanding the rural perspective. Reciprocating, the rural people also get enriched with the access to developmental informations from governmental machinery as well as scientific fraternity.

Country has been working to generate Knowledge-driven economy. We want to establish knowledge society. It requires societal enriching at every level, including the women, the youth, the laggards, the marginal farmers and the landless labourers. The smooth and multi-directional flow of information is a requirement for this. The crucial role of Development communication in this respect is prominent.

Thus, Development Communication is crucial for any assessment, analysis, strategy formulation, implementation or evaluation. Extension planning and management also needs communication support for success at local or national level. It is the time when communication and extension should be taken more seriously as a critical input of development to generate and strengthen sustainable growth at micro as well as macro level.

Shivendra Kumar Kashyap

Contents

List of Contributors

Aakansha Melkani. College of Agriculture, G.B.P.U.A.T., Pantnagar, Uttarakhand

Akanksha Rastogi. Department of Environmental Science, College of Basic Sciences and Humanities, GB Pant University of Agriculture and Technology, Pantnagar – 263145, Uttarakhand, India.

Anup Prakash Upadhyay. Department of Extension Communication and Management, College of Home science, CAU, Meghalaya

Archana Negi. Department of Plant Pathology, GBPUA&T, Pantnagar

Arpita Sharma. Dept. of Agricultural Communication, College of Agriculture, G. B. Pant University of Agriculture and Technology, Pantnagar – 263145 (Uttarakhand)

B.B. Singh, Ex-Professor and Head, Dept. of Agricultural Communication, College of Agriculture, G. B. Pant University of Agriculture and Technology, Pantnagar – 263145 (Uttarakhand)

B. Kumar, Dean Post-Graduate Studies, Bihar Agricultural University, Sabour, Bhagalpur, Bihar

Bipin Kumar. Department of Environmental Science, College of Basic Sciences and Humanities, GB Pant University of Agriculture and Technology, Pantnagar – 263145, Uttarakhand, India.

Biswajit Lahiri. Department of Extension Communication and Management, College of Home science, CAU, Meghalaya

Ganesh Prasad Pokhariyal. School of Mathematics, University of Nairobi, P.O.Box 30197, Nairobi, Kenya.

Gaurav Papnai. Community Radio Station, Directorate of Communication G.B.P.U.A.&T., Pantnagar, Uttarakhand

Goldi Tiwari, College of Agriculture, G.B.P.U.A.&T., Pantnagar, Uttarakhand

Gulehayat. Department of Agricultural Communication G.B.P.U.A.&T., Pantnagar, Uttarakhand

J.C. Badola. Deputy Comptroller (associated with Agri-business Management faculty). GB Pant University of Agriculture and Technology, Pantnagar-263145, Uttarakhand, India.

J.K. Patel. C. P. College of Agriculture, S.D.A.U, Sardarkrushinagar Dist: Banaskantha (Gujarat)

Kalyan Ghadei. Department of Extension Education, Institute of Agricultural Sciences, BHU, Varanasi.

Kamala Kant. Dairy Extension Division, NDRI, Karnal (Haryana)

Kiran Arya. Department of Agricultural Communication G.B.P.U.A.&T., Pantnagar, Uttarakhand

Kuldeep Choudhary. Department of Human Resource Management), Agriculture Cooperation, Banking & Marketing Polytechnic, Navsari Agricultural University, Navsari (Gujarat)

Lathiya Amit. Department of Marketing Management, Agriculture Cooperation, Banking & Marketing Polytechnic, Navsari Agricultural University, Navsari (Gujarat)

M.A. Ansari. Department of Agricultural Communication G.B.P.U.A.&T., Pantnagar, Uttarakhand

M.R. Prajapati. C. P. College of Agriculture, S.D.A.U, Sardarkrushinagar Dist: Banaskantha (Gujarat)

Madhur Jain. PGP-ABM, Final Year IIM Ahmedabad

Mamta Rautela, College of Agriculture, G.B.P.U.A.&T., Pantnagar, Uttarakhand

Manish Kumar Singh. Dairy Extension Division, NDRI, Karnal (Haryana)

Manmeet Kaure. Department of Agricultural Communication, G. B. Pant University of Agriculture & Technology, Pantnagar, Uttarakhand, India

Mohan Singh. Department of Agronomy, College of Agriculture, GB Pant University of Agriculture and Technology, Pantnagar-263145, Uttarakhand, India

Mukesh Kumar. Department of Botany, Sahu Jain P.G. College, Najibabad- 246763 U.P.

Neelam Bhardwaj. Professor & Head, Department of Agricultural Communication G. B. Pant University of Agriculture & Technology, Pantnagar – 263145 (Uttarakhand) INDIA

Neelima Patel. College of Veterinary Science & AH, Jabalpur

Pankaj Kumar Ojha. Department of Extension Education, Institute of Agricultural Sciences, BHU, Varanasi; e-mail: pankajojhabhu@gmail.com

Poonam Prajapati. Department of Agricultural Communication G.B.P.U.A.&T., Pantnagar, Uttarakhand

Raj Kumar Patel. Dairy Extension Division, NDRI, Karnal (Haryana)

S.K. Badodiya. College of Agriculture RVSKVV Gwalior M.P.

S.K. Garg, College of Agriculture RVSKVV Gwalior M.P.

S.K. Kashyap, Department of Agricultural Communication G.B.P.U.A.&T., Pantnagar, Uttarakhand

Sonu Fartyal. Department of Agricultural Communication G.B.P.U.A.&T., Pantnagar, Uttarakhand

Vir Singh. Department of Environmental Science/ Directorate of Communication, GB Pant University of Agriculture and Technology, Pantnagar-263145, Uttarakhand, India

Chapter 1

Concept and Strategies Toward Sustainable Rural Development

☆ *Archana Negi*

Sustainable development is development that meets the needs of the present without compromising the ability of future generations to meet their own needs. It contains within it two key concepts, first the concept of 'needs', in particular the essential needs of the world's poor, to which overriding priority should be given; and second the idea of limitations imposed by the state of technology and social organization on the environment's ability to meet present and future needs. It is impossible to achieve sustainable development without applying sustainable agriculture on a large scale. Agriculture can be sustainable when it not only produces a lot of high-quality food, but also generates income for poor people. That means rural development: improving transport, development of market facilities and linkages, improving (access to) information, participation of the rural poor in decision making, providing access to credit, and so on. In a scenario of shrinking land and depleting water resources, the challenge of the new millennium is to increase biological yields to feed the ever-growing population without destroying the ecological foundation. It is thus important not to package this challenge as a demand or imposition of society on farmers, for which farmers would bear the cost, but as a necessity and methodology to also sustain their welfare and incomes. Agriculture is directly linked to very many facets of sustainable development, including poverty eradication, sustainable consumption and production, management of natural resources, energy, freshwater, health, education, trade and market access, as well as technology transfer and capacity building. Agriculture centers on integrated use of natural resources such as soil, water, climate and biological diversity. The integration of agriculture with other aspects of land management and ecosystem conservation is essential in order to promote both environmental sustainability and agricultural production.

Dimensions of Sustainable Development

Sustainable development is a multinational concept aiming at benefits derived from interactions between the legitimate interests of business and the economy, government and the, policy, civil society and culture, environment and living systems. While discussing the dimensions of sustainability, different criteria have been used depending on the context and the level of decision making. However, all the existing models that describe the sustainability dimensions focus on three major dimensions namely, social, economic, and environmental. Thus sustainable agriculture is required to maintain the environmental, economical and social integrity of nation

Ecological Sustainability

Ecological sustainability requires certain practices and it has following major advantages in sustainable agriculture:

1. *Soil fertility*: Sustainable agriculture improves fertility and soil structure and prevents erosion, so would be an answer to this problem.
2. *Water*: Sustainable agriculture increases the organic matter content of the topsoil, so raising its ability to retain and store water that falls as rain.
3. *Biodiversity*: Sustainable agricultural practices frequently involve mixed cropping, so increasing the diversity of crops produced and raising the diversity of insects and other animals and plants in and around field

4. *Pollution*: Pesticides are hazardous to human health as well as to the local ecology. Sustainable agriculture reduces or eliminates the use of hazardous chemicals; instead it controls pests with a variety of biological and agronomic measures and the use of natural substances.
5. *Landscape*: Sustainable agriculture avoids problems like Erosion, landslides and flooding, by improving productivity, conserving the soil, avoiding the expansion of farming into unsuitable areas, and preserving rural jobs.
6. *Climate* The way agriculture is practiced contributes significantly to global climatic changes Conventional agriculture contributes to the production of greenhouse gases in various ways: by reducing the amount of carbon stored in the soil and in vegetation, through the production of methane in irrigated field, and through energy intensive activities such as the production of artificial fertilizers. Adopting sustainable agriculture would reduce these impacts significantly.

Economic Sustainability

Agriculture cannot be sustainable unless it is economically viable over the long term. The advantages are as follows.

1. Creation of new markets and opportunities for sales growth. Focusing on exports alone involves hidden costs: in transport, in assuring local food security, etc.
2. Creation of additional added value.
3. Cost reduction through efficiency improvements and reduced energy and raw material inputs.
4. The demands for certified organic products is increasing quickly, opening opportunities to expand sales of such products and to explore niche markets.

Social Sustainability

The social sustainability of farming techniques is related to the ideas of social acceptability and justice, having following advantages

1. Health and safety
2. Impact on local communities, quality of life

3. Benefits to disadvantaged groups *e.g.*, disabled
4. Sustainable agricultural practices usually are based on local social customs, traditions, norms and taboos, so local people are more likely to accept them and adapt them to their own needs.

Strategies for Sustainable Rural Development

- Natural resources have to be accessible to the poor, which in the farm sector means secure rights to land, water and genetic resources. For this, there is a need to develop public-private partnerships.
- Policies for land and water resource management, biodiversity protection, infrastructure investment, strategy on institutional market reforms, reduction of tariffs and phasing out of possible commodity control are integral to achieving sustainable agriculture.
- Sustainability should be seen in the context of different agro-climatic zones as well of as the country as a whole. Suitable technologies should be developed and indicators for sustainable agriculture should be identified for both.
- It is essential to provide funding for integrated rural development plans, programmes and strategies, at national and regional levels, with particular emphasis on investment in economic and social infrastructure in rural areas, enterprise development, human resource development, and capacity building for local governance.
- An efficient credit policy regime with the required rural banking and credit system will play a major role in the future. The government should encourage investment in vital agriculture infrastructure, credit linkages, and use of new and appropriate techniques towards this end.
- More than 70 per cent of the country's agriculture is under small and marginal farmers with limited resources. A nationwide crop insurance scheme will provide such farmers the needed confidence to invest and gain from technological advances in agriculture.
- The focus on accelerated food grains production on a sustainable basis and free trade in grains, as well as on

rural employment opportunities will lead to faster economic growth and give purchasing power to the people, which in turn would help increase household food security.

- Concerted efforts should be made at national, regional and local levels to pool, distil and evaluate traditional practices, knowledge and wisdom and to harness them for sustainable agricultural growth.
- It should be recognized that information is a critical input for agricultural development. It is as important as other key inputs including credit, seeds, nutrients and water. Information can be efficiently converted into economically rewarding opportunities.
- It is critical to recognize that the challenge to world agriculture is both technological (requiring the development of new, high productivity, environmentally sustainable production systems), and political (requiring policies that do not discriminate against rural areas in general, and agriculture in particular)

Approaches to Sustainable Agriculture

Sustainable agriculture is a broad concept that covers a number of different approaches. All Try in one way or other to achieve environmentally sound, economically profitable, acceptable and socially responsible form of land husbandry. Some of the approaches are discussed as follows:

- *Organic agriculture*: Organic agriculture was developed as a holistic, ecosystem-based approach, conceived as an alternative to what proponents see as the ecologically unsound practices of conventional agriculture. It is necessary to distinguish between certified agriculture, and agriculture which is practiced in an organic way but without certification
- *Traditional organic practices*: Many traditional agricultural practices around the world refrain from using chemical fertilizers and pesticides. They do this for various reasons: by tradition, because farmers cannot afford agrochemicals, they cannot buy them locally, or they do not know how to use them. This traditional form of organic agriculture is

not necessarily sustainable, even if it has been adapted to local conditions over many generations. Population growth, declining prices, insecure land tenure and water-use rights, along with many other factors, have often led to overuse, loss of diversity, soil degradation and other environmental problems. Sustainable agriculture can be met by using various organic sources like- Vermicompost, Biofertilizers, Legumes and green manure, etc. Hence then urgent need for more sustainable approaches. There are numerous modern attempts to update these traditional forms of land use. Some of them are described below.

- *Site-appropriate agriculture or ecofarming*: This tries to cut down on costly inputs and minimize negative environmental impacts by making intelligent use of existing ecological factors.
- *Integrated pest management*: This approach reduces the use of synthetic pesticides by integrating a range of ways to control pests and disease pathogens, from crop rotations to determining damage thresholds before applying plant protection products.
- *Integrated nutrient management*: This approach makes a special effort to minimize fertilizer inputs.
- *Watershed management*: Watershed management aims to adapt land management practices in ecologically vulnerable hill and mountain regions to the natural carrying capacity by means of systematic management. It emphasizes adapting technical solution to the socio-economic circumstances of users, respecting the needs of different resource users and attempting to reconcile their interests.
- *Conservation agriculture and minimum tillage*: This aims to conserve the soil structure and improve the water storage capacity of the soil. Introduced on a large farm level it is often combined with weed management through pesticides. Because it eliminates ploughing, conservation agriculture needs less labour, so is a viable option for areas with labour shortages.

References

GTZ Sustainet. 2006. Sustainable agriculture: A pathway out of poverty for India's rural poor. Deutsche Gesellschaft für Technische Zusammenarbeit, Eschborn.

Masters, G.M.2007, Introduction to Environmental Engineering and Sciences,pp. 92-96.

Mishra, B.B., and K.C. Nayak. 2004. Organic farming for sustainable agriculture. Orissa Review, Oct 2004.

Nair, G.K. Tap domestic market potential for organic products. Hindu Business Line, 2 Feb 2005

Pretty, J. 1995. Regenerating agriculture: An alternative strategy for growth. Earthscan, London

Rai, Manggala. 2005. Organic farming: Potentials and strategies. Millennium Guest Lecture, S.V. College, Tirupati, 3 June 2005.

Shiva. V., Biodiversity-based sustainable agriculture, Navdanya, Uttaranchal

Veeresh, G.K. 1998. Organic farming: Ecologically sound and economically sustainable. Man and Development, pp. 142-48.

Chapter 2

Community Radio as an Alternative Tier of Broadcasting: Scripting a New Role for Development

☆ *Arpita Sharma*

"Community radio is a social process or event in which members of the community associate together to design programmes and produce and air them, thus taking on the primary role of actors in their own destiny, whether this be for something as common as mending fences in the neighbourhood, or a community-wide campaign on how to use clean water and keep it clean, or agitation for the election of new leaders. The emphasis is on the ownership of democratic and development efforts by the members of the community themselves and the use of media, in this case radio, to achieve it. In every sense, this is participatory communication (not programmes made about them by somebody else!). It is above all a process, not a technology, not merely a means, because the people are part of that means, and so is the message and the audience. Community radio is most relevant to a group of people who live and act as a community, and this could be several families, several neighbourhoods, or even several villages or communities, but the important thing is that they interact. That is why I think of community radio as the community speaking to each other and acting together for common goals." Carlos A. Arnaldo. Community radio has grown since the New Order Era was over (1998). Since then, there are hundreds community radio exist but none of them affiliated or gather in one big association which has a clear division of community empowerment. Many of community radio exist because of hobby, specific interest, and only run temporary. Even so, the government has recognized their existence through defined community radio in the new Broadcasting Law. According to Broadcasting Law No. 32 year 2002, Article 21-249: **Section 6 Community Broadcasting Institutions. Article 21** (1) Community Broadcasting Institutions as referred to in Article 13 clause (2) point c, are broadcasting institutions in the form of Indonesian legal entities that are founded by certain communities. The Community Broadcasting Institutions are independent and non-commercial for they provide services to their community. The transmitters are low in power. (2) The Community Broadcasting Institutions as referred to in clause (1) operate on the following bases: a. Non profit oriented and not a part of a profit oriented company; and b. To educate and teach the community to increase welfare by promoting programs in the field of culture, education and information that reflect national identity. (3) The Community Broadcasting Institution is a non partisan community organization that: a. is neither a representative of a foreign organization or institution nor a member of international community; b. is not related to illegal organizations; and c. is not a tool for the propaganda of certain groups or factions. **Article 22** (1) A Community Broadcasting Institution is established by the fund contributed by a certain community and belongs to the community. (2) A Community Broadcasting Institution receives funding from donation, grants, sponsors and other legal sources with no string attached. **Article 23** (1) Community Broadcasting Institutions are not allowed to receive foreign initial fund to establish the stations and operational fund. (2) Community Broadcasting Institutions are not allowed to run advertisings and/or other commercials except the PSA's. **Article 24** (1) A Community Broadcasting Institution is obliged to develop codes of ethics and regulations that must be known widely by the community and other members of the society. (2) In the case of the existence grievance from the community or other members of the society on the violation of code of ethics and/or regulations, the Community Broadcasting Institution is obliged to take actions in accordance to guidelines and prevailing provisions. There are 3 unique points clear from the above articles: (1) the community radio should educate and teach the community to increase welfare by promoting programs in the field of culture, education and information that reflect national identity; (2) A Community Broadcasting Institution is established by the fund contributed by a certain community and belongs to the community: (3) Community Broadcasting Institutions are not allowed to run advertisings and/ or other commercials except the PSA's. From these 3 points we can conclude that the strength of a community radio is coming within the community and have more intimate relationship with its listener.

Concept of Community Radio

Community radio, as distinct from public service broadcasting, serves to bring small communities together, focuses on common man's day-to-day concerns and helps in realizing local aspirations. In this sense it aims to contribute to the lives of the local community, through the content that is created by the people and for the people of the community. Community radio reflects the interests and needs of the community it serves. It challenges the traditional division between the broadcasters on one side and the listeners on the other. Non-profit organisation and communities stand to benefit from this inexpensive yet effective means of communication. Community radio can be defined as having three aspects: non-profit making; community ownership and control; and community participation. It is not about doing something for the community but about the community doing something for itself, which means the community is owning and controlling its own means of communication. Community radio is also defined as non-profit distributing which is designed to serve specific communities of location and interest, thereby providing programming that is relevant to the community, and with management structures that represent the community the station serves.

Community Radio in the Context of the Globalization of Media

"George Orwell in Nineteen Eighty-Four warned us of a society controlled by Big Brother. Is that what we are encountering today when we see so many people in poor communities tuning into western dominated ideals of the rich consumer society? Orwell was very concerned about the socialist drives of the industrial age. But perhaps he was also warning about the takeover of society by a democratic political power driven to degradation by these very industrial drives and by the easy resort to globalization of media." Recent years have seen a strong trend towards the globalization of media. Colossal media enterprises of a commercial nature have been formed and increasingly span the globe with their programmes. Certain countries have also become centres of highly successful media production, mainly of an entertainment character, and sell their output to TV channels worldwide. Obvious examples are soap operas from the USA. However, audience research has shown that people prefer to watch programmes with their own cultural orientations, rather than those imported from others. For this reason, media productions from developing countries, such as Brazil, China, Egypt, India, and Indonesia, are now gaining wider distribution in large-scale commercial media. While some people argue that the globalization of the media disrupts local cultures, others state that global media intensifies the consciousness of the world as a whole and is therefore beneficial. They see global media and community media as complementary, each forming important functions that the other cannot. And this is certainly the case. By definition, global media are commercial and need to attract large audiences for their advertising content. Thus, they broadcast programmes that attempt to satisfy a common thread of sensitivities among large numbers of people, using well-tried and rather standard if not banal entertainment formats. The lack of variety in programme orientation is, therefore, generally attributed to the 'self-censorship' of the market, which uses entertainment as the sole criterion for selection. However, it is also true that governments tend to be more comfortable with private broadcasters limiting themselves to entertainment, rather than becoming involved in the more problematic area of news and current affairs. For these reasons, themes reflecting socio-political interests are often insufficiently covered, or deliberately ignored, by private broadcasters. Clearly, given their characteristics and orientation, commercial and global media can hardly meet socio-economic and development needs of the countries they cover. The excessive entertainment provided by commercial television has often provoked a call for a reappraisal of the potential of public broadcasting, stressing the need for quality programmes and demanding more possibilities of choice and access for audiences. A logical step in this direction is to expand the democratization of media to the community level, especially through community radio, in which accessibility is the norm. Furthermore, community radio works in the cultural context of the community it serves; it deals with local issues in the local language or languages; it is relevant to local problems and concerns; and its aim is to help the community to develop socially, culturally and economically.

Community Radio Worldwide

Here are some elaborate definitions of community radio by experts worldwide: A particularly philosophical definition of community radio is provided by José Ignacio Lopez Vigil, in the 1997 Manual urgente para Radialists Apasionados: "When radio fosters the participation of citizens and defends their interests; when it reflects the tastes of the majority; when it truly informs; when it helps resolve the thousand and one problems of daily life; when all ideas are debated in its programs and all opinions are respected; when cultural diversity is stimulated over commercial homogeneity; when women are main players in communication and not simply a pretty voice; when no type of dictatorship is tolerated; when everyone's words fly without discrimination or censorship; that is community radio." Louie Tabing (2002) defines a community radio station as "one that is operated in the community, for the community, about the community and by the community." According to Tabing, "the community can be territorial or geographical – a township, village, district or island and can also be a group of people with common interests, who are not necessarily living in one defined territory." Carlos A Arnaldo distinguishes community radio as a social process in which members of a community federate design and produces programmes, and air them. (UNESCO, 2001) Community radios have been consistently gaining ground over the last few years worldwide. In the western countries, community radio fulfils the needs of self-expression for those groups who have negligible access to the mass media. The potentiality of community radio as an agent of social change have been experienced in Latin America back in the mid 1940s, with the advent of miner's radios of Bolivia in Latin America in 1949. Community radio is now an emergent force in many African countries, mainly in South Africa.

In Europe most probably the first independent and non-commercial radio station was set up by the students of the University of Ljubljana, Slovenia in 1969, named Radio Student. In most of the parts of North America and Australia, there are locally owned and managed community radio stations, which are licensed by an independent broadcast regulator, which are meant to serve their communities. In Asia, Philippines, Sri Lanka, Nepal, Thailand, and Indonesia provide important examples of community radio stations. The very first community radio station that was set up in Asia was in the Philippines in the 1990s, as a part of the Tambuli Community Radio Project. The Community Radio Association (now known as the Community Media Association) wanted to make sure that in Britain the best model for community radio was adopted and they commissioned a special report to examine potential models. The report – Community Radio in a Global Context by Eryl Price Davies and Jo Tacchi – compared the legal and regulatory frameworks for community radio in six countries. The Community Radio Association argues that specific legislation is needed to aid the development of community services. They pointed out the example of France's Community Radio, which has a separate license category for providing protection from takeovers by networks and profit-making organisation. Community radio has drastically changed rural radio in the countries where there was only one Government radio system in the country.

Community Radio in India

- ☆ **1935-** Agriculture institute of Allahabad got permission to establish a campus radio.
- ☆ **1956-** Farm radio was established in Pune as a joint venture of UNESCO and AIR. It was medium web broadcasting by 1 Kw transmitter. The main purpose of this radio station was to broadcast programme related to agriculture so that farmers could get latest information and improve their farming. It was a successful project.
- ☆ **1960-** Pantnagar Agriculture University (Uttarakhand) established a campus radio. After initial success it was closed due to lack of enthusiasm and interest of University employee.
- ☆ **1970-** In 1970 AIR started to established local radio station.

These FM station were equipped with 1 to 6 Kw transmitters. They were established to focus on the problems of local communities. They used to broadcast information about Government development projects.

- **1995-** In a decision Supreme Court of India declared Air Waves or frequencies as a public property and denied any possibility of monopoly on it. Court directed to use air waves in public interest. This decision prepared the legal base for Community radio.
- **2000-** Government opened the FM broadcasting for private sector.
- **2002-** Government allowed Universities and reputed educational instates to established Community radio station.
- **2006-** Government allowed the nonprofit civic organization to established Community radio station.
- **1 February 2004** -Anna FM is India's first campus 'community' radio, launched on 1 February 2004, which is run by Education and Multimedia Research Centre (EM^2RC), and all programmes are produced by the students of Media Sciences at Anna University
- **16 November 2006-** On 16 November 2006, the government of India notified new Community Radio Guidelines which permit NGOs and other civil society organizations to own and operate community radio stations. About 4,000 community radio licenses are on offer across India, according to government sources.
- **30 November 2008-** By 30 November 2008, the ministry of Information and broadcasting, government of India, had received 297 applications for community radio licenses, including 141 from NGOs and other civil society organizations, 105 from educational institutions and 51 for 'farm radio' stations to be run by agricultural universities and agricultural extension centers ('Krishi Vigyan Kendras'). Of these, 107 community radio stations have been cleared for licensing through the issue of Letters of Intent. 13 Grant of Permission Agreements (GOPA) have been signed with license applicants under the new scheme.

By 30 November 2008, there were 38 operational community radio stations in the country. Of these, two are run by NGOs and the rest by educational institutions.

- ☆ **15 October 2008-** The first community-based radio station, licensed to an NGO (as distinct from campus-based radio) was launched on 15 October 2008, when 'Sangham Radio' in Pastapur village, Medak district, Andhra Pradesh state, was switched on at 11.00am. Sangham Radio, which broadcasts on 90.4 MHz, is licensed to Deccan Development Society (DDS), an NGO that works with women's groups in about 75 villages of Andhra Pradesh. The community radio station is managed by 'General' Narsamma and Algole Narsamma.
- ☆ **23 October 2008 -** The second NGO-led community radio station in India was launched on 23 October 2008 at 'TARAgram' in Orchha, Madhya Pradesh state. Named 'Radio Bundelkhand' after the Bundelkhand region of central India where it is located, the radio station is licensed to the Society for Development Alternatives (DA), a Delhi-based NGO. Radio Bundelkhand also broadcasts on 90.4 MHz for four hours a day, including two hours of repeat broadcast.
- ☆ **1 November 2009-** According to the Ministry of Information and Broadcasting, 47 community radio stations were operational in India by 1 November 2009, including 45 campus-based stations and two CRS run by NGOs. By December 2009, the number of CR stations run by civil society groups had probably gone up to seven, including Sangham Radio (Pastapur, Medak District, Andhra Pradesh), Radio Bundelkhand (Orchha, Madhya Pradesh), Mann Deshi Tarang (Satara, Maharashtra), Namma Dhwani (Budikote, Karnataka), Radio Mattoli (Wayanad, Kerala), Kalanjiam Samuga Vanoli (Nagapattinam, Tamil Nadu) and Barefoot (Tilonia, Rajasthan).
- ☆ **4 December 2009-** By 4 December 2009, the Ministry of Information and Broadcasting had issued 'Grant of Permission Agreements' (GOPA) for 62 community radio stations. Most of the GOPAs were issued to educational

institutions. Among the fully functional campus-based community radio stations started in 2009 **Community Radio SARANG 107.8MHz** (simultaneously used with FM) is the only one in Karnataka, though there are a few more which have received SACFA (Standing Committee Clearance for Frequency Allocation) and started broadcasting. Two other campus-based stations are already operational in Bangalore, one each in Tumkur, Gulbarga, and Dharwad (Agricultural University). The last two are situated in North Karnataka. Community Radio SARANG 107.8 is managed by the Mangalore Jesuit Educational Society (MJES) and is run by St. Aloysius College (Autonomous), Mangalore, a coastal town in the southern part of Karnataka. In a way, Radio SARANG is a campus radio in that it is based in an educational institution campus. But it is more oriented towards local communities of people than mere the host institution, producing programs with,for and by local people such as ordinary farmers, fisher folk, patients, vendors, small farmers, service providers like bicycle repairers, cobblers, etc. **SARANG** 107.8 FM means 'beautiful blending of all colours' signifying various social, religious, linguistic communities and their harmonious existence of Mangalore - which is a requirement now after the disturbance in the context of attack on churches (post 14 September 2008) by radical saffronists, and later assault on women in a pub in the name of moral policing by similar groups. The Mangalore community is a boiling pot of cultures and languages. Hence, Dr Richard Rego, its founder, felt SARANG felt that it is the most appropriate name - to symbolise harmony and peaceful coexistence. The local communities of farmers, fisher folk, medical/legal experts, students, workers contribute regularly to this radio. The radio also spreads messages of peace and harmony among people through programs based on the need for the same. Health and hygiene, agricultural messages, fisher folk issues, road safety, water conservation, rain water harvesting, folk culture and life, women and children's rights and privileges, original entertainment by locals and students are the hall mark of this radio.

- **20 June 2010-** As on 20 June 2010, Radio SARANG 107.8FM broadcasts in Konkani, Kannada, Tulu, and English languages daily, besides broadcasting in Malayalam, Beary (mother tongue of local Muslims), and Hindi languages on weekly basis. In addition, Community Radio SARANG 107.8MHz also broadcasts in Punjabi, on the request of the local Sikh community. Since 15 June 2010, Community Radio SARANG 107.8FM broadcasts 14 hours non-stop, from 6.30 to 20.30 hours. The content includes programs on health and hygiene, sanitation, agriculture, fisher folk issues, education, local cultures, inter-religious harmony issues, legal aid, talks, interviews, entertainment, etc. The programs are produced both by the regular staff, members of local communities, students of mass communication (MCMS or MS Communication, equivalent to MCJ with specialisations) and others students of St Aloysius College and neighboring schools and colleges. The program formats include talks, interviews, phone-ins, songs, poetry, stories, chat-shows, etc. Dr Richard Rego SJ is both the founder and director of this campus based community Radio SARANG 107.8FM.
- **11, March 2010-** With the aim to create a common platform for local communities of Supi in Uttarakhand, TERI launched 'Kumaon vani', a community radio service on March 11, 2010. Uttarakhand Governor Margaret Alva inaugurated the community radio station, the first in the state. The 'Kumaon Vani' aims to air programmes on environment, agriculture, culture, weather and education in the local language and with the active participation of the communities. The radio station covers a radius of 10 kms reaching out to almost 2000 locals around Mukhteshwar. Under the new (2006) community radio policy, any not-for-profit 'legal entity' - except individuals, political parties and their affiliates, criminal and banned organizations - can apply for a CR license. Central funding is not available for such stations, and there are stringent restrictions on fundraising from other sources. Only organisations that are registered for a minimum of three years old and with a 'proven' track record of local community service can apply. License conditions implicitly favour well-funded stations as against

inexpensive low power operations, several of which (*e.g.* Mana Radio in Andhra Pradesh and Raghav FM in Bihar) ran successfully on shoe-string budgets before the imposition of any community radio policy. The licence entitles them to operate a 100 watt (ERP) radio station, with a coverage area of approximately 12 kilometres radius. A maximum antenna height of 30 meters is allowed. Community radio stations are expected to produce at least 50 per cent of their programmes locally, as far as possible in the local language or dialect. The stress is on developmental programming, though there is no explicit ban on entertainment. News programmes are banned on community radio in India, as also on commercial FM radio. However, the government recently clarified that certain categories of news are permitted on radio, including sports news and commentaries, information on traffic and weather conditions, coverage of cultural events and festivals, information on academic events, public announcements pertaining to utilities like electricity and water supply, disaster warnings and health alerts. Five minutes of advertising per hour is allowed on community radio. Sponsored programs are not allowed except when the program is sponsored by the Government at the Centre or State.

☆ **26 February 2008-** Activists and community workers from across the country have banded together under the aegis of the 'Community Radio Forum' in order to coordinate training and support for community radio stations, as well as to continue to petition for a more proactive community radio policy. The Community Radio Forum, India, was registered as a 'Society' and 'Trust' on 26 February 2008. In the meantime, mobile telephone operators have begun to offer commercial broadcast services over GSM, evading completely government restrictions built around traditional concepts of broadcasting technology.

Community Radio Programmes

Women Speak to Women

The Deccan Development Society (DDS) works in Zaheerabad of Medak district in Andhrta Pradesh. Zaheerabad, which falls in the backward Telangana region, is contiguous with other least developed districts of North Karnataka. A semi-arid region sans industrilisation, people migrate during summers in large numbers since development schemes hardly reach the targeted population. It is in this geo-political and developmental context that the Deccan Development Society's efforts are centered. The society works with about 100 Dalit women's groups (Sangams) consisting of nearly 4,000 members in 75 villages. Having working on areas like sustainable Agriculture and empowerment of Women, DDS established a media centre and its Women Speak to Women project is carried out through community radio and a community video project.

The DDS community radio station was set up with part funding from UNESCO.A total of Rs.22 lakhs has been spent on the building and equipment including acoustics treatment, recorders, mixers, microphones, cables and installation. The FM station is designed to work on the audiocassette technology. It has two FM transmitters and a 100- metre transmission tower, which has a capacity to broadcast to a radius of 30km roughly, the coverage area of DDS. With this installation and the nominal amounts paid to community members who the programme costs currently amount to about Rs.500 per hour. It is estimated that if and when the station goes on air, it may be able to operate at Rs.1000-Rs.1500 per hour. A five members technically trained team visits villages in the NGO's constituency and records programmes on a simple cassette recorder and edits it again on a cassette editor. The team has already prepared 200 hours of programmes and is awaiting a nod from the Government to switch on the transmitter that has a radius of about 30 Km covering some 70-oddd villages.

Kunjal Panjee Kutch Ji (Sarus Carne of Our Kutch)

The arid Kutch district of Gujrat has seen a silent revolution in the area of community radio. The Kutch Mahila Vikash Sanghatan and Drishti Collective decided to harness the potential of community radio to create awareness among women on Panchayat functions. All India Radio, has leased weekly air time to the NGO working with rural women. The all-women team produces a 30 minute serial every Thursday at 8 pm called Kunjal Panjee Kutch Ji. it began with 20 minutes but was increased to 30 minutes after the first three months after AIR loweresd its royalty rates. It completed a year of broadcast and then recently, in the post-air. Programmes scripted rehearsed and performed by the rural women with help of Drishti Collective are recorded and given to AIR in digital format for broadcast. The United Nations Development Programme funded this project for two years and its costs come over the period of broadcasting. The programmes are recorded and edited of broadcasting. The programmes are recorded and edited on digital audio format. Says one of the directors of the programme, "Just because it is for a rural audience, it should not be lacking in quality.

Chala Ho Gaon Mein

Palmau district of the newly formed state of Jharkhand, carved out of Bihar, is one of the most backward areas of northern India. Tribal and non tribal groups constitute majority of the population. They earn their livelihood out of minor forest produces and grow basic crops like paddy, Wheat and lentils. Ecological affected both the natural wealth of the region and the poverty with a sizable number of men dependent on more than 70 per cent of women illiterate. Poverty, however, has not hampered their natural aptitude for song- writing, musical compositions, folk theatre and non formal information dissemination.

Alternative for India (AID) and National Foundation for India (NFI) the two NGOs working in this area decided to dovetail the creative potential of the people with that of community radio to create awareness among prople in Palamau. Trained in the basics of audio production, volunteers chosen from various villages of Paamau recorded quite a few field based programmes, including the signature tune being composed by the villagers themselves. The recorded programmes were then "narrowcast" in various villages. Enthused by the response, the team then bargained for by the Palamau team focus on empowerment of the tribal communities with women as the focus. A few other significant initiatives by civil society groups in other parts of the country have given a fillip to the movement demanding space for communities in the FM spectrum.

Purpose and Importance of Community Radio

Mainstream media is unable to cater to the basic information needs of the community, as it mainly runs with profit-making motives and is market driven, so here comes the need for the community radio. Community radio narrows down the differences between the broadcaster and the audience. Its approach is towards empowerment at the grassroots, which automatically strengthen the democracy. The chief characteristic of community radio is that it is non-profit making and whatever profits are gained, are put back into the running of the station. The success of this kind of rural radio station is that it complements the oral tradition of communication, and it is built on the tradition of participatory development. Decentralized community radio maintains close ties with the local community and provides local people the opportunities to voice their opinions and ideas, share their knowledge which enables them to solve their own problems. Community radio is also important as a training ground for new entrants to radio, and as a place where new ideas can be tried. The historical philosophy of community radio is to use this medium as the voice of the voiceless, the mouth-piece of the oppressed and generally as a tool of development. Community radio became popular as an alternative media to public and commercial radio in the late 70s. Community radio is an essential partner in community development. It can be characterised by its access, public participation in production and decision making, management by listeners, and its operations rely mainly on the community's very own resources. Community radio incorporates new languages, inventive formats, novel music and innovative ways of pressuring the authorities. It works as a cultural broadcast mechanism that adapts perfectly to reflect the interests and needs of the community it serves.

Strategies for Consideration

Deepen Linkages with Development

There is a need for community radio to deepen its linkages with development and build synergies with social movements like Freedom of Information, Freedom of Expression, Food Security, Gender issues etc. The experience of Sangam Radio in India is a case in point. Sangam Radio India is India's first grass root community radio station to go on air. It is also the country's first Dalit Radio managed by the Community Media Trust – a team of Dalit women. The radio station's programmes on traditional systems of agriculture have played a significant role in addressing the issue of food scarcity in a drought prone area. The radio station recently initiated an innovative mechanism of a shareholder concept to address sustainability and income generation. In October 2009, a plan to strengthen its sustainability was formalized by the Community Media Trust. Accordingly, each of the 5000 sangham members would contribute Rs 5 every month towards the radio station resulting in an annual contribution of Rs 2, 50,000. Already 2,000 are active members and contribute the requisite amount which helps to take care of staff and radio production. In doing so, it ensures that it is not dependent on advertising, but exhibits and practices a shareholder model

Innovative Use of Mixed Media/Technology

Community Broadcasting needs to strategically combine old and new communication technologies and develop mixed media media models. Some examples below illustrate the point. ARRnet is short for the Aceh Radio reconstruction Network that started in November, 2005 in Indonesia. Comprising a membership of 46 community radio stations in Aceh and North Sumatra, the network was dedicated to community based rehabilitation and reconstruction posts the 2004 Tsunami. It used a mixed media model that combined community radio, website, telephone and fax lines to enable it to reach out to the last mile, last post. The operational strategy was a direct process whereby the member stations sent information to the ARRnet hub in Banda Aceh, from where it was uploaded directly on to the internet. There are other interesting examples that demonstrate how a mixed media model has been effectively used to reach the last mile, last post. Prior to community radio legitimacy in India, the Namma Dhwani community media centre (in the southern state of Karnataka) used a mix of cable technology and loudspeakers to function as a cable radio station and also regularly narrowcast information through loud speakers on market prices. The same technology was used by the YCMC Centre in Bangladesh. With climate change and disaster mitigation assuming criticality, the case for community based mobile broadcasting and examples like the E Tuk Tuk in Sri Lanka, and Doko Radio in Nepal assume additional significance.

Strengthen Relationship between Community and Public Broadcasting Sectors

There needs to be more engagement between the community broadcasting and public broadcasting sectors. In India, community based groups have (especially in the pre 2006 period) bought time and broadcast programmes produced by the community over the Government owned All India Radio which also has a substantial local radio network across the country.

Engage with Academia

There is a need to build linkages with Academia. There needs to be more research and impact assessment studies that track and evaluate performance of Community Radio stations and study their co-relation with development. The Ethnographic Research programmes initiated by UNESCO in South Asia exemplify this point. At the same time, there needs to be more support provided for training in community radio and develop a pool of country/regional resource persons that undertake community radio capacity building.

Explore Funding Mechanisms

Funding support from government also needs to be explored. The example of France throws up the up the possibility of a support mechanism like a community radio fund. Closer home, in the Philippines, there are collaborative alliances like the Local Government Units (LGU) initiative.

Strengthen Networking

Even while community radio may be a recent entrant in some countries in Asia Pacific, there needs to be a greater emphasis on networking both at the country and regional levels. Networks comprising community radio practitioners, advocates and community media production groups at the country and regional are required to strengthen the case for legal reform, technology access and fund raising. Examples like ACORAB in Nepal, CRF in India and JRKI in Indonesia are examples of efforts in the Asia Pacific region to advocate for enabling environments and judicious legislation in their countries. They are also valuable mechanisms for content sharing and dissemination, awareness and capacity building. The experience of AMARC strengthens the case for building cross regional and global networks. AMARC today is a network of about 6,000 community radio stations in 110 countries. The network comprises members from diverse and marginalized communities with expertise in advocacy, capacity building, technology facilitation and content sharing.

Conclusion

The impact of Community radio is clearly visible in every bit of personal and social life of Indian people. It has brought about fundamental changes in the patters of our personal and social interaction. More than five decade have been found to be inadequate to draw concrete conclusions on the role of media in social change as research findings facilitates between the two extremes of media having "powerful effects" and marginal effects". But role of community radio in driving social change has been established "beyond doubt" with in less than two decades. In fact, community radio driven social change have amazed the humanity across the globe. Some changes are fast as the changes in the technology itself. Community Radio depends on stimulating a single semse that is sense of hearing to convey learning. It is more abstract than television and video. It is not confined to language but music. Appropriate mix of language, volume, vocal variety, music and background sound stimulate imagination of listener to comprehend messages being conveyed. Community radio is catalyst as the social change in the society through broadcasting different programmes on the various aspects.

Community radio creates a public sphere that can urge each people to speak and argue, as long as it comes from the society, independent, not controlled by one's institution propaganda. The role of community radio is increasing especially in India. Although, they still try to find the best way to improve their function and role. That is why, in my point of view, we need to support their existence as an alternative way to create a participative communication model that comes within the society. As young generation who will be responsible for the future of mankind with all its inheritances, we have to seek alternative way as to solve grass root problems. That is why; I want to show to all young generations that community radio can and will play an important role in the future. All in all, community radio as the media is the tool for us to make changes in our society especially poor living community. We can use this chance and idea to improve our way in disseminating, advocating, consulting, capacity building, or other forms as long as we use this tool for the best of our community and humanity. Therefore, let us make a change to make our world better. The world where there will be less hunger, less trafficking, less illiteracy, less global warming, less information divide, and so on, the world of democracy, the world of ours. Let us turn NOT KNOWING INTO KNOWING

References

Colin F. and Sonia R. (2006). Community Radio for Change and Development. *mediaresearchhub.ssrc.org/resource.2006-07-15.062009-2*

Center for International Media Assistance (CIMA) (2007). Community Radio: Its Impact and Challenges to its Development. http://www.ned.org/cima/cima.html.

Dragon, A. G. (2001). Making Waves Stories of Participatory Communication for Social Change. New York. The Rockfeller Foundation. Pp.63-72.

Prasad K. (2004). Information and Communication Technology. B. R. Publishing Corporation. New Delhi. pp.415.

Sharma A. (2010). Community Radio for Rural Development. Yojana (A Development Monthly). Vol.54. pp.60-63.

Sharma A. (2009). Effectiveness of Media Mix in imparting Nutritional Education among Rural women in District Udham Singh Nagar of Uttarakhand. Unpublished thesis. G.B.P.U.A and T Pantnagar.

Srivastavsa, H. O. (2009). Community Radio for education, farming and livelihood generation: Challenges before existing CR initiatives. World Development Foundation.

Chapter 3

Cyber Extension: A New Extension Approach for Sustainable Rural Development

☆ *S.K. Badodiya and S.K. Garg*

Agricultural extension played a very vital role in achieving the targets of green revolution. The post green revolution scenario is witnessing emergence of new paradigms like sustainable agriculture, agribusiness and contract farming. The advances in info-communication technology (ICT) are poised to complement extension efforts for transfer of technology. The paper conceptually visualizes the cyber (virtual) extension in future development of Indian agriculture.

Cyber extension is an agricultural information exchange mechanism over cyber space, the imaginary space behind the interconnected computer networks through telecommunication means. Cyber extension using power of online networks operates through various tools like internet, e-mail, telnet, file transfer protocol, gopher and websites. It helps the farmers by providing opportunity for interaction with research scientists and extension workers through e-mail, up-to-date news and information services such as market price and weather conditions, online questions and answers, launching online agricultural and rural development publications and magazines. In India there were 55, 00,000 (0.50 per cent) internet users in 2000; 4,20,00,000 users (03.70 per cent) in 2009 and went up to 88,000,000 (**88 million**) active Internet users in 2010.Total penetration rate of internet users is **6.9 per cent** (6.9 persons using Internet out of 100).India has **10.52 million broadband users** (till Oct.2010), constituting 6.0 per cent of the population. More than 200 websites related to agriculture and allied subjects are available for access by farmers which requires less money, time, efforts and steps for extension process as compared to traditional extension methods. Agri-cyber extension makes information available continuously for 24 hours. Agri-cyber extension can therefore play significant role in dissemination of farm information without deteriorating messages. It also provides feedback and opportunity for interaction between the source and targeted audience and help in meeting challenges of liberalization and globalization in the field of agriculture.

Indian agriculture is presently standing at the cross roads. Under the regime of globalization, liberalization, free economy and open market system Indian agriculture is facing tough challenges. In order to cope up with the challenges Indian agriculture need improvement in terms of cost, quality and output. To fulfil these needs Indian farmers needs to be well informed about the latest trends in respect of farm techniques, methods of cultivation, crops, seeds, insecticides, pesticides, water management, nutrient management and marketing. Presently the farmers meet their farm information needs through information received from various agencies. The received information however, is not adequate and up-to-date.

Access to information and improved communication is therefore a crucial requirement for sustainable agricultural development and social and economic development of the farming community. It is observed that farmers still have difficulty in accessing crucial information in forms they can understand in order to make timely decisions. Modern communication technologies when applied to the agriculture can help to improve communication, increase participation and disseminate farm information and share knowledge and skills. They also generate possibilities to solve farm problems inequality and giving an opportunity to bridge the gap between information-rich and information-poor and support sustainable development in agriculture.

Agri-Cyber Extension

Agri cyber extension may be defined as the farm technology transfer programme over the cyberspace, the imaginary space behind the interconnected telecommunication and computer networks, the virtual world. Agri cyber extension means "Using the power of online networks, computer communications and digital interactive multimedia to facilitate dissemination of agricultural technology".

Important Tools of Agri-Cyber Extension

E-mail

Electronic mail, commonly called email or e-mail, is a method of exchanging digital messages from an author to one or more recipients. E-mail (electronic mail) is the most frequently used application in the cyber extension. E-mail allows sending and receiving text message to and from other user of the internet. Modern email operates across the Internet or other computer networks. Today's email systems are based on a store-and-forward model. Email servers accept, forward, deliver and store messages. Neither the users nor their computers are required to be online simultaneously; they need connect only briefly, typically to an email server, for as long as it takes to send or receive messages.

Telnet

Telnet is an application that allows us to log on to a remote computer. It is like a terminate emulation programme. Telnet session present text based data as a terminal would.

Telnet is a network protocol used on the Internet or local area networks to provide a bidirectional interactive text-oriented communications facility using a virtual terminal connection. User data is interspersed in-band with Telnet control information in an 8-bit byte oriented data connection over the Transmission Control Protocol (TCP).

FTP (File Transfer Protocol)

FTP (File Transfer Protocol), is the simplest way to exchange files between computers on the Internet. FTP is commonly used to transfer Files back and forth for your personal homepage. It is commonly used to download shareware or other files to your computer from other networks. To use FTP you should acquire an FTP client or to put it in simple terms "a ftp browser". Your web browser can also make FTP requests to download programs you find on a web page. Using a ftp client you can rename, add or remove files. Doing this generally applies to your personal account ftp. Most internet services provide free web space. Contact your internet service provider to find out how to use your ftp account for a web page.

Gopher

Gopher is a menu-oriented way to "cruise and browse" the Internet Gopher presents you with lists of the Internet's files, programs, resources, services, and other menus, in the form of easy-to-read point-and-click menus. By simply positioning the cursor or entering the appropriate item number, you make selections and thereby cruise much of the Internet using nothing more than a few keystrokes.

WWW (World Wide Web)

The World Wide Web (abbreviated as WWW or W3 and commonly known as the Web), is a system of interlinked hypertext documents accessed via the Internet. With a web browser, one can view web pages that may contain text, images, videos, and other multimedia and navigate between them via hyperlinks. The WWW has become so popular that it has almost replaced all the above internet tools and become the most important tool of cyber extension. WWW is an organization of hyper text documents containing text, images, animations, sound, video and increasingly interactive programmes.

Use Net News Groups

The Usenet stands for "user's network", and is sometimes called just "the newsgroups". Usenet newsgroups are thousands of virtual bulletin boards on a wide range of different subjects available around the world. Anyone with access to the *Internet* can post a message to any newsgroup, read any message, and post a response to any message, making the Usenet a unique global common space covering a wide range of subjects.

Types of Websites

Static Websites

web sites which provide only information. It displays the same information for all users, from all contexts, providing the classical hypertext, where navigation is performed through 'static' documents.

Dynamic Websites

Dynamic websites are the most popular kind of websites for the companies, where in they have all the flexibility to change the content of the website. This kind of website is very useful for the companies trading in commodity items or the items in which content, prices, specification changes frequently, even the website with regular product addition/updating requires a dynamic website. Most business websites these days are dynamic meaning that the web pages are dynamically built pages that allow user interaction. This is required for example for an online shopping cart.

Interactive Websites

Interactive Websites provide standards-based cross curricular web resources designed to enhance online learning opportunities. These sites interact with the user usually through either a text-based or graphical user interface. Choose from the links above to explore a collection of interactive resources. Interactive web sites provide information and interaction between group of individuals like chatting, question and answers.

Type of Farm Information Provided on Cyber

The World Wide Web can help in following ways:

1. Provide opportunity for interaction among research scientist, extension workers, farmers and other rural people through e-mail.
2. Provide up-to-date news and information services such as market prices and weather conditions.
3. A question and answer on-line service among scientist, extension workers and farmers, where expert respond to quires on specialized subjects. (Interactive expert system)
4. Hosting websites by major institutions participating in agricultural extension, putting latest packages of practices for various agro-climatic regions.

5. Launching online agricultural and rural development publication, magazine, books etc.
6. Providing information regarding agricultural programmes, trainings, schemes.
7. Providing mechanism of user/beneficiary feedback for public sector schemes.
8. Opening cyber cafes to enable education rural people, farmers and extension worker at village level to have direct access to World Wide Web for having market information.
9. Creation and maintenance of statistical data base on critical agricultural parameters.
10. Provide internet access at district and block level agriculture and rural development offices.

Present Status of Internet Users

The following information pertaining to internet connections and its users as well as development and availability of websites throws light on the present status of internet and websites:

Internet Connection and its Users in India

Table 3.1: Internet Usage and Population Statistics

Sl.No.	*Year*	*Users*	*Population*	*Population %*
1	1998	1,400,000	1,094,870,677	0.1
2	1999	2,800,000	1,094,870,677	0.3
3	2000	5,500,000	1,094,870,677	0.5
4	2001	7,000,000	1,094,870,677	0.7
5	2002	16,500,000	1,094,870,677	1.6
6	2003	22,500,000	1,094,870,677	2.1
7	2004	39,200,000	1,094,870,677	3.6
8	2005	50,600,000	1,112,225,812	4.5
9	2006	40,000,000	1,112,225,812	3.6
10	2007	42,000,000	1,129,667,528	3.7
11	2009	81,000,000	1,156,897,766	7.0
12	2010	100,000,000	1,173,108,018	8.5

Source: http://www.internetworldstats.com/asia/in.htm.

The Worldwide Internet Users report provides an overview of 15 Internet markets worldwide and ideally complements the more focused marketing and demographic reports eMarketer publishes.

Table 3.2: Internet Users and Penetration in Select Countries Worldwide, 2006 (millions and per cent of population)

Sl.No.	*Country*	*Internet Users*	*Penetration*
1.	US	181.9	63.6
2.	China	133.5	10.2
3.	Japan	87.2	68.4
4.	Germany	39.4	47.8
5.	UK	35.1	57.9
6.	South Korea	34.4	70.5
7.	France	28.7	47.1
8.	Italy	28.6	49.2
9.	India	25.5	2.3
10.	Brazil	21.2	11.3
11.	Canada	21.0	63.4
12.	Mexico	20.0	18.6
13.	Spain	16.5	40.8
14.	Australia	13.1	64.5
15.	Agentina	7.9	19.8
16.	Rest of World	368.0	13.2
17.	Worldwide	1080.0	16.6

Source: e Marketer, January 2007

Information in Local Language

The information is stored in the form of local languages which is an easy way to spread the information to the farmers. In India there are about 40 languages spoken by the people living in different parts of the country. Out of them 19 languages are known to be more popular including international language English. Disseminating information in all local languages is very difficult. The software which can capture scripts of all Indian languages is about available. The software developed by Centre of Development of Advanced Computing (C-DAC) supports only 12 Indian languages.

Languages Supported by the C-DAC Software

1. Assamese
2. Bengali
3. Gujarati
4. Hindi
5. Kannada
6. Malayalam
7. Marathi
8. Oriya
9. Punjabi
10. Sanskrit
11. Tamil
12. Telugu

Table 3.3: Availability of Websites According to their Subjects

Sl.No.	*Subjects*	*Number of Websites*	*Percentage*
1.	Agriculture	150	74.35
2.	Veterinary	27	13.37
3.	Horticulture	17	08.41
4.	Dairy science	04	01.98
5.	Fishery	02	00.99
6.	Forestry	02	00.99
	Total	**202**	**100.00**

Source: Velumani, 2003 and Deshmukh *et al.*, 2010.

Difference between Traditional Extension Method and Cyber Extension

The traditional and cyber extension differs on the number of counts. Major points of differentiations is given in Table 3.4.

Strengths of Agri Cyber Extension

Agri Cyber Extension will Save Money, Time and Efforts

Scientists will prepare electronic version of messages themselves. These versions are not to be printed or posted. This will

Table 3.4

Sl.No.	General Characters	Traditional Extension	Cyber Extension
1	Requirement on money, time and efforts	More	Less
2	Requirement of steps for extension process	More	Cut steps
3	Interaction between farmers and subject matter specialist	Limited time	Available time or continuous
4	Message	Eroded	As such
5	Availability of information	Limited time	Continuously (24 hours)
6	Communication capacity	Poor	Strong
7	Coverage	Limited	Wide
8	Requirement of experts/extension personal	More	Less
9	Incorporation of new vision and ideas	Difficult	Easy

save efforts, money and time. Cyber messages will be updated online and that saves time too.

Agri Cyber Extension will Save Time, Cut Steps from Extension Process

Agri cyber extension will remove number of steps all together from the traditional extension process. In the context of Agriculture, the zonal workshop, monthly workshop and training to subject matter specialists (SMS) can eliminated all together. All concerned will get the information immediately and queries/classification will also be addressed equally fast, without involving a chain of extension machinery.

Agri Cyber Extension will be Information Rich and Interactive

It appeals to the curious extension workers and analytical farmers. It will allow them to search and locate the information they need quickly. The extension workers can talk to concern scientist for more information on the subject.

Agri Cyber Extension will Offer Instant International Reach

Online networks have created an instant global village. Cyber extension will eliminate the time and distance barrier that come in the way of knowing the latest information on any particular problem from any part of the world.

Agri Cyber Extension will be Continuously Available

One of the key attributes of an online information service in that it is available all the time, 24 hours a day. If you have connectivity you can get information from wherever it is available.

Some Important Cyber Extension Projects in India

1. AGMARKNET a project provides current pricelist and arrivals of commodities from major markets.
2. E-chaupal provides weather information and market information.
3. Warna wired village project in Maharashtra.
4. The information village project of the MS Swaminathan research foundation in Pondicherry.
5. Tarahaat.com for all round rural development.
6. Information-villagers project of MANAGE in Ranga Reddy District of Andhra Pradesh.
7. Gyandoot.net initiatives of District Dhar M.P.
8. The Computer Aided Administration of Registration Department (CARD). A project of Andhra Pradesh.

Chapter 4

Extent of Adoption of Recommended Water Management Practices by the Beneficiary Farmers of Participatory Irrigation Management Society of Mehsana District, Gujarat

☆ *J.K. Patel and M.R. Prajapati*

Since 1985 Ministry of Water Resources has been inspiring farmers' participation in water distribution and management of tertiary system in the projects covered under the Centrally Sponsored Command Area Development Programme. The concept of involvement of farmers in management of the irrigation system has been accepted as a policy of the Government of India and has been included in the National Water Policy adopted in 1987.

The Gujarat Government had enacted the Gujarat Water Users Participatory Irrigation Management Act, 2007. Gujarat has been giving high priority to PIM and has been systematically promoting, it by facilitating through Government resolutions from time to time since 1980. So far, 576 number of Water User Associations (WUAs) covering an area of 96680 ha. The implementation of PIM in Sabarmati Reservoir Project on June 1st, 1995 by Government of Gujarat. The Sabarmati Reservoir Project is one of the major irrigation projects in North Gujarat. The Sabarmati Reservoir Project comprises of two stages, the first (the major one) served by the Sabarmati Right Bank Minor Canal (SRBMC) and second stage is Sabarmati Left Bank Minor Canal (SLBMC). The Sabarmati Reservoir Project covers area under irrigation in Mehsana and Sabarkantha Districts is 48,105 ha. and 12,980 ha. respectively. The total area under irrigation in the project is 61,085 ha.

Though, Participatory Irrigation Management is an accepted concept for the country, but the operationalisation of this concept in a systematic manner has been a major weakness since last two decades. Through this PIMS, it would be assumed that by adopting water management practices and management system of PIMS, there should be techno-economic change and extent of adoption of recommended water management practices among the members of PIMS. Hence there is an urgent need to study the extent of adoption of recommended water management practices by the beneficiary farmers of Participatory Irrigation Management Society.

Objectives

1. To study the extent of adoption of recommended water management practices followed by the members of PIMS for major crops. (Wheat, Tobacco and Cotton)
2. To ascertain relationship between selected independent variables and extent of adoption of recommended water management practices by the members of PIMS.
3. To know the direct and indirect effect of the independent variables on extent of adoption of recommended water management practices by the members of PIMS.

Methodology

The Mehsana District of Gujarat state was purposively selected for the study as the district has taken lead in introducing PIMS in the state. Among the seven talukas of the district three talukas *viz.*, Visnagar, Vijapur and Vadnagar were leading talukas for participatory activities carried out by the irrigation department and other institutions. For the selection of talukas, villages/PIMS and respondents, multistage random sampling technique was employed. Total 200 respondents from 20 selected PIMS were selected using proportionate random sampling method. Adoption is a decision to make full use of innovation at the best course of action available. Adoption in present study was operationlized as the recommended water management practices actually put into practices by the respondents during last five years wheat, cotton and tobacco. Totally, there were 36 questions pertaining to the water management practices (for wheat 13, cotton 11 and tobacco 12) in the schedule and each of them was given a score of 0 and 1 for no adoption and complete adoption, respectively. A respondent's adoption level was determined by adopting the adoption quotient (Aq) developed by Sengupta (1967). For the collection of data field survey by personal contact using structured schedule was used. The data were collected, coded, classified, tabulated and analyzed in order to get meaningful findings.

Results and Discussion

A perusal of data presented in Table 4.1 indicates that more than three-fifth (64.00 per cent) of the respondents of beneficiary farmers had medium level of adoption of recommended water management practices. While, 19.00 per cent beneficiary farmers were found high level of adoption of recommended water management practices and 17.00 per cent of the beneficiary farmers were found with low level of adoption of recommended water management practices.

It can be inferred from the above finding that a great majority (83.00 per cent) of the respondents had medium to high level of adoption of recommended water management practices by the PIMS beneficiaries.

The probable reason for this finding might that the beneficiary farmers had favorable attitude toward PIMS, medium level of knowledge, frequent extension contact and utilization of information sources which led them to higher adoption of recommended water management practices. Another reason might be due to sincere effort put forth by implementing agency *i.e.,* Participatory Irrigation Management Society (PIMS) and Irrigation Department (I.D.). This finding coincides with the finding reported by Patel (1997) and Dabhi (2002).

Table 4.1: Distribution of the Respondents According to their Extent of Adoption of Recommended Water Management Practices (n = 200)

Sl.No.	*Extent of Adoption of Recommended Water Management Practices*	*Frequency*	*Percentage*
1.	Low (Below 48.212 scores)	34	17.00
2.	Medium (48.212 to 66.580 scores)	128	64.00
3.	High (Above 66.580 scores)	38	19.00
	Total	200	100.00
	Mean = 57.396	S.D. =	9.184

It is evident from the data presented in Table 4.2 that there are seventeen variables used for the study, out of them 15 variables namely education, caste, social participation, socio-economic status, occupation, size of land holding, cropping intensity, annual income, economic motivation, scientific orientation, risk-preference, attitude towards PIMS, knowledge of recommended water management practices, contact with extension agency and utilization of information sources were positively and significantly correlated with extent of adoption of recommended water management practices. While credit orientation was positive and non-significant correlation with extent of adoption of recommended water management practices. Whereas, age was negatively and significant correlation with extent of adoption of recommended water management practices.

The probable reasons might be that aged farmers have less risk taking capacity, innovativeness and enthusiasm, education improves ability to comprehend and interpret new ideas and majority of respondents belongs to general caste, highly educated and good economic condition. Social participation play important role in getting acquaint with various extension agencies and helps to broaden their intellectual horizon. Higher income through more numbers of occupation, more intensity of land used, the farmers

Table 4.2: Relationship of Independent Variables with Extent of Adoption of Recommended Water Management Practices (n = 200)

Sl.No.	*Independent Variables*		*Correlation Coefficient ('r')*
[I]	**PERSONAL :**		
	1. Age	**(X_1)**	-0.1499*
	2. Education	**(X_2)**	0.5138**
	3. Caste	**(X_3)**	0.1836**
[II]	**SOCIAL :**		
	1. Social participation	**(X_4)**	0.3259**
	2. Socio-economic status	**(X_5)**	0.6488**
[III]	**AGRO-ECONOMIC :**		
	1. Occupation	**(X_6)**	0.5259**
	2. Cropping intensity	**(X_7)**	0.2367**
	3. Size of land holding	**(X_8)**	0.4262**
	4. Annual income	**(X_9)**	0.6108**
	5. Credit orientation	**(X_{10})**	0.0233^{NS}
[IV]	**PSYCHOLOGICAL :**		
	1. Economic motivation	**(X_{11})**	0.5112**
	2. Risk-preference	**(X_{12})**	0.4515**
	3. Scientific orientation	**(X_{13})**	0.5184**
	4. Attitude toward PIMS	**(X_{14})**	0.5586**
	5. Knowledge of recommended water management practices	**(X_{15})**	0.9096**
[V]	**COMMUNICATIONCAL :**		
	1. Contact with extension agency	**(X_{16})**	0.5935**
	2. Utilization of information sources	**(X_{17})**	0.5719**

NS: Non-Significant.

* Significant at 0.05 per cent level of significance.

** Significant at 0.01 per cent level of significance.

with large size of land holding are generally sound in economic position resulting into high risk bearing capacity and higher extent of adoption. Further higher income facilitates in optimum and procurement of inputs and desired technological guidance. Credit orientation shown negative relationship as respondents might have oriented for availing credit facility but not used properly. The economically motivated farmers have better contact with extension

Table 4.3: Multiple Regression Analysis of Independent Variables with Extent of Adoption of Recommended Water Management Practices (n = 200)

Sl.No.	*Variables*	*Regression Co-efficient (b_i)*	*S.E. of (b_i)*	*'t' Value*
[I]	**PERSONAL :**			
	1. Age	0.0197	0.0355	0.5549
	2. Education	0.8054	1.1264	0.7150
	3. Caste	-1.9916	1.1115	-1.7918
[II]	**SOCIAL :**			
	1. Social participation	-0.6712	1.1979	-0.5603
	2. Socio-economic status	1.2965	1.0684	1.2349
[III]	**AGRO-ECONOMIC :**			
	1. Occupation	-0.8845	1.2675	-0.6978
	2. Cropping intensity	0.0003	0.0034	-0.0882
	3. Size of land holding	-1.7361	1.2392	-1.4009
	4. Annual income	0.0002	0.0001	1.8533
	5. Credit orientation	-0.0709	0.1127	-0.6291
[IV]	**PSYCHOLOGICAL :**			
	1. Economic motivation	0.1649	0.1203	1.3707
	2. Risk-preference	-0.1122	0.1379	-0.8136
	3. Scientific orientation	0.0293	0.1427	0.2053
	4. Attitude toward PIMS	0.1136	0.0412	2.7572*
	5. Knowledge of recommended water management practices	0.8480	0.0389	21.7994**
[V]	**COMMUNICATIONCAL :**			
	1. Contact with extension agency	-0.1355	0.1368	-0.9944
	2. Utilization of information sources	0.1097	0.1295	0.8471

* Significant at 0.05 per cent and ** Significant at 0.01 per cent level of probability.

Multiple R = 0.9292 R^2 = 0.8633.

agencies, higher risk preference among PIMS and scientifically oriented farmers are likely to have more inclination to use scientific farming practices. Likewise favourable attitude and knowledge understood main features of ideas or things increase their adoption. Actual participation of farmers in various activities may to interact with extension personnel result into higher extent of adoption. This finding is in line with the finding of Vankar (2000) and Dabhi (2002).

It can be concluded from Table 4.3 that 86.33 per cent total variation in extent of adoption of recommended water management practices was explained by a set of 17 independent variables together. Further, out of 17 variables, two variables *viz.*, Knowledge of recommended water management practices and attitude towards PIMS had significant contribution in extent of adoption of recommended water management practices. The probable reasons might be that favourable attitudes towards PIMS and knowledge understood main features of ideas increase their adoption.

Table 4.4: Stepwise Variation Accounted by Selected Independent Variables with Extent of Adoption of Recommended Water Management Practice (n = 200)

Sl.No.	*Independent Variables*	*Multiple R*	*Total Variation Accounted R^2*	*Variation between Step*
1.	Knowledge of recommended water management practices (x_{15})	0.9097	0.8275 (82.75%)	82.75
2.	Attitude toward PIMS (x_{14} + x_{15})	0.9235	0.8528 (85.23%)	2.53

It is also clear from Table 4.4 that the variable, knowledge of recommended water management practices alone accounted 82.75 per cent variation in adoption of recommended water management practices, followed by knowledge of recommended water management practices + attitude towards PIMS (85.23 per cent).

The data in the Table 4.3 indicates the Results of path analysis inferred that out of 16 variables analysed 8 variables exerted direct positive effect and 8 variables expressed negative direct effect. The variables *viz.*, knowledge of recommended water management practices, socio-economic status and attitude towards PIMS showed highest positive direct effect. With respect to highest indirect positive

Table 4.5: The Direct, Total Indirect and Substantial Indirect Effects on Independent Variables on Extent of Adoption of Recommended Water Management Practices (n = 200)

Sl.No.		Variables	Direct Effect	Total Indirect Effect	Substantial Indirect Effect (First)
1.	**(X_1)**	Age	0.0186	-0.1685	-0.1133 **(X_{15})**
2.	**(X_2)**	Education	-0.0963	0.6101	0.3799 **(X_{15})**
3.	**(X_3)**	Caste	-0.1133	0.3029	0.1852 **(X_{15})**
4.	**(X_4)**	Social participation	-0.0433	0.3688	0.2283 **(X_{15})**
5.	**(X_5)**	Socio-economic status	0.3687	0.2801	0.4842 **(X_{15})**
6.	**(X_6)**	Occupation	-0.0760	0.6019	0.3810 **(X_{15})**
7.	**(X_7)**	Cropping intensity	-0.0032	0.2399	0.2110 **(X_{15})**
8.	**(X_8)**	Size of land holding	-0.1811	0.6073	0.3244 **(X_{15})**
9.	**(X_9)**	Annual income	0.0148	0.5960	0.4492 **(X_{15})**
10.	**(X_{11})**	Economic motivation	0.0554	0.4558	0.3577 **(X_{15})**
11.	**(X_{12})**	Risk preference	-0.0321	0.4836	0.3294 **(X_{15})**
12.	**(X_{13})**	Scientific orientation	0.0086	0.5098	0.3766 **(X_{15})**
13.	**(X_{14})**	Attitude toward PIMS	0.1267	0.4319	0.3674 **(X_{15})**
14.	**(X_{15})**	Knowledge of recommended water management practices	0.8007	0.1089	0.2299 **(X_5)**
15.	**(X_{16})**	Contact with extension agency	0.0740	0.5195	0.4412 **(X_{15})**
16.	**(X_{17})**	Utilization of information sources	-0.0699	0.6418	0.4405 **(X_{15})**

Multiple R = 0.9293; R^2 = 0.8633

effect on adoption of recommended water management practices, the key variables were utilization of information sources, education and size of land holding, while in case of first substantial effect all above variables were important and found affecting through variable *i.e.*, knowledge of recommended water management practices.

Conclusion

1. A great majority (83.00 per cent) of the beneficiary farmers were found medium to high adoption of recommended water management practices.

2. The variables *viz.*, education, caste, social participation, socio-economic status, occupation, size of land holding, cropping intensity, annual income, economic motivation, scientific orientation, risk-preference, attitude towards PIMS, knowledge of recommended water management practices, contact with extension agency and utilization of information sources were positively and significantly correlated with extent of adoption of recommended water management practices. While credit orientation was positive and non-significant correlation with extent of adoption of recommended water management practices. Whereas, age was negatively and significant correlation with extent of adoption of recommended water management practices.
3. Multiple regression analysis indicated that all variables exerted as much as 86.33 per cent of total variation in. The result of stepwise regression analysis indicated that 85.23 per cent of the total variation in extent of adoption of recommended water management practices was accounted by a set of two variables *viz.*, knowledge of recommended water management practices and attitude towards PIMS.
4. Results of path analysis inferred that out of 16 variables analysed 8 variables exerted direct positive effect and 8 variables expressed negative direct effect. The variables *viz.*, knowledge of recommended water management practices, socio-economic status and attitude towards PIMS showed highest positive direct effect. With respect to highest indirect positive effect on adoption of recommended water management practices, the key variables were utilization of information sources, education and size of land holding, while in case of first substantial effect all above variables were important and found affecting through variable *i.e.*, knowledge of recommended water management practices.

References

Dabhi, R.A. (2002). Impact of PIMS on techno-economic change of farmers of Anand District in Gujarat State. Ph.D Thesis (Unpublished).Gujarat Agricultural University, Anand.

Patel, A.A. (1997). Extent of utilization of canal irrigation water in Anand taluka of Kadana Command Area in Gujarat State. M.Sc (Agri.) Thesis (Unpublished).Gujarat Agricultural University, Anand.

Sengupta, T. (1967). A simple adoption scale used for farmers for high yielding varieties programme in rice. Indian J. Ext. Edn., **3** : 22-25.

Vankar, P.M. (2000) Impact of canal irrigation on schedule caste farmers in Khambhat taluka of Anand District of Gujarat State. M.Sc (Agri.) Thesis (Unpublished).Gujarat Agricultural University, Anand.

Chapter 5

Role of ICT in Higher Education and its Challenges in Developing Nations

☆ *Anup Prakash Upadhyay, Gaurav Papnai and Biswajit Lahiri*

Higher education provides people with an opportunity to reflect on the critical social, economic, cultural and spiritual issues facing humanity. It contributes to national development through dissemination of specialized knowledge and skills. It is therefore a crucial factor for survival. Being at the apex of the educational pyramid, it has also a key role in producing teachers for the education system. In the context of the unprecedented explosion of knowledge, higher education has to become dynamic as never before, constantly entering uncharted areas.

Higher education has to adapt continuously to meet the emerging needs of the society. Growing complexity of modern culture is making increasing demands on the capabilities of a teacher. The preparation of such an important functionary therefore must get the highest priority. Country's best talents need to be encouraged in the teaching profession if it is desired to produce leader of thought and action in every walk of life. The status of teachers reflects the socio-cultural ethos of a society. It is said "No pupil can rise above the level of its teachers" (N.P.E. 1992). The profound shifts undergone in the academic field must be viewed by thoughts on the new possibilities with new technologies evolving. Traditional teaching and learning paradigms have been affected by the impact of the integration of Information and Communication Technologies (ICT) into educational practices.

In the knowledge driven economy education is going to be tremendously influenced. Education and all related activities like teaching, learning, evaluating research, materials production, management of education etc. should therefore have to be geared up to meet the emerging needs. Development in various fields combined with adroit innovation revolves around a teacher, so one can aptly remark that teacher is a mechanism for dissemination of knowledge for the progression.

In view of the current reality that new learning environment is taking place in the emerging knowledge-based society are impinging on the roles of teachers. These are characterized by the paradigm shift in education from the old concept of 'education' to learning. These changes have generated new types of learners, new process of learning and new approaches to evaluation of learning, which in turn have contributed to the changed roles of teachers from the conventional one to a series of new roles. Teachers' role shifted to work as facilitator of knowledge. They are also now a proactive agent of change and active participant in transformation. A teacher is specialist in teaching with new technologies, and a continuous learner throughout life (National Policy on Education, 1992).

The impact of internet in education in recent years fosters the vision of an open, global and flexible learning, leading to radical shifts in the teacher's role and competencies. Indian Council of Agricultural Research (ICAR) through the State Agricultural Universities (SAUs) has taken innovative decisions which include modernization of laboratories, classrooms, updating curriculum, preparation of course manuals.

The acquisition of technical, organizational, conceptual skills together with the new literacy: technical, scientific, digital, and cultural literacy is essential. The widespread use of computers in all areas has a direct effect upon the way in which the world is perceived. New profile of teachers developed according to the following functions: assessor and guide of the autonomous learning process, resource facilitator, designer of new technology-rich learning environments, adapter of different materials, producer of new didactic materials in ICT-based settings, evaluator of the different processes in which these environments and resources are involved and finally ability to acquire a professional viewpoint on ICT (Cobb, 1992).

Teacher of today is not a mere purveyor of lessons in a classroom. He is instead an individual who is not only interested in student's acquiring knowledge and skills but also equally involved in his total development Kakkar (2001). Preparing the teachers to meet these challenges and enhancing quality of teacher is currently an essential need. Conventional methods have been used to train teachers, which have several limitations. Modern communication technologies can play an important role in the training of teachers. ICT based technologies have immense potential in improving agricultural education. Information and communications Technology (ICT) has the potential to improve all aspects of our social, economic and cultural life. The introduction of ICT into universities clearly changes the way education is conducted. ICT also paves way for a new pedagogical approach, where students are expected to play more active than before (Alabi, 2004) ICT focuses on the crucial issues of how people communicate and learn in electronic environment. ICT in learning depends on effective communication of human knowledge, which may either occur in synchronous or asynchronous and blended learning situation as the case may be. The role of Information and Communications Technology (ICT) in human development has received growing attention among development practitioners, policy makers, government and civil society in recent years due to the growing proliferation of the Internet, convergence in IT and telecommunications technologies and increasing globalization. While issues of access and the adoption of new ICTs have tended to revolve around utopian themes of empowerment and the development potential of ICT, it has also raised the accompanying issue of digital divide and the challenges for developing countries to participate in the global information society. ICT, when adopted as one of many complementary strategies in development projects such as health, education and rural development, has the potential to empower communities with improved access to knowledge networks and services. On the other hand, any meaningful participation in this ICT 'revolution' is also challenged by very apparent discrepancies, imbalances and inequalities that currently characterize issues of ICT access and adoption. ICT has become a fashionable acronym borne largely out of the Internet and telecommunications 'revolution' to describe an electronic means of capturing, processing, storing and disseminating information. Little attention, however, is placed on the fact that ICT is not a recent phenomenon since its broader definition also includes print-media, radio, telephone.

Role of ICTs in Pedagogy for Quality Teaching Learning

Another most important dimension of higher education sector influenced by ICT integration is improving quality of teaching-learning. Also, the changes taking place due to globalization and internationalization attach premium to knowledge and information. Therefore, the integration of ICTs would not only help in promoting personal growth but also in developing "knowledge societies". The call of the hour is the need to provide education for everyone, anywhere, and anytime. Lifelong learning has become the driving force to sustain in the contemporary competitive environment. Therefore to strengthen and/or advance this knowledge-driven growth, new technologies, skills and capabilities are needed. In this regards however the research available is scarce, though the efforts for improving pedagogical practices/approaches are being undertaken in many countries. The scope includes development of infrastructures, content and trained personnel. Adoption of ICTs in education requires establishment of infrastructural facilities, acquisition of technologies and their periodic updating, management and professional support services. However, initial investments for the process of developing interface between technology tools and delivery of education are exorbitant. Conventional teaching-learning processes are undergoing a paradigm shift. Focus of instruction is now on education programs/practices that promote competency and performance. Such curricula tends to require access to variety of information sources, information forms and types; student centered learning settings based on information access and inquiry; learning environments centred or problem-centred and inquiry-based activities, authentic settings and examples; and teachers as coaches and mentors rather than content experts (Oliver 2002). The shift towards development of educational programs whose curricula is competency and performance-based is well supported by and encouraged by the emerging instructional technologies. In addition, ICTs lend themselves strongly to educational programmes offered by open and distance learning universities and provide a choice to students who are otherwise unable to attend the campuses. Integration of ICTs would thus lead to quality learning settings not only within the classrooms/institutions but also through online distance learning modules. Some of the Indian universities/institutions namely IIMs, IGNOU, BITS Pilani, MAHE, NIIT are already offering online programs and many more have emerged in the recent period. Although such a learning module will lack face-to-face teacher-learner interaction but at the same time provide a participatory experience of higher order learning. Apart from enhancing student's learning experience, role of ICTs in capacity building/training of educational personnel has very large potential. National level institutes can provide leadership role in enhancing technical and managerial manpower in different disciplines through ICT networks and collaborations. Technology facilitated learning would result in preparation of staff regarding innovative pedagogic methods, new ways of learning and interacting, easy sharing of new practices among teaching community and result in widening the opportunities for their participation. The capabilities of competent and trained teachers/academic experts can be made available to larger audiences/students through flexible and virtual settings.

Problems Associated with Use of ICT in Higher Education System

Policy Structure of the Government

The growth of any communication technology in a society and hence its applicability for Distance Education depends to a very great extent on the degree to which policy makers recognize the importance of ICTs in promoting a knowledge based society. Many Developing Countries like India have realized the importance of giving a boost to New Information and Communication Technologies for the general betterment of the society. The New Information Technology Act 2000 passed by the Indian Parliament is a step in the right direction. Many Countries have bestowed tax incentives on Communication technology based industries. Some Countries that have paid relatively scarce attention to the area of information technology are lagging behind in the field of spreading education using the latest technology. The failure of Distance Education in many African Countries can be attributed to this. Not only are policies important but also their implementation deserves greater attention. The road to failure is often paved with good intentions. Many structural factors make the implementation of technology a daunting task. At the planning stage the enormity of such factors are often not recognized.

Use and Access to Internet

The low levels of Internet penetration in India are clearly visible from the data presented in the table. The percentage of Internet users is just.05 per cent, which compares unfavorably with countries like Thailand (.26 per cent) and China (.27 per cent). The same scenario holds true for most basic infrastructure needed to make ICT usage more viable in Developing countries. Further the waiting time for obtaining access to basic ICT is also very long. Even after liberalization, the average waiting time for obtaining telephone access in India is more that 8 months in India. Access to even the most basic of electronic devices like the Television is also highly limited in countries like India. In India the TV penetration is only 80 per 1000.Coupled with these is the fact that, for most modern information and communication technologies, the user charges are very high that makes their use for Distance Education a very costly affair. A case in view is that of the cost of Internet connectivity for Indian homes. It still costs as much as Rs.30 per hour for Internet access in Indian homes. Such prohibitive costs make the use of such technology for imparting Distance Education, a luxury.

Political Factors

The perceptions and attitudes of a political system greatly affect the acceptance and growth of technology in any society. The same holds true for all the ICTs relevant to Distance Education. A political system conscious of the payoffs of ICT for the enhancement of the educational profile of a country will frame appropriate policies for the adoption and dissemination of ICT through out the length and breadth of the country. Political factors of various hues affect the application of ICT in various ways. The political will of the ruling elite can at times pave the way for the growth of a particular type of communication technology in a country. The current phase of buoyancy related to computer technology and information technology can be attributed to the energetic steps taken by the late Prime Minister Mr.Rajiv Gandhi and his scientific advisor, Mr. Sam Pitroda. They were also instrumental in initiating a series of Technology missions. Further, if there is decentralization of communication technologies, it will lead to making the country a well-informed one. Such a scenario can help the people to make well-informed choices about the political scenario. This may even result in a topsy-turvy period of transition.

Cultural Factors

Language is one of the major factors that hinder the easy assimilation of ICTs by many developing countries. This hinders transfer of technology. The radio and TV programmes, computer software and the printed texts are produced in different countries bearing different cultural backgrounds. As such, such tools may fail to impress students of another country. For example, a zoology text can safely give the example of a koala in Australia, but the same cannot be replicated in India. With regard to cultural patterns there are two groups of policy makers. Policy makers can be Pro-implementation or Anti- implementation. It is precisely the cultural moorings of a society that makes people either in favour of implementing technology or to reject it. Japanese have over the years built up a reputation of being quick to adapt and implement new technology. This can be linked to the way in which a new culture of receptivity to new ideas was built up after centuries of stagnation when commodore Perry forced the Japanese to open up their society. Again, in recent times it has been seen that the culture of class room teaching and learning has been so strongly built into the psyche of the teaching community that they often exhibit resistance in the way of implementing technological change that forces a change in the role of the teacher from being a store house of all learning to a manager of the teaching-learning process (Bansal, et.al, 1999).

Technological Factors

Very often, technology becomes the determining factor in the growth of ICT in any society. One would be justified in applying the

Bates criteria for media selection as an appropriate parameter for selecting appropriate technology for educational purposes.With regard to the acceptance of a particular technology, the factors such as access, cost, teaching functions, interactiveness and user-friendliness, organizational issues and speed afforded to change are important issues. In the case of Media selection, Bates regards Novelty of a media as the least important criterion on which a particular media should be selected or rejected. However, in the case of many third world countries, it is novelty of a media that attracts the attention of policy makers. For example, in the late70s and 80s, the novelty of TV as a medium influenced the UGC to initiate the Country-Wide Class room programme for the benefit of the college students. However much care was not taken to ensure whether, the programme could generate enough interest in the student community to make the programme a success. Moreover, at the time of its initiation, access to TV sets was also a major problem. Even today the tele-density in India stands at a low 80 per 1000. The end result was that UGC's CWC generated a utilization rate of less than 10 per cent (Sukumar, 2001).

Apart from the factors mentioned above, once a technology is selected, there are certain other factors that need the concern of policy makers. Handling of New technology needs care and technical proficiency. For this training is an important aspect. Many developing countries lack enough personnel to train manpower in new technology. Moreover, constant retraining of manpower to acquaint them with changing technology is also important. These often act as constraints before the smooth growth of ICT. Maintenance of equipment also needs sufficient care. Frequent snags may render equipments unusable. Maintenance as a function also needs sufficiently trained staff, high quality spare parts and machine friendly attitude from the users.

The Human Element

The Human Element is also major importance in the growth and application of new ICT. In many cases, it is seen that the teachers act as a major roadblock against the implementation of new technology. They are not ready to accept any change in their role. With the advent of new ICT teachers are no longer the storehouse of all knowledge, but are more of managers of education. Communication policies of various countries also play a major role in deciding the application of various communication technologies. These policies are a product of social pressure. Policy formulations are based on the kind of role the political elite want that media to play in the process of development of the country. In the Educational field policies should be formulated in such a way that the inter – regional disparities as well as the inter- strata disparities are overcome and equal access is made available to all the segments in their quest for education.

Strategies for Introducing ICTs in HEI (Higher Education Institutes)

Apart from having enabling telecommunications and ICT policies, governments and higher education institutions will need to develop strategies for effective ICT and media deployment and sustainability. A relatively less costly medium that has not been fully exploited in some jurisdictions for educational purposes is the radio. Recognizing the potential reach of this medium, 27 tertiary education institutions in Nigeria have received government licences to operate campus radios for teaching, research and entertainment. Where capacity is lacking for the proper assessment of ICTs and their benefits, institutions would do well to, first, mount training workshops in the areas of ICT procurement, contracting and the total cost of owning particular systems, which includes acquisition, installation, power supply, maintenance, allied material and equipment, replacement, training, recycling, etc. Such training should be undertaken within the context of a technology plan that includes long term budgeting or funding scenarios, acquisition, maintenance, replacement and possible sharing, at least coordination, of ICT usage with other institutions. For governments, it is important for an education ministry to liaise and coordinate efforts with other departments in the country, *e.g.*, Finance, Telecommunications, Industry and Commerce and Economic Development. In developing internal capacity in the use of ICT in teaching, learning, and research, teachers need to be involved in designing particular ICT initiatives to ensure their relevance and effectiveness. Rather than introducing ICT wares across the institution all at once, it is prudent to test the efficacy of a technology at, say, the departmental level before deploying it institution-wide. Such piloting, if successful, will reassure

Institutional policymakers of the soundness of the technology in facilitating improved teaching and, on the part of students, more and better learning outcomes. On the other hand, this must not lead to each department adopting its own IT solutions. Students appreciate having some consistency in the platforms (say for eLearning) that they will find in different parts of the HEI.

The Key Points Emerging from the Review

- The integration of ICTs in higher education is inevitable. The very high demand for higher education has stimulated significant growth in both private and public provision. Open universities, which depend on technology-mediated learning, are expanding and multiplying and many conventional HEIs are adopting dual-mode or blended program delivery systems, creating a new dynamic in flexible and lifelong learning.
- ICT is moving beyond personal computers to mobile technology, Virtual World, Cloud Computing etc. HEIs should integrate these emerging technologies into their ICT policies and programmes. The choice between open sources and proprietary software can sometimes be hijacked by interest groups and ideologies. The sensible policy is to do what is appropriate when it is appropriate after a careful analysis of long-term costs and benefits.
- Institutional and sector-wide higher education ICT policy and planning should identify the specific role of ICT in enhancing research capabilities and provide for adequate infrastructure backed by capacity building. Digital libraries, access to online databases, networking, etc., can be enhanced through interinstitutional collaboration to ensure optimal usage of ICT expertise and resources.
- ICTs in the form of Management Information Systems are increasingly universal. The wide adoption of ICTs calls for mindsets and skill sets that are adaptive to change. An attitude of resistance to change is often caused by the lack of appreciation of the benefits brought by ICTs and the fears about the displacement of people by technology.

Conclusion

Although the use of technology in web-based forms of higher education has grown exponentially in the past decade, it is becoming increasingly obvious that traditional university teaching can also benefit from its advantages. Universities all over Europe invest heavily in course management software, expanded networks, and training and support capabilities to introduce web enhancements to traditional courses. There are at least two fundamental reasons that justify this increased investment. The first is that university education has a responsibility to ensure that future graduates are well versed in the use of ICTs, since, in a knowledge economy, such technologies are an indispensable tool of everyday life in the world of work they hope to enter. There can hardly be a single profession or area of academic endeavour, in which progress is possible without recourse to technology, at some level. This in itself would justify efforts made to ensure the omnipresence of ICTs in universities, the incorporation of specific ICT skills subjects as for instance this reason is obvious: in the knowledge society, ICTs are everywhere, and must therefore be present in university education. One of the best ways of incentivating the use of ICTs as university teaching tools is by providing clear evidence that this technology helps to increase educational benefits, *i.e.*, that students learn more and more effectively – in conditions of equivalent efforts by both teachers and students. The point, however, is that little has been reported on the specific impact of Web enhancements on classroom activities – the face-to-face component of traditional courses – and the nature of that impact.

References

Alabi. (2004). Evolving Role of ICT in Teaching, Research and publishing. Nigeria Tribunal, 30-31.

Bansal, Kiron and Chaudhary, Sonvir, S. (1999), "Interactive radio for supporting distance education: an evaluative study", Indian Journal of open learning.

Balasubramanian, K., Willie Clarke-Okah., Daniel, J., Kanwar, A. (2009). ICT for higher education., UNESCO World Conference on Higher Education, Commonwealth of learning.

Cobb, G. (1992). Teaching statistics. In Heeding the Call for Change: Suggestions for Curricular Action. L.A. Steen, Ed. Washington DC: Mathematical Association of America.

IGNOU (2001). Growth of Communication Technology. Communication Technology for Distance Education, ES- 318, pp.34-40.

IGNOU (2001). Media in Distance Education. Communication Technology for Distance Education, ES-318, pp.28-31.

Kakkar, S.B. (2001). Educational Psychology. Prentice-Hall of India (Pvt.) Ltd., New Delhi.

Oliver, Ron (2002). "The role of ICT in higher education for the 21st century: ICT as a change agent for education. Paper presented in HE21 Conference,

Rajesh, M. (2003). A Study of the problems associated with ICT adaptability in Developing Countries in the context of Distance Education. Turkish Online Journal of Distance Education-(TOJDE), ISSN 1302-6488 Volume:4 Number:2

Sukumar, B.(2001). IGNOU Interactive Radio Counselling: a study, IJOL,10 (1), pp.80-92.

Chapter 6

Agricultural and Sustainable Development Models

☆ *Ganesh Prasad Pokhariyal*

Accurate and timely communication of farm related information enhances knowledge of farmers about the inputs for growing various crops. This in turn injects wisdom to handle marketing aspects of the outputs, which then assists in attaining the cherished goal of sustainable rural development. Communication is derived from the Latin word "communis", meaning to share and is defined as the exchange or imparting of thoughts, ideas, messages, opinions or information by speech, visuals, writings, signals, feelings, gestures or behaviors. Communication requires a sender (source), information and recipients, mostly in an area of common interest. The communication process is assumed to be complete, once the recipient has understood the information by the sender.

Agricultural Communication

Agricultural communication being a subset of communication, is a field of study and work which focuses on communication about agricultural related information among agricultural stake holders and between agricultural and non- agricultural stake holders.

Agricultural stake holders include: farmers; farm laborers; sellers of seeds, fertilizers and grown products; transporters; warehouse owners; insurance companies and consumers. Non-agricultural stake holders include: industries; local, state and central government organizations; international bodies and non-governmental organizations (NGO). Agricultural communication is done formally and informally by agricultural extension and addresses all subject areas related to complex enterprises of food, feed, fiber, renewable energy, natural resource management, rural development and others locally to globally. Furthermore, it spans all participants from scientists to consumers and all stages of enterprises, from agricultural research and production to processing, marketing, consumption, nutrition and health (Wikipedia).

Effective communication is that which produces effect and serves the purpose for which it was planned or designed and ensures that distortion of information does not take place during communication process. It can be achieved through the use of words that are understood by the involved parties. Nonhuman communication which includes cell signaling, cellular communication and chemical transmissions between primitive organisms like bacteria and within the plant and fungal kingdom. The study of animal communication, called zoosemiotics, has played an important part in the development of ethology, sociobiology and the study of animal cognition. It is a rapidly growing field and the areas such as personal symbolic name use, animal emotions, animal culture and learning and even sexual conduct has been revolutionized.

Plants and Fungi Communication

It is observed within plant organisms, especially in the root zone. Plant roots communicate in parallel with rhizome bacteria, with fungi and with insects in the soil. These parallel sign-mediated interactions are governed by syntactic, pragmatic and semantic rules and are possible because of the decentralized "nervous system" of plants. Recent research has shown that most of the inter-organismic plant communication processes are neuronal like. Plants also communicate via volatiles when exposed to herbivore attack behavior, thus warning neighboring plants. In parallel they produce other volatiles to attack parasites which attack these herbivores. In stress situations plants can overwrite the genomes they inherited from their parents and revert to their grand or great-grand parents.

Fungi communicate and organize their growth and development such as formation of mycelia and fruiting bodies. Fungi communicate same or related species as well as with non-fungal organisms in a great variety of symbiotic interactions, especially with bacteria, unicellular eukaryotes, plants and insects through semi-chemicals of biotic origin. Fungal organisms can differ between molecules taking part in biotic messages and similar molecules being irrelevant in the situation. So far five different primary signaling molecules are known to coordinate different behavioral patterns, such as filamentation, mating, growth and pathogenicity.

Bacteria quorum sensing communication is the tool used by microorganism like bacteria, apart from humans, animals and plants. Through quorum sensing, bacteria are able to sense the density of cells and regulate gene expression accordingly (Wikipedia).

Adequate knowledge of human and nonhuman communications could be useful in designing effective strategies for the production and marketing of various types of farm commodities.

Communication Models

The first major model for communication was given by Shannon and Weaver (1949) for Bell Laboratories. The original model was designed to mirror the functioning of radio and telephone technologies and consisted of three primary parts: sender, channel and receiver. This simple model often referred to as the transmission model or standard view of communication, information or content and is based on the following elements like Information source; transmitter, which encodes the message into signals; channel, to which signals are adapted for transmission; receiver, which decodes (reconstructs) the message from the signal and destination, where the message arrives.

However, there are three levels of problems in the implementation of this theory: Technical, which is due to accuracy of message transmission; semantic, which is due to the precision of meaning being conveyed; effectiveness, dealing with how effectively does the received meaning affect behavior.

There is likelihood of the following types of communication noises being involved in using this theory: environmental;

physiological – impairment; semantic; syntactical; organizational; cultural and psychological. The transactional model of communication, developed by Barnlund (2008), has the basic premise that individuals are simultaneously engaging in sending and receiving the messages.

The incorporation of the characteristic features of these two models is adequate enough for efficient agricultural communication, even in the current situation and environment.

Marketing

The discipline of marketing covers the services involved in moving the agricultural products from the farms to the consumers. Many interconnected activities are involved in doing this, such as planning production; growing and harvesting; grading; packing; transport; storage; agricultural, dairy, poultry and meat processing; distribution; advertising and sales. Marketing has to be customer oriented and should be capable of providing profit to the farmer, transporter, trader, processor and all others involved in it.

In various countries considerable agricultural marketing support to farmers is often provided. In the United States the Agricultural Marketing Services (AMS) has programs for cotton, fruits and vegetables, livestock and seed, poultry and tobacco. These programs provide testing, standardization, grading and market new services and oversee marketing agreements and orders, administer research and promotion programs and purchase commodities for federal food program. The AMS also enforces certain federal laws. In the United Kingdom support for marketing of some commodities was provided before and after Second World War by boards such as Milk Marketing Board and Egg Marketing Board, but these were closed in the 1970s. Britain established marketing boards in many former colonies, some of which continue to exist, but many were closed down during 1990s at the time of the introduction of structural adjustment measures. Currently European Union has its own marketing arrangements.

In recent years, many developing countries have established government sponsored marketing or agribusiness units. South Africa, for example, started the National Agricultural Marketing Council (NAMC) as a response to the deregulation of the agriculture industry and closure of marketing boards in the country. India has the long established National Institute of Agricultural Marketing (NIAM). These are primarily research and policy organizations, but other agencies provide facilitating services for marketing channels, such as the provision of infrastructure, market information and documentation support. In Kenya the support to the farmers is provided by various boards, such as: National Cereal and Produce Board, Sisal Board, Tea Board, Pyrethrum Board, Cotton Board, Kenya Dairy Board and Kenya Meat Commission. These boards assist in procurement and sale of the commodities in the local and international markets. There has been considerable interest recently in various countries by NGOs to carry out activities to link farmers to markets.

Efficient marketing infrastructure such as wholesale, retail and assembly markets and storage facilities, is essential for cost effective marketing to minimize post-harvesting losses and to reduce health risks. Markets play an important role in income generation, rural development, food security and establishing linkages with other markets.

Efficient market information provides benefits to farmers and traders. Up to date information on prices and quantities, along with other market factors assist farmers to negotiate with traders and also facilitates spatial distribution of products from rural locations to towns and between markets. Modern communication technologies open up the possibilities for market information services to improve information delivery through SMS on cell phones and FM radio stations. Internet, in future would become an effective way of delivering information between farmers and stakeholders. Marketing training of farmers and enabling environment would also contribute positively towards achieving optimum results.

Sustainable Development

United Nation released the Brundtland report in 1987 by defining, "sustainable development is development that meets the needs of the present without compromising the ability of future generations to meet their own needs". Sustainable development ties together concern for the carrying capacity of natural systems with the social challenges faced by humanity. The concept of sustainable development is often broken out into three constituent parts: environmental sustainability, economic sustainability and sociopolitical sustainability. A Venn diagram has been drawn to represent the intersection between these three parts (Barbier, 1987).

- *Environmental sustainability* requires that human activity only uses nature's resources at a rate at which they can be replenished naturally. Long term result of environmental degradation is the inability to sustain human life. Such degradation on a global scale could imply extinction for humanity.
- *Economic sustainability* involves using the assorted assets of the unit effectively to allow it to continue functioning in a profitable manner over time and is concerned with seeking durable growth solutions. Economic sustainability is about meeting diverse needs as well as providing livelihood and services to communities.
- *Social-political sustainability* is concerned with engagement, modification and advancement of institutional mechanisms. It seeks pathways to durable social enrichment and development through vibrant and healthy political processes of society.

Agriculture in India

India is ranked second worldwide in farm output. Agriculture and allied sectors accounted for 16.6 per cent of GDP in 2009 and about 50 per cent of total workforce. As per 2010 FAO world agriculture statistics, India is world's largest producer of many fresh fruits and vegetables, milk, major spices, selected fresh meats, jute, millet and castor oil. India is the second largest producer of wheat and rice. India is also second or third largest producer of several dry fruits, agriculture based textile raw materials, roots and tuber crops, pulses, farmed fish, eggs, coconut, sugarcane and numerous vegetables. India is ranked within the world's five largest producers of over 80 per cent of agricultural produce items, including many cash crops, such as tea and coffee, in 2010. India is also one of the world's five largest producers of livestock and poultry meat with one of the fastest growth rate, as per 2011. Recent studies claim that India can easily feed its growing population, plus produce wheat and rice for global exports, if it can reduce food staple spoilage, improve its infrastructure and raise its farm productivity to those achieved by other developing countries such as Brazil and China (Wikipedia).

India's arable land area of 159.7 million hectares is the second largest in the world, after United State. Its gross irrigated crop area of 86.6 million hectares is the largest in the world. Although agricultural growth in India increased (doubled in few cases) from 1970-71 to 2010-2011, but as compared to world's most productive farms, average yield (tons per hectare) in India, in most cases is half to one third (2010).

There are many problem areas for agriculture in India. Slow agricultural growth is a concern for policy makers as nearly two third of India's people depend on rural employment for a living. Current agriculture practices are neither economically nor environmentally sustainable. Poorly maintained irrigation systems and almost universal lack of good extension services are problem areas. Farmers' access to markets is hampered by poor road network, rudimentary market infrastructure and excessive regulations (World Bank, 2008).

The required level of investment for development of marketing, storage and cold storage infrastructure is estimated to be too huge. Government has not been able to implement various schemes (like construction of rural godowns, market research and information network, grading and standardization). In this year (2012) summer, due to 19 per cent drop in monsoon rains added further problems to farmers. In response, Bihar government offered farmers over $100 million in subsidized diesel to operate their pumps. Now the delayed rains in August and September, 2012 are causing additional problems to farmers as well as governments.

India's vision 2030 envisages the potential challenges and opportunities in the economic, socio-political and environmental spheres over the next 2 decades. India's vision 2030 argues that there are five broad desired objectives of India's growth and development (meta-outcomes) that are critical for India to achieve: end of endemic poverty and reduction of inequality; progress around social transition; further political consolidation; economic integration and regional geopolitical engagement.

Conceptual Framework

The study in such areas is usually accomplished through the conceptual framework by identifying independent variables, moderating variables, intervening variables and dependent variable (with its determinants).

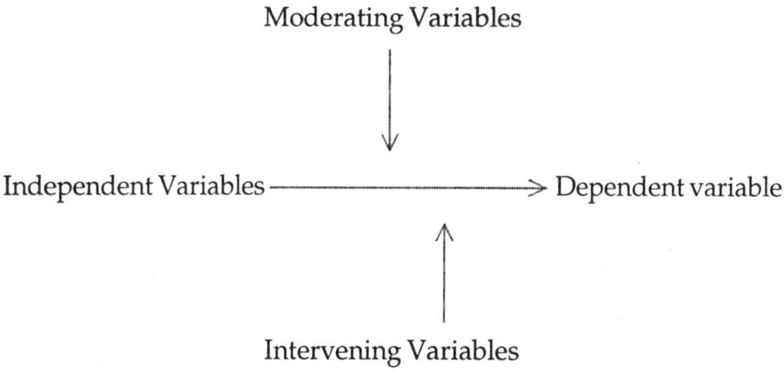

General Model for Sustainable Development

Let Y denote sustainable development, whose determinants are: economic wellbeing; environmental care and protection; competitiveness; healthcare; quality of life and ethical norms followed in the society. Let the independent variables be denoted by X1(seed quality), X2 (fertilizers), X3(labor/machinery), X4 (irrigation), X5(power supply), X6(soil type), X7(communication system), X8(storage facility) and X9(marketing system). Let the moderating variables be denoted by X10(mixed crop), X11(shared labor/machinery) and X12(ethical processes used). Let the intervening variables be denoted by X13(government policies), X14(international economy/market) and X15(regional and international communication systems).

The general model for sustainable development is given by the following multiple regression equation:

Y= a0 + ai Xi + e, where e denotes the error term and i goes from 1 to 15.

Data has to be collected through well designed questionnaire and using Likert's scale of suitable order, so that with data analysis coefficients of model parameters are estimated. In addition, various research hypotheses can be formulated and tested for the undertaken study.

Model for India

India has cultural diversity and as a consequence of this, its agriculture has fairly high degree of variability in terms of agro-ecological zones, inputs, the markets as well as needs. Yet there is good unity at national level even in the diversity and desire for sustainable development. This could be best accomplished through a stratified agricultural and development integrated model. The model consists of three interconnected systems: farm, market and society. Each system has its components that assist in running the system. Some of the developing countries like India require such a model.

Farm system consists of land (its quality and agro-ecological zone); seed quality and its suitability; chosen crop and its maturity duration; irrigation facilities; manpower and machinery; communication facilities in the farm; electricity and other energy sources and weather forecast facility.

Market system consists of proximity to market; road and other transportation network; demand and supply mechanism; economic status of people in and around the market; communication mechanism at the market and ethical practices followed in the market.

Society system consists of people's attitude (their desire and participation in development activities); environment for sustainable development; level and quality of education of people; short term and long term development plans; government and private support for sustainable development; suitable infrastructure and ethical behavior of people.

The functioning of each system, which would be represented by a factor, is governed by its independent variables. Effective interface between these systems is established with the help of efficient and adequate communication mechanism and is considered necessary for the steady state for the stratified integrated model. With the help of factor analysis for the collected data the extent of sustainable development can be determined in the following manner:

$$SD = b0 + b1\,F + b2\,M + b3\,S$$

where, SD denotes sustainable development, F, M and S denote farm, market and society factors respectively. Analysis of variance is then conducted to check the difference in the effectiveness of the factors towards their contribution to sustainable development.

Discussions and Recommendations

The general model can be applied to the countries, where agricultural communication systems are fairly well established and people constitute reasonably good homogenous society. The developers and executors of the systems are knowledgeable and are assumed to follow ethical norms. The countries which consist of dissimilar groups having specific needs and lifestyle require stratified agricultural and development integrated model. Through this model all the people in the country can develop collectively. In a previous study (Pokhariyal, 2007), development strategies for Sub-Saharan Africa with emphasis on attitudes as well as ethical behaviors (dharma) of leaders, administrators and business groups were analyzed and their consequences on development efforts were discussed.

Excessive materialist thinking, attitude of self- interest and inflated ego prominently prevalent in society in India and some other countries hamper efforts for sustainable development. Mechanism of performance measurement for all persons involved would motivate people to work efficiently in achieving the set targets. In this manner the objectives of vision 2030 could be accomplished.

Knowledge gained by researchers and scientists about nonhuman communication should be transmitted to farmers through extension services, seminars and conferences to develop adequate farming strategies and get optimum production. This would supplement the knowledge about human communication and advances in science and technology of communication.

Special care should be taken to develop strategies for India and other countries, as the formulators and executors of short as well as long term policies, in some cases, cannot be absolutely trusted from ethical dimensions.

In future, communication is going to use "Cloud-based system" and "Data farms" for efficiency and bigger volumes. The areas of chemical foods, nano-technology and experiences from outer space would influence all aspects of development on our earth.

References

Baluska F; Marcuso, Stefano and Volkmann, Dieter (2006). Communication in plants: neuronal aspects of plant life; Taylor and Francis US, p 19 ISBN 3-540-28475-3

Barbier, E. (1987): The concept of sustainable economic development. Environmental conservation, 14(2); 101-110.

Barnlund, D.C. (2008). A Transactional Model of Communication. In C.D. Mortensen (Eds.); communication theory (2nd ed., pp47-57), New Brunswick, New Jersey: Transaction.

FAO STAT, 2010 data. Faostat.fao.org; (Wikipedia: retrieved on May 1, 2012)

Handbook of Statistics on Indian Economy (2011). Reserve Bank of India.

Pokhariyal, Ganesh P (2007): Development strategies for sub-Saharan Africa; International Jour. On world peace, vol XXIV No.1, 83-102.

Shannon, C.E. and Weaver, W (1949). Mathematical Theory of Communication, Urbana Illinois; University of Illinois Press.

United Nations (1987): "Repot of the world commission on environment and development" General Assembly Resolution 42/187, 11th December, 1987.

United Nations (2009) Faostat. "Top Production, in India.

United States Department of Agriculture (October, 2011). Livestock and Poultry: World markets and trade".

Wikipedia. Retrieved on May 1, 2012.

World Bank (2008). India Country Overview.

Chapter 7

Indigenous Technical Knowledge (ITK) for Sustainable Agriculture Development in Chhattisgarh

☆ *Poonam Prajapati, Sonu Fartyal and Gulehayat*

Sustainable agriculture includes the practice of low input agricultural production technologies, which attempts to ensure the profitability of farms while preserving the environment. And from the market point of view, these products obtained are sold at profitable prices which would provide incentives for farmers to adopt the necessary methods (Niamh Dennehy *et al.*, 2000). In addition, the farmers also need to be convinced that achieving such production systems for future generations is as crucial as, it is necessary to find a way to prioritize different programs and goals and then allocate resources towards those goals (Kristi N. Hughes and Ledbetter, 2009). Sustainable agriculture is a complex issue associated with producing food while maintaining our biophysical resources including soil, water and biota with no adverse impact on the wider environment.

According to FAO (1991), "Sustainable rural development is the management and conservation of natural resource base and the orientation of technological and institutional change in such a manner as to assure the attainment and continued satisfaction of human needs for the present and future generations.

There is an urgent need to develop farming techniques, which are sustainable from environmental, production and socio-economic point of view. That means to guarantee sufficient food production in the next decades and beyond is critical because modern agriculture production throughout the world does not appear to be sustainable in the long-term. The agricultural community is thus setting it hopes on sustainable agriculture, which will maintain the cycle of input-output and ecosystem balance.

India is the land of diversity. Many cultures, many societies with different ways of living, live in a variety of agro-climatic and geographical situations. It has the long tradition of various settlements *viz.*, Harappan and Mohenjodaro. Fertile rich soils here have given birth to and sustained till to date, many cultures. While in the last thousand years, when many dynasties in the country rose and fell and the society underwent many transformations in its structure, form and group dynamics, a simultaneous slow and steady process of observation, experimentation, understanding and invention was taking place, in these days on the number of farmyards and homesteads of the farmers, all over the country. Several experiments by the farmers, on trial and error basis have been taking place in the field of agriculture and allied fields over thousands of years. They made a wise use of available natural resources and deviced many technologies to increase the quality and quantity of the output of various enterprises, they had undertaken. The knowledge thus generated over the years is time tested and has the attribute of eco-friendliness. Such knowledge is called the 'indigenous technical knowledge (ITK)' or 'local knowledge' or 'traditional knowledge'. This knowledge is based on experience, often tested over centuries of use, adapted to local culture and environment and is dynamic and changing.

People's technology is local wisdom that is unique to a given culture or society. It is the basis for local level decision making in agriculture, health care, food preparation, natural resource management and a host of other activities in rural society. Such knowledge is passed down from generation to generation, in many societies by word of mouth. India has a rich tradition of oral knowledge that goes back to the Vedic times. Much of that wisdom is being rediscovered by modern world. This is true of Indian agriculture as well; a rich heritage of accumulated indigenous agriculture knowledge is being practiced.

Definition of ITK

"It is the systematic body of knowledge by local people through the accumulation of experiences, informal experiments, and intimate understanding of the environment in a given culture" (Rajasekaran, 1993).

The term "indigenous knowledge" has been defined as "the unique, traditional, local knowledge existing within and developed around the specific conditions of women and men indigenous to a particular geographic area." (Gremier, louise 1998).

The Special Features of Indigenous Knowledge

- ☆ Local in that it is rooted in a particular community and situated within broader cultural traditions; it is a set of experiences generated by people living is those communities. Separating the technical from the non-technical, the rational from the non-rational could be problematic. Therefore, when transferred to other places, there is a potential risk of dislocating indigenous knowledge.
- ☆ Tacit knowledge and, therefore, not easily codifiable.
- ☆ Transmitted orally, or through imitation and demonstration. Codifying it may lead to the loss of its properties.
- ☆ Experiential rather than theoretical knowledge. Experience and trial and error, tested in the rigorous laboratory of survival of local communities constantly reinforce indigenous knowledge.
- ☆ Learned through repetition, which is a defining characteristic of tradition even when new knowledge is

added. Repetition aids in the retention and reinforcement of indigenous knowledge.

- Constantly changing, being produced, discovered as well as lost; though it is often perceived by external observers as being somewhat static.

Principles of ITK

1. Holistic view
2. Community based farming
3. Optimal use of local resources
4. Reliance on genetic and physical diversity
5. Soil protection and recycling natural nutrient
6. Risk minimization
7. Location specific techniques

ITK principle also similar with sustainable agriculture principles so we can say that ITK promotes sustainable agriculture techniques also but scientific systems of knowledge *i.e.* use of chemical, high cost new technology etc. are not based on the sustainable agriculture. Following difference between tradition knowledge system and western scientific system help us to understand how tradition knowledge is similar to sustainable agriculture.

Differences between Traditional Knowledge System and Western Scientific System

Differences between Traditional Knowledge System and Western Scientific System is given in Table 7.1.

Thematic Areas of ITK

In the book of ICAR Inventory of Indigenous Technical Knowledge in Agriculture Document: 1, identified and classified different indigenous knowledge of India in different theme that are giving in Table 7.2.

ITK of Chhattisgarh

The Chhattisgarh state is popularly recognized as rice bowl of the country as rice is the principal crop of this state and about 70 per cent of net sown area is covered under rice. Other major crops are

Table 7.1: Differences between Traditional Knowledge System and Western Scientific System

Traditional Knowledge System	*Western Scientific System*
All parts of the natural world are regarded as animate, all life forms as interdependent.	Human life is generally regarded as superior, with a moral right to control other life forms.
Knowledge is transmitted largely through oral media.	Knowledge is transmitted largely through the written word.
Knowledge is developed and acquired through observation and practical experience	Knowledge is generally learned in a situation, which is remote from its applied context.
All parts of the natural world are regarded as animate, all life forms as interdependent.	Human life is generally regarded as superior, with a moral right to control other life forms.
Knowledge is transmitted largely through oral media.	Knowledge is transmitted largely through the written word.
Knowledge is developed and acquired through observation and practical experience	Knowledge is generally learned in a situation, which is remote from its applied context.

Table 7.2

Theme	*No. of ITK*
Veterinary and animal husbandry	556
Pest and disease management	232
Grain/seed storage	177
Horticultural crops	164
Crops and cropping systems	148
Ethno-botany and bio-diversity	102
Ethnic food	92
Farm implements	89
Food product development	61
Weather forecasting	55
Soil and water conservation	48
Rain water management	43
Soil fertility management	35
Tillage practices	33
Fishery	31
Housing material	29
Natural yarns,dyes and weaves	24
Thermal efficiency	12
Fuel management	09
Garbage disposal and management	09
Wind erosion	05
Waste water management	05
Post-harvest technology	04
Unclassified	35
TOTAL	**1998**

Source: (2000) Inventory of Indigenous Technical Knowledge in Agriculture. Document 1 and 2. 2000. ICAR, Delhi.

wheat, maize, pulses and oil seeds. Horticulture crops such as mango, banana, guava, jackfruit, custard apple, ber and vegetables are successfully grown in large areas of state. The cropping intensity of the state is 137 per cent. Due to rice based farming system, many of the ITKs of Chhattisgarh are related with rice farming.

Table 7.3

Code No.	Title of ITK	Description of the ITK
1759	Preparation of bunds in rice field	Chhattisgarh region receive heavy rainfall during July and August. For that time, rice is the only crop suitable for that area. But at later stages terminal drought condition affected crop severely at reproductive stage. For water management practices, farmers constructed huge rice dykes (bunds) and impounded water for 30-40 cm in the rice field after vegetative phase. To tolerate this condition, traditionally tall rice varieties cultivated.
1767	Summer ploughing in rice field	Summer ploughing of rice fields is adopted by farmers after receiving rains during summer. This is practiced to reduce insect and weed population in the field. Farmers of Raipur/districts/ of Chhattisgarh are practicing this method.
1779	Direct seeding of rice	Beushening operation followed by gap filling and weeding in rice practiced by small holding farmers of Chhattisgarh region. The direct seeding of rice with beushening operation give sustainable yield when compared to transplanting rice under rain fed conditions. Normal transplanting is required, analysis shows most of the areas does not have stable rainfall during July in Chhattisgarh, and farmers of Chhattisgarh region have adopted this practice to over come the drought problem, since many years.
1780	Rice based cropping system in rainfed condition	Traditional tall and long duration varieties are being cultivated under the beushening system by the farmers of Chhattisgarh region. If the plant population under beushening system became low after beushening, lathyrus seeds or linseed are broadcasted as a relay crop in the paddy field. About 60kg/ha lathyrus seeds are sown in standing water in the rice field 15 to 20 days prior maturity and harvested 5q/ha lathyrus without using any other inputs and tillage operations. A farmer taking bonus crop and the lathyrus husk is used for animal feed.
1781	Crop rotation practices	Colocasia and other vegetable crops are raised in the sweet potato harvested field. Due to this crcp rotation, life cycle of sweet potato weevil got disrupted. Farmers of Raipur districts in Chhattisgarh have been adopting this method, since several years.

Contd...

Table 7.3–Contd...

Code No.	*Title of ITK*	*Description of the ITK*
1822	Pest management in rice	Farmers of Raipur district in Chhattisgarh are practicing some methods to control pests in rice which are indicated here. Kodo straw is spreaded over stagnated water to control pests and salfi palm and karla sticks are installed in stagnated water to reduce the insects. Salfi palm, kodo straw and karla sticks have some insecticidal properties which reduce the insect population.
1865	Method of wheat seed storage	Wheat seeds are stored in gunny bags in houses and these are covered with dried straw of about 3 inches thick layer from all the direction including bottom. This practice ensures 100 per cent seed protection from all storage pests including rodents. This is due to coverage of straw all around the seed material creating an anaerobic condition in the vicinity of seeds resulting in unfavorable condition for development and multiplication of storage pests.
1866	Storage of vegetable seeds	Vegetable seeds like bhindi, tomato, brinjal etc. are stored in bamboo, wrapped with shevni leaves. This practice of storage of vegetable seeds lasts for one year. Farmers of Raipur district in Chhattisgarh have adopted this practice.

Source: Inventory of Indigenous Technical Knowledge in Agriculture. Document 1 and 2. 2000. ICAR, Delhi.

Inventory of Indigenous Technical Knowledge in Agriculture. Document 1 and 2. 2000. ICAR, Delhi is given code no. to each ITK and also describes ITK from particular area. These are ITK of Chhattisgarh given in Table 7.3

Conclusion

It could be concluded that majority of the farmers have significant adoption of those indigenous agricultural practices which involve low cost or almost no cost and not much scientific technique. Indigenous crop cultivation practices are generally organic in nature; do not cause damage to air, water and soil and safe to human beings. Indigenous practices differ considerably from region to region depending on soil type, rainfall, topography etc., and often show modification by local farmers.

Indigenous knowledge, therefore, becomes important, which would otherwise be lost soon, not be regained at any cost. Abstracting the science of indigenous knowledge system would certainly help us to understand the concepts and practices depicting the elements of sustainability to integrate with the modern information system, for efficient resource management. In recent years, there has been a growing scientific interest in these indigenous practices as a source of sound ideas that could lead to sustainable use and management of natural resources.

References

Anonymous, (2000). "Inventory of Indigenous Technical Knowledge in Agriculture." Document 1 and 2. ICAR, Delhi.

Barik, M.K. and Parasar,B.(2000), "Indigenous knowledge of Farmers on Agriculture and Animal Husbandary in North-Western Agro-Climatic Zone of Orrisa." J. Ext. Edu. Vol. V Nos.1 and 2, (2000),:107-110.

Kalaivani,S.,Seetharaman Netaji, R. and Oliver, J. (1998) "Effect of Indigenous Knowledge on Adoption of Gardenland Technologies." J. Ext. Edu. Vol.9 Nos.3 1998. 2075-2079.

Nagnur,Shobha, and Channal Geeta (2004), "Indigenous knowledge System for Sustainable Rural Healthcare." Ind. Res. J. Ext. Edu. Vol.4, No.1 and 2, Jan. and July 2004: 233-236.

Narayanagowda, K., Ranganath, M. and Siddaramaiah, B.S. (2004), "People's Technologies in the Farm sector – A Scientific Approach for sustainability. Manage Ext. Res. Review, July-Dec. (2004).

Pal Singh, Mahendra (2001), "Indigenous Technologies for Safe Storage." Intensive Agriculture, March-April (2001); 17-19.

Pavathi,S., Chandrakandan,K. and Karthikeyan (1996); "Adoption of Indigenous and Modern Post Practices followed by Dry land Farm Women." J. Ext. Edu. Vol. 7 No.1 (1996). 1322-1326.

Pradhan, L., Nayak, M.P.,Mahapatra, A. K. and BaliarSingh,A. (2003) "Indigenous Grain Storage Practices: A Study at Bhadrakh District." J. Ext. Edu. Vol.VIII,Nos. 1 and 2, 2003.

Prasad,M.V. (2009), "Indigenous knowledge use in Maize cultivation in Andhra Pradesh." Indian Res. J. Ext. (1), January 2009: 65-70

Savaliya, V. J., Kanani, P. R. and Popat, M. N. (2003), "Indigenous Plant Protection Measures Adopted by Farmers." Ag. Ext.Review, Sep- Oct (2003): 3-5

Shinde,P.S.,Vaidya,V.R.,and Satpute, S. K. (2000). "Identification and adoption of Indigenous Agricultural practices by Dryland Farmers." Maharashtra J. Exten. Edu. XIX, 2000: 259-263.

Singh, R. P. and Tiwari Amberish, (2004), "Wood and Stone Houses : An ITK to Disaster management." Ind. Res. J. Ext. Edu. Vol-4, No.-3, Sep-2004 :10-13.

Somasundaram, E. and Amanullah Mohamed, M.(2008), "Indigenous knowledge (ITK): Organic resource of sustainable agriculture", Green Farming 1(6): 37-39,March 2008.

Thorat, V. S., Patil, V.G. and Dhekale, J. S. (2003) "Indigenous technological Knowledge about Nutrient management in Coconut Production." Maharashtra J. Ext. Edu. XXII (2),2003: 156-157.

Chapter 8

Using Information and Communication Technologies for Agricultural Extension in India

☆ *Kiran Arya, M.A. Ansari and Manmeet Kaure*

In India, the role of agricultural extension in improving agricultural growth is today being recognized with increasing investment. India's 10th and 11th five-year plans emphasize agricultural extension as a key to increasing agricultural growth by reducing the yield gap in farmer fields, and therefore stress the need to strengthen agricultural extension in India **(Planning Commission 2001, 2005, 2006)**. The efficiency and effectiveness of agricultural extension, in the context of poverty alleviation, is directly related to the achievement of precise and measurable sustainable rural livelihoods outcomes. Agriculture defined as the production, processing and distribution of food, fish, and forest products. Traditional public-sector programs have attempted to overcome barriers to technological adoption by using agricultural extension services at the village or farm level. Yet despite decades of experience with a variety of extension programs and new technologies, adoption rates still remain relatively low in low-income countries ICT interventions that directly relate to the agricultural sector and that contribute to sustainable rural livelihoods outcomes.

The rapid spread of mobile phone coverage in developing countries provides a inimitable opportunity to facilitate technological adoption via ICT-based agricultural extension programs. This paper provides a review of using ICT for agriculture, with a particular focus on agricultural extension.

Recent global food price increases and high levels of inflation have provided an opportunity to increase farmers' profitability. However, to realize the benefit of higher prices, farmers need to access a wider range of information, related not only to production technologies but also to postharvest processes, access to remunerative markets, price information, and business development (Sulaiman and van den Ban 2003). This information could be integrated with services that support the use of the information. For example, technology information needs to be supported with information about reliable sources for that technology, and where credit can be accessed.

Background

Today governments and public extension institutions are challenged to adopt diversified and pluralistic national strategies to build dialogue and collaboration among a variety of public, private, non-governmental and community based entities to promote extension to improve rural livelihoods.

Extension brings information and new technologies to farming communities, allowing them to improve their production, income and standard of living. In the past, extension was seen primarily as a public service, institutionalised and organised by national governments. Several emerging challenges confront Indian farmers. These include limited land and water availability, which is further exacerbated by degradation of natural resources; climate changes; changes in demand and consumption patterns, moving toward high-value agriculture; increasing population pressure; and liberalization of trade (Lele *et al.*, 2010).

ICTs and Agricultural Extension

ICTs are those technologies that can be used to interlink information technology devices such as personal computers with communication technologies such as telephones and their telecommunication networks. The PC and laptop with e-mail and Internet provides the best example. Michiels and Van Crowder (2001) have defined ICTs 'as a range of electronic technologies which when converged in new configurations are flexible, adaptable, enabling and capable of transforming organisations and redefining social relations'. The range of technologies is increasing all the time and 'there is a convergence between the new technologies and conventional media' (Michiels and Van Crowder, 2001:8).

An increase in the use of Information and Communications Technology (ICT) in almost all spheres of life, and this will continue to influence every aspect of human endeavour in the knowledge era. ICT potential and its ability to support integrated development with long-term social and economic benefits have been recognized globally, and policy guidelines are being framed for its use despite problems of access, connectivity, literacy, contents and costs. Extension, which depends to a large extent, on information exchange, has been identified as one area in which ICT can have a significant impact.

The dimensions and scope of extension services are changing due to socio-economic factors; and face challenges in areas of relevance, accountability and sustainability. Agriculture is becoming knowledge-based and future agricultural growth would largely accrue from improvements in productivity of diversified farming systems. Information requirements of the farmers and rural youth are increasing and linear information flows that dominated the traditional model of technology transfer are being replaced by pluralistic information flows.

Arokoyo (2005) reported that a strong agricultural extension linkage complimented by flawless information flow enhanced by the effective use of information and communication technologies (ICT) will significantly boost agricultural production and improve rural livelihoods. As Carl Greenridge (2003) highlighted the importance of focus on participants, the important question is how to harness ICTs meaningfully to remedy the many ailments and challenges facing the rural poor.

This focus on rural livelihoods over agriculture-specific extension services was also a key theme of the pre-consultation email dialogue (Ballantyne and Bokre, 2003) which defined extension as aiming to:

- Improve the wellbeing of individuals and communities
- Change production systems so that they improve rural livelihoods and sustain the resource base
- Improve agriculture and the social, economic and political status of rural communities
- Improve the wellbeing of farm families
- Improve productivity and livelihoods for farmers
- Increase and improve farmers' incomes and productivity on a sustainable basis Enhance farmers' production

Extension is typically seen as a service – public or private – that responds to the needs of farmers and rural people for knowledge they can use to improve their productivity, income and welfare, and to manage the natural resources on which they depend in a sustainable way. Lightfoot (2003) challenged Observatory participants to develop operational procedures and guidelines, harnessing

ICTs where Appropriate

- Facilitate multi-stakeholder collaboration and bring together partners – farmers
- NGOs
- Private and public service providers
- Local government- for demand driven extension Nurture different approaches so that stakeholders organize demand-driven extension services in their own way Prioritise farmers' demands and target groups to maximize impact on poverty reduction Build local capacity – for farmers to articulate and communicate their demands
- Extension service providers to respond to those demands
- Stakeholders to form multi-stakeholder collaborative partnerships Reach the poor – who are rarely well organised, who have little or no voice, and who need

services such as health, education and credit that can be coordinated with the assistance of extension managers.

Information Needs and Preferred Information Medium

Agricultural extension, or agricultural advisory services, comprises the entire set of organizations that support people engaged in agricultural production and facilitate their efforts to solve problems; link to markets and other players in the agricultural value chain; and obtain information, skills, and technologies to improve their livelihoods (Birner *et al.*, 2009; Davis 2009).

Agricultural extension is now seen as playing a wider role by developing human and social capital, enhancing skills and knowledge for production and processing, facilitating access to markets and trade, organizing farmers and producer groups, and working with farmers toward sustainable natural resource management practices (Swanson 2008).

Farmers Require Information Related to the Following (Van den Ban 1998)

- Most appropriate technological options
- Management of technologies, including optimal use of inputs
- Changing farm system options (mixed farming and diversification, animal husbandry, fisheries)
- Sourcing reputable input suppliers
- Collective action with other farmers
- Consumer and market demands for products
- Quality specifications for produce
- Time to buy inputs and sell produce
- Off-farm income-generation options
- Implications of changing policies (input subsidies, trade liberalization)
- Access to credit and loans
- Sustainable natural resource management and coping with climate change

How ICTs could affect Agricultural Extension

ICT is an umbrella term that includes any communication device or application, such as radio, television, mobile phones, computers and network hardware and software. Over the past decade has introduced a new search technology that offers several advantages over other alternatives in terms of cost, geographic coverage and ease of use (Aker and Mbiti 2010).

- ✰ *Mobile phones*: Mobile phones can improve access to and use of private information about agricultural technologies, thereby potentially improving farmers' learning. As previously discussed, farmers have information needs at various stages and on various topics for the agricultural production process. Traditionally, farmers in developing countries have obtained such information from personal visits, radio and to a lesser extent, landlines and newspapers. Mobile phones, by contrast, can reduce costs of obtaining this information as compared with other information mechanisms.
- ✰ *Voice-based information delivery services*: Voice-based information delivery services include a telephonebased information delivery service that provides advice on farming methods and market access (*e.g.*, a hotline). Some use callin centers for agricultural extension support (ie, Cameroon). More complex voice technology uses a simple telephone – community fixed phone or mobile – as the medium of information exchange while sophisticated communication technology and computing applications have been configured at the backend platform for the provision of the requisite information service.
- ✰ *Radio dial-up and broadcasts*: Radio dial-up and broadcasts include regular radio broadcasts that provide market prices or other agricultural information and dialup radio that feature a series of short segment audio programs that provide smallscale farmers telephone access to relevant information through an automated voice system. This radio system is an information hub featuring a regularly updated, diverse menu of prerecorded agricultural content. In some cases, the systems allow farmers to ask

questions via SMS and the responses are disseminated via the radio.

- *SMS-based extension* services: SMS-based extension services essentially use message-based platforms to collect and disseminate information. This includes data collection via a simple SMS-based questionnaire; sending an SMS-based code to request potential information (on market prices or for simple agricultural questions) and receiving the response via SMS; and receiving mass SMS on agricultural topics.
- *E-learning*: A telecentre is a public place where people can access computers, the Internet, and other digital technologies that enable them to gather information, create, learn, and communicate with others while they develop essential 21st-century digital skills. While each telecentre is different, their common focus is on the use of digital technologies to support community, economic, educational, and social development – reducing isolation, bridging the digital divide, promoting health issues, creating economic opportunities, and reaching out to youth. According to the International Telecommunication Union (ITU), the magnitude of the digital divide has remained unchanged from 2002 to 2007, in spite of significant improvement in ICT development among the developing nations (ITU 2009).
- *Voice calls and SMS*: Voice calls and SMS between farmers and extension agents can be used to collect data on the use of new technologies, costs and yields on a more frequent basis, rather than waiting for annual agricultural surveys, when recall data on costs and production are often subject to measurement error. In addition, mobile phones can be used to verify agents' visits, as has been done with cameras in schools in India (Duflo, Hanna and Ryan 2007).
- *e-Choupal*: e-Choupal is a commercial agricultural communication and information dissemination network for Indian farmers. It was developed by ITC, one of India's leading private companies, with annual revenues of over US$2bn (Annamalai and Rao, 2003). The word choupal means 'village gathering place' in Hindi. Farmers recruited

by the company act as kiosk operators. The model is designed to assist lead farmers (who act as local extensionists) at the frontline (the company providing the service) of the ITC supply chain with a variety of agricultural extension and market information.

Farmers often have little information about real market prices, price trends and market conditions. 'As a result, traders are well positioned to exploit both farmers and buyers through practices that sustain system-wide inefficiencies.' (Annamalai and Rao, 2003) Farmers access e-Choupal at village Internet kiosks, and use the system primarily for ecommerce. According to one report (Sawhney, 2002) the results have been impressive: In 2000, the Indian Tobacco Company (ITC) launched an initiative called e-Choupal. The project is a private commercial initiative in agricultural extension. The e-Choupal initiative, which consists of 6,500 kiosks, serves four million farmers in 40,000 villages in 10 states (ITC 2010a). Essentially, e-Choupal is a kiosk located in a village and equipped with computers with Internet access. To manage the e-Choupal, ITC identifies and trains a local farmer (Sanchalak), who bears the operative costs.

The Impact of ICTs on Information, Agricultural Adoption and Agricultural Extension

The power of knowledge for development can be greatly enhanced by ICTs if they are harnessed to improve access and break down barriers to knowledge because 'while education develops cognitive skills, information gives content to knowledge' (UNDP, 2001:35). In this sense the use of ICTs is integral to realising the potential of collective knowledge as the technologies themselves represent tools for achieving development and not merely the rewards of it (UNDP, 2001).Broadly speaking, technology is the "relationship between inputs and outputs" (Foster and Rosenzweig 2010), or the set of hardware (physical) and software (techniques) tools that allow for a different mapping of inputs to outputs. In the context of agriculture, hardware refers to improved cultivars (seeds), fertilizers and pesticides, whereas software refers to practices such as inter-cropping, mulching, and integrated pest management.7 In this context, technology adoption is therefore defined as the "use of new tools or techniques that relate inputs to outputs and the allocation of inputs" (Foster and Rosenzweig 2010).

Effective adoption of Information and Communication Technologies (ICT) now has a proven record in many parts of the world and a demonstrated potential to attain significant economic, social and environmental benefits at local, national and global levels. Rogers, (1962) provides a general framework, user acceptance of ICT is discussed by Venkatesh et.al. (2003) and the economics of specific agricultural technologies are reviewed by Grilliches, Z, (1957, 1988) and Gelb, Kislev, Voet (1996).

Conclusion

The growth of ICT in developing countries offers a new technology and new opportunities for accessing information in poor countries. One of the mechanisms is sharing information via agricultural extension, which has long been plagued with problems related to scale, sustainability, relevance and responsiveness. ICTs can be harnessed to have a direct impact on enhancing both rural livelihoods and the agricultural sector in which the rural poor are immersed. However, ICTs can truly enhance rural livelihoods, are to be avoided. The growth of ICT in developing countries offers a new technology and new opportunities for accessing information in poor countries. One of the mechanisms is sharing information via agricultural extension, which has long been plagued with problems related to scale, sustainability, relevance and responsiveness.

References

Annamalai, K. and Rao, S. (2003) What Works: ITC's e-Choupal and Profitable Rural Transformation. University of Michigan, Ann Arbor, MI, USA: World Resources Institute, Digital Dividend Project. Annual Review of Economics. 2: 395-424.

Ballantyne, P. and Bokre, D. (2003) Report from the 'PrepCom' (for CTA's Sixth Consultative Expert Meeting of its Observatory on ICTs). Wageningen, the ICTS – Transforming Agricultural Extension? Development. Washington, D.C.

Duflo, Esther, Rema Hanna and Stephen Ryan. 2007. "Monitoring Works: Getting Teachers to Come to School." BREAD Working Paper No. 103.

Foster, Andrew and Mark Rosenzweig. 2010. "Microeconomics of Technology Adoption."

Gelb, E., Kislev, Y., Voet, H. (1996). A computer in the milking parlor. Working paper 9805. The Center for Agricultural Economic Research, Rehovot, Israel.

Greenridge, C. (2003) Welcome Address: ICTs Transforming Agricultural Extension? Presentation to CTA's Sixth Consultative Expert Meeting of its Observatory on ICTs. Wageningen, the Netherlands: CTA.

Grilliches, Z. (1957). Hybrid Corn: An Exploration in the Economics of Technological Change. Econometrica, Vol. 25, p. 501-522

Grilliches, Z. (1988). Hybrid Corn: An Explanation in the Economics of Technological Change." Technology, Education, and Productivity. New York: Basil Blackwell, page 28.

ITC (Indian Tobacco Company). 2010. e-Choupal. < http://www.itcportal.com/rural-development/echoupal.htm>. Accessed June11, 2010.

ITU (2009) "New ITU ICT Development Index compares 154 countries", ITU Press Release, 2 March 2009 (http://www.itu.int/newsroom/press_releases/2009/07.html).

Lele, U., *et al.*, 2010. Transforming agricultural research for development. Paper presented at the Global Conference on Agricultural Research for Development, Montpellier, France.

Lightfoot, C. (2003) Demand-driven extension: some challenges for policy makers and managers. Presentation to CTA's Sixth Consultative Expert Meeting of its Observatory on ICTs. Wageningen, the Netherlands: CTA.

Michiels, S.I. and Van Crowder, L. (2001) 'Discovering the 'Magic Box': Local Appropriation of Information and Communication Technologies (ICTs).' SDRE, FAO, Rome.

Planning Commission 2006. Towards faster and more inclusive growth: An approach to the 11th five year plan (2007–2012). New Delhi: Yojana Bhavan.

Planning Commission. 2001. Approach paper to the tenth five year plan (2002–2007). New Delhi: Yojana Bhavan.

Planning Commission. 2005. Midterm appraisal of the 10th five year plan (2002–2007). <http://planningcommission.nic.in/plans/mta/midterm/midtermapp.html>. Accessed July 14, 2010.

Rogers, E. (1962). Diffusion of Innovations. Free Press ISBN 0-7432-2209-1

Sawhney, M. (2002) Fields of Digital Dreams: E -commerce can flourish anywhere if you build the right business model. CIO Magazine, 15 October 2002.

Sulaiman, R., and A.W. van den Ban. 2003. Funding and delivering agricultural extension in India. Journal of International Agricultural and Extension Education 10(1): 21–30.

UNDP (2001) Human Development Report 2001. Making Technologies Work for Huma

www.cta.int/observatory2003/keynote_papers/Challenges_in-demanddriven_extension.pdf

www.cta.int/observatory2003/keynote_papers/Welcome.pdf

Chapter 9

Emerging ICTs and their Potential in Fortifying Small Scale Agriculture in India

☆ *Choudhary Kuldeep and Lathiya Amit*

The agricultural sector has been described as the engine for economic growth and improved livelihoods in India. The majority of the population in India lives in rural areas and depends directly or indirectly on agriculture. Agriculture contributes about 17 per cent to the Gross Domestic Product (GDP) of India.

India has made significant strides in agriculture and associated activities. The Green, Yellow, White and Blue revolutions are testimony to the progress made. Concurrently India has successfully embarked upon a "Cyber revolution". Despite the progress made in agriculture, information technology and the Cyber revolution integrating them to alleviate the above constraints is still incomplete. Without doubt agricultural information technology has the potential and will play a vital role in transforming India into a stable and prosperous democracy within this 21st century.

Small-scale agriculture and the harvesting of natural resources provide livelihoods for majority of the Indian population. Small-scale farmers have certain defining characteristics: they derive their livelihood from holdings of less than 2-5 hectares.(usually less than 2 hectares), in normal circumstances they own between 10 to 20 heads of livestock, although often, they have less than 2 or none at all (Hirst *et al.*, 1988). Small-scale farmers also tend to practice a mix of commercial and subsistence production (in crops and/or livestock). The family provides the majority of labour, while the farm provides the principle source of income (Narayanan and Gulati 2002; Davis 2006).

To improve productivity, these smallholders need access to improved technologies, best practices, and to appropriate, timely and comprehensive information and knowledge on production, value addition and markets. The FAO (2000) asserts that 'information and knowledge play a key role in ensuring food security and sustainable development'. Thus, ICTs are considered to be cross-cutting drivers of change for rural and agricultural development, by connecting rural and remote communities, and improving healthcare, education and agricultural productivity (Richardson 1997). ICTs can, for example, speed up the extension of development services, can be instrumental in strengthening partnerships and in providing a framework for shared learning. A networked information economy helps to achieve competitiveness, and although it cannot in itself solve poverty, hunger and disease, it provides new avenues for cultural production, creates new economic opportunity, and facilitates the sharing and dissemination of scientific outputs and innovative linkages between farmers, scientists and other actors (Benkler 2006). It is not surprising, therefore, that ICTs have led to increased use of a networked information environment and the development of platforms for better sharing and exchange of information and knowledge.

The system of modern farming system has recognized the importance of ICT initiatives in India, and noted that relatively little attention had been paid to the potential benefits in the broader use of ICTs to small-scale agriculture. In this paper aspects of the scoping study are presented, which focus on the challenges faced by small-scale farmers, and the potential of emerging ICTs in revitalizing small scale agriculture in India.

ICT adoption in agriculture in other countries over the past years is reviewed by Gelb *et al.*, 1999. Within this context the Indian agricultural scene is still in the process of rationalizing production and adopting itself to the graduation of the economy from a traditional farming society to an industrialized, market oriented economy. The process includes adopting modern practices, new crops and varieties of traditional staples, information utilization as a production factor and management tool, response to supply and demand on local and international markets and integration of agriculture into broader national environmental and other policies. ICT is now accepted as a dominant tool to achieve national and individual goals for agricultural production and sustained rural economic viability. In order to get a rough outline and information on ICT adoption and constraints in India a study was undertaken to identify the information needs of farmers and bottlenecks in the use of ICT.

ICT and Indian Agriculture

Indian Agriculture contributes 17 per cent of our GDP, and approximately 55 per cent Indians derive their livelihood from the agricultural sector. Today's farmers want not only the two-time bread for their families from their hard sweat, but also surplus food production, which can be sold in the market to get sufficient money to fulfill their other daily needs. Also, private sector initiatives like contract farming have commercialized the Indian agricultural sector. It has also seen many new concepts and theories substituting the traditional methods. Introduction of Information and Communication Technology (ICT) is one of them, which enables the dissemination of requisite information at the right time. This revolution in information technology has made access to the information easy and cost-effective.

Need of ICT in Indian Agriculture

At present, the ratio of the farmers to the extension worker is 1000:1, which is really very less. Although the appointed Village Local Workers (VLWs) disseminate the information, they hardly accept any accountability. These two issues have created the urgency to help and guide the poor farmers properly. The cost factor in face-to-face information dissemination at the right time, and the difficulties in reaching the target audiences, has also created the urgency to introduce ICT. It is only by the introduction of ICT that information can also be upgraded at the least cost. There are several models of ICTs in Indian agriculture, which have made a significant difference in the delivery of services in Indian agriculture like, the establishments of Kisan Call Centers, Gyandoot project, Bhoomi project, Village Knowledge Centers, and AGMARKNET.

India's Position in Use of ICTs

India is positioned as the highest English speaking population in Asia with the highest number of Information Kiosks implemented across rural sectors. 45 per cent of the worlds' ICT projects are implemented in India. India also has a proposal for Rural Info Kiosk project where in one Rural Info Kiosk in each of the 600,000 villages will be established.

Unique Features of Successful ICT Projects in India

- The "Bhoomi" project (digitalized land records) in Karnataka today serves as an excellent example of governance in its ideal form, transparent and accountable.
- e-Shringula, a one-stop, Web-enabled portal for information and services relating to the government-citizen interface creating an "e-Shringula" ("electronic chain") of information and e-governance.
- 'Drishtee' besides providing technical expertise and management consultancy to build the IT infrastructure and the human capacity to link service providers (government department and private firms) with rural citizens.
- 'Info-Village' of Puducherry by MSSRF developed community ownership and collective action with a "pro-poor", "pro-nature" and "pro-women" approach to development.
- In Gyan Ganga project, Gujarat all comprehensive education, support and services including agriculture and veterinary services were provided.
- 'e-Choupal' is a huge private sector investment by ICT, which revolutionized agricultural commodity marketing in India procuring Soya, Coffee, and Prawns at the doorsteps of the villagers and provides all real time data on crop prices, products and services and facilitate supply of high quality farm inputs in partnership mode.

- ICT devices into the management of operations of the National Dairy Development Board and their milk collection centres in Gujarat and the Swayam Krishi Sangram (SKS) smart cards project use of ICT to reduce transaction costs and reduce the cost of credit are other two successful examples of commercial ventures of ICT in India.
- Info knowledge Village at Puducherry, Warna Wired Village project in Maharashtra, Krishi Vigyan Kendras of ICAR at Ahmednagar and Baramati provided quality offline, static content including packages of practices, recommendations, locally relevant technologies, government schemes, FAQ etc. in local languages.
- Women empowerment through SEWA in Gujarat, mobile classrooms through IT buses in rural Pune, Project Shiksha – computer literacy, Action Aid at Bolangir, Orissa, Akshaya at Malappuram, Kerala, and EDUSAT address the issue of capacity building and empowerment of farmers, farm women, rural artisans and also large number of extension personnel and use of ICT for education and alleviation of poverty from rural sector.
- SATCOM, Madhya Pradesh, Teja TV in Andhra Pradesh and E-TV telecasted programmes on location specific agricultural technologies integrated and Interactive live question answer sessions in local languages resulting in high percentage of farmer-viewers.

Issues in ICT implementation in Indian Agriculture

There are various issues of importance which has to be considered for successful implementation of ICT in Indian agriculture. The most important ones are:

1. *Regional priorities*: The remote regions of India, especially the North East is to be given priority for launching the S and T based Agricultural development programme using ICT in a significant way. The 'e-connectivity' programme implemented by Government of India in KVKs would have been more beneficial to the remote regions like NE region since other connectivity options are also limited or nil for KVKs here.

2. *Information, knowledge and skill empowerment of SHGs.*
3. *Every village knowledge centre*: ICT to all the 6, 00,000 villages by 2007.
4. *Domestic Software Development and Application*: Government Projects mainly provides static information. Hence, dynamic information like wealth, markets, health, and other day to day information needs to be given priority.
5. *Community Radio*: For *e.g.* Fishermen in Catamarans; Government of India should liberalise policies for the operation of community and farm radio thus reaching the unreached through the integrated ICT system.
6. *Technology upgradation in villages*
7. *Content creation*: consortium of content providers will have to be developed for each agro climatic zones.
8. *Women and ICT*
9. *Participatory knowledge system*: E-governance is invariably a passive system of information empowerment. Hence, there is a need for promoting participatory methodologies of content creation and knowledge management. The present approach is of partnership and not patronage. Farmer Participatory Knowledge System (FPKS) could replace the existing beneficiary and patronage approach to knowledge dissemination.
10. *Sustainability and replicability*: should be the bottom line in the development of National Action Plan for the 'every village a knowledge centre movement with involvement of Gram Sabha and Panchayat.
11. *Virtual Academy for Food Security and Rural Prosperity.*
12. *Political commitment.*

Methodology

The study was carried out through secondary sources of information covering small scale agriculture and a wide range of ICT-related experiences and initiatives of government as well as private sector. The reports of the international organizations like FAO, UNDP also used for the documentations of the challenges faced by the small scale farmers.

Findings and Discussion

Challenges Faced by Small-Scale Farmers

Small-scale farmers in India face many problems that are often complex and multi-faceted. The most pronounced challenges facing small scale farmers included the farm sizes, which have been declining over time. Because of this factor, rural people have insufficient land to eke a living (Jayne 2001). Some of the rural community members are landless or near landless, leading to major social and economic problems. The smallness of their lands leads to challenges of diseconomies of scale, and considering that most small-scale farmers are resource-poor, they find it difficult to access affordable credit and inputs for their produce. Most of these farmers have little experience in produce marketing (Mukhwana, Nyongesa and Ogemah 2005), and lack good and efficient markets (Mukhebi 2007). Typical examples include the very high transport and transactional costs, small inefficient markets, low agricultural productivity, low levels of irrigation and erratic rainfall, vulnerability to high seasonal and inter-annual fluctuations, high rates of evapo-transpiration and very slow adoption of new technologies.

According to the FAO reports in India Millions of peoples living in chronic hunger, smallholder farmers, consequently, they cannot re-invest and continue to face the demands of declining production and productivity. National policies have not adequately addressed the needs of small-scale farmers.

The (ECA 2006) cites problems of weak backward and forward linkages between agriculture and other sectors. Further, small-scale farmers contend with inadequate subsidies and unfair trade (Karaan 2006), limited access to animal and mechanical power, reduced availability of labour due to rural-urban migration, weak information systems, a poor regulatory framework that does not facilitate investment and specialization in new and high value products, inadequate market information and lack of agricultural information (Kidane, Maetz and Dardel 2006). There are also challenges of low uptake of research products, counter productive policies and insufficient investment in market infrastructure (Jones 2006).

In addressing these issues, many emerging technologies are being examined for their potential in transforming agricultural development in India. As outlined below, the use and application of modern ICTs could occupy a pivotal position in this line of engagement, especially in the context of small scale agriculture.

So we have to concentrate on high value agricultural (HVA) products, focus on improvement in productivity, considering the options for commercial agriculture, paying increased attention to new markets and marketing strategies and increasing agricultural production through biotechnology.

Some of the emerging ICTs that were identified include GIS and decision support systems, mobile mapping and hand held personal computers (personal digital assistants (PDAs)), precision agriculture and mobile (cellular) phone applications, community radio stations, radio frequency identification tags, World Space satellite radio, and more generally, access to the internet and web-based applications.

GIS-Based Decision Support Systems

A Geographical Information System (GIS) makes visual comparisons between different types of data possible. It helps to establish relationships between different data sets and is important in the production of maps, and charts and additional information associated with coordinates and time. It helps in the analysis of post harvest variation in crop yield measures, and provides a holistic view of the production system.

Mobile mapping is a component of GIS systems which provides the ability to collect field data, including unique geospatial time tags and attributes, for integrating into/updating a GIS (GIS Development 2007).

Handheld Personal Computer (HPC) or Personal Digital Assistants (PDAs)

HPCs are small, light and robust have been used for providing access to information, mobile mapping and other data gathering activities (GIS Development 2007). This cuts down face-to-face contacts and reduces telecommunication and transport costs.

Mobile (Cellular) Phone Applications

The cellular phone has provided market links for farmers and entrepreneurs. This has reduced transaction costs, broadened trade networks and facilitated searches for employment. The cellular phone applications such as the SMS to be one of the most important emerging

ICT applications in India. This helps in dissemination of the market related services like the provision of market information and electronic trading platforms, where farmers and traders access information on commodities being sold, their prices and the identity of their buyers and extension messages.

Community Radio Stations

Radio is an important mechanism for disseminating knowledge and information in different languages and formats (Bobbili *et al.*, 2006), especially to poor people. Radio is the most highly used media in accessing development and agricultural information. The convergence of ICTs, such as the internet with rural radio can provide powerful support to help harness and communicate knowledge for development.

Radio Frequency Identification (RFID)

RFID can be used to capture data on individual livestock that is then transmitted to a central database as part of a repository of information for livestock farmers, state veterinary services and health authorities.

Internet and Web-Based Applications

The internet, e-mail, web sites and web-based applications are becoming increasingly important in sharing and in disseminating agricultural information and there are many ongoing web-based application initiatives in India. The FAO and partners are implementing e- Agriculture – aimed at the intersection of agricultural informatics, agricultural development and entrepreneurship, focusing on agricultural services, technology dissemination and information delivered through the internet. Agriculture is intended to promote the integration of agricultural stakeholders and technology with multimedia, knowledge and culture, and aims to improve communication and learning processes (FAO 2006).

In India, Agmarknet, Kissan Call Centres etc. uses a web portal to provide market information services and a question and answer service to small scale farmers. Internet cafes, telecentres, information kiosks, market information centres have attracted the attention of rural information brokers who disseminate agricultural information on the web.

Precision Agriculture (PA)

PA has been described as the 'next great revolution in agriculture'. PA is also known as 'precision farming, information-intensive agriculture, prescription farming, target farming' (Srinivasan 2006)' Taylor and Whelan define PA as 'an integrated information and production-based farming system that is designed to increase long-term, site-specific and whole farm production efficiency, productivity and profitability, while minimizing unintended impacts on wildlife and the environment'. PA has 'the ability to manage land by the square meter instead of the square mile'. It adapts to variability: spatial – changes across farm, temporal – season to season and predictive – difference between predicted and actual results (Wikipedia 2006). Through PA, local situations of disease or lodging can be assessed to enable a farmer to optimize use and vary the rate of inputs, such as fertilizer, across a field based on the need identified by GPS guided grid sampling. Satellite positioning and navigation have played a catalytic role in the evolution of PA. The technology encompasses four key information technologies, namely location determination (via GPS), GIS, computer-guided controllers for variable rate application (VRA) of crop inputs, and sensing technologies for automated data collection and mapping. Among the four, GPS and GIS have been more widely established and used (Swinton and Lowenberg-Deboer 2001). PA has been used to increase yields for row crops, hay production, pasture management, animal grazing and other agricultural activities (GIS Development 2006). PA also has the inherent capacity to provide an effective forum for disseminating research and experience and for assessing natural resources variability such as soil and landscape variability, weather forecasting and remote sensing.

Conclusion

India is a country with over 1 billion population and 5 million computers. 80 per cent of the 5 million computers used in offices and hardly, 20 per cent are available for use in development work. Despite all the barriers, the Indian agriculture is bound to adopt and implement ICT to double the agricultural production. This aim can be achieved only when there is proper utilization of ICT and more investment in it.

ICTs has grown steadily in India but weak ICT policies and poor implementation capacity are among the biggest obstacles to wider use. One of the key factors affecting the use of ICTs in agriculture is inappropriate ICT policies, especially those that address rural communities and rural development. Sustainability is another key requirement for the use of ICTs, yet most ICT initiatives were project-based, and were disjointed and uncoordinated. The use of ICTs further calls for good ICT infrastructure, adequate ICT skills, good and affordable connectivity, and appropriate ICT policies

In addition, there is a need for high bandwidth despite these problems; there has been massive rollout of basic information communication infrastructure in India, partly spurred by the introduction of cellular technology that has reduced subscriber costs. Indian governments have also continued to support ICT initiatives in under-served areas by offering incentives to the lowest competitive bidders for infrastructure provision.

Findings of the present study have shown that radio stations and the cellular phone have become important tools in improving small-scale agriculture in rural areas. The internet and web-based applications are becoming increasingly important in the sharing and disseminating agricultural information and knowledge and marketing of goods and services. The livelihoods of farmers could be enhanced through adoption of modern technologies such as PA, online markets and the application of appropriate ICTs in information and knowledge dissemination. The creation of 'one-stop centres' for training and for linking farmers to markets and restructured extension services that target farmer groups to improve agricultural production and assist in the exchange of knowledge and information. However, the study established that there is low capacity and usage of ICTs and the ICT infrastructure in rural areas is a major problem. These challenges and their causes need to be addressed if ICTs are to benefit the small-scale farmer in India.

There is a great scope to implement ICT in order to communicate and integrate the complete agri-food supply chain, as the e-choupals are doing in Madhya Pradesh to procure soyabean. The other beneficiaries of ICT can be food-processing companies, and suppliers within the agri-food sector. On the other hand, the need to market the agricultural produce at reasonable prices will also change the farmers' attitude, and they will be more dependent on ICT. ICTs will, thus, definitely help in fortifying Small Scale agriculture in India.

References

Benkler, Y. (2006). The wealth of networks: how social production transforms markets and freedom. London: Yale University Press. 8

Bobbili, R., M. Luczynska, S. Miyagawa and M. Gaudi. (2006). Radio farm forum and Afronet: learning from successful ICT projects in Zambia.

Economic Commission for Africa (ECA). (2006). Economic report on Africa 2005: meeting challenges of unemployment and poverty in Africa. Addis Ababa: ECA.

Food and Agriculture Organization of the United Nations (FAO). (2000). The role of information and communication technologies in rural development and food security. Rome: FAO.

Food and Agriculture Organization of the United Nations (FAO). (2006). "e-agriculture" a definition and profile of its application. <http://www.fao.org/rdd/doc/eagriculture per cent 2014-10-051.pdf> (Verified December 10 2006).

GIS Development. 2006. GIS application.

Hirst, J., J. J. Overton, B. Allen and Y. Byron (eds.) (1988). Small-scale agriculture. Canberra: Australia Commonwealth Geographic Bureau.

Jayne, T. S. (2001). Smallholder income and land distribution in Africa: implications for poverty reduction strategies. Michigan: Michigan State University, Department of Agricultural Economics.

Jones, M. (2006). An agricultural research perspective on poverty, innovation policies and agricultural development in sub-Saharan Africa. Paper presented at the EGDI Policy, Poverty and Agricultural Development in sub-Saharan Africa Workshop, Frosundavik, Sweden, 8-9 March 2006.

Karaan, M. (2006). Market access for South African producers. Paper presented to the 26th Conference of the International Association of Agricultural Economists (IAAE), Gold Coast, Australia, 12-18 August 2006.

Kidane, W., M. Maetz and P. Dardel. (2006). Food security and agricultural development in sub-Saharan Africa. Building a case for more public support. Main report. Rome:

Mukhebi, A. (2007). Linking farmers to markets through modern information and communication technologies in Kenya.

Mukhwana, E., M. Nyongesa and V. Ogemah. (2005). Facilitating small-scale farmer collective marketing activities in Africa: the case of cereals banks in Kenya. Nairobi

Narayan, S. and A. Gulati. (2002). Globalization and smallholders: a review of issues, approaches and implications. IFPRI MSSD Discussion Paper 50.

Richardson, D. (1997). The internet and rural and agricultural development – an integrated approach. Rome: FAO<http://www.fao.org/docrep/w6840e/w6840e00.htm>(Verified December 15 2006.

Richardson, D. (2006). ICTs – transforming agricultural extension. Report of the 6th

Consultative Expert Meeting of CTA's Observatory on ICTs. CTA Working Document no. 8034. CTA. 86p.

Srinivasan, A. (ed.) (2006). Handbook of precision agriculture: principles and applications. New York: Haworth Press Inc.

Swinton, S. M. and J. Lowenberg-Deboer. (2001). Global adoption of precision agriculture technologies: who, when and why.

Wikipedia. (2006). Precision agriculture.

World Bank. (2006a.) 2006 information and communications for development: global trends and policies. Washington: World Bank.

Chapter 10

Sustainable Rural Development through Forward and Backward Integration and Technological Intervention in India

☆ *Madhur Jain*

India's massive agricultural sector employs about 60 per cent of the population, yet accounts for only about 17 per cent of total GDP. Growth in agriculture has stagnated relative to other sectors: last year the agricultural sector grew at a rate of 2.7 per cent, relative to 11 per cent growth in both the service and industry sector. Agricultural incomes are lower and growing slower than incomes in other sectors (kumar).

India produces 180 MT of fruits and vegetables a year. Farmer has to sell immediately due to perishability and absence of proper infrastructure to store it for longer period. Owing to this, post harvest wastage of fruits and vegetables is valued at around 45000 crore. These losses in India are more than consumption in United Kingdom. The farm gate prices in India are 25 per cent of the cost that the end consumer pays for the product. It is very less compared to countries like US where it is around 60 per cent (Agriwatch, 2012).

The use of fertilizers, pesticides and other chemicals led to the increase in production during green revolution, but its extensive use in certain regions of the country, for example Punjab has led to a decrease in the productivity. These areas have also witnessed problems like leaching due to which drinking water has become unfit for consumption.

There is an imminent need to have systems in place so that the problems of Indian agriculture could be addressed. There is no doubt that communication in the form of extension services, etc., whether through government or private channel is going to be the way forward.

Various Models and Agencies in Action to Counter the Problems in India

Globally, emergence of successful business models in the food industry has been based on their ability to ensure substantial level of efficiency and product innovation. Looking at the performance of the Indian companies in food, one can find that successful initiatives have been characterized by reasonable levels of performance on either the efficiency or innovation axes.

Some of the models that have been established are as follows:

Contract Farming followed Successfully by Pepsi in Punjab

When Pepsi food ltd. installed a Rs. 22 crore state-of-the-art tomato processing plant at Zahura in Hoshiarpur district of Punjab, The total Punjab tomato crop was 28000 tons, available over a 25-28 day period, while PepsiCo required at least 40000 tons of tomato to operate its factory, which had a gigantic capacity of 39 tons fresh fruit per hour.

The PepsiCo model of contract farming, measured in terms of new options for farmers, productivity increases, and the introduction of modern technology, has been an unparalleled success. The company focused on developing region- and desired produce-specific research, and extensive extension services. It was thus successful in bringing about a drastic change in the Punjab farmers' production system towards its objective of ensuring supply of right produce at the right time in required quantities to its processing plant.

The PepsiCo model of contract farming, measured in terms of new options for farmers, productivity increases, and the introduction of modern technology, has been an unparalleled success. The company focused on developing region- and desired produce-specific research, and extensive extension services. It was thus successful in bringing about a drastic change in the Punjab farmers' production system towards its objective of ensuring supply of right produce at the right time in required quantities to its processing plant (Singh).

Key Elements of PepsiCo's Success

- ☆ Core R&D team
- ☆ Unique partnership with local agencies including a public sector enterprise
- ☆ Execution of technology transfer through well-trained extension personnel
- ☆ Supply of all kinds of agricultural implements free of cost to contracted farmers
- ☆ Supply of timely and quality farm inputs on credit
- ☆ Prompt dispatch/delivery/procurement of the mature produce from every individual contracted farmer through the system of 'Quota Slips'
- ☆ Effective adoption/use of modern communication technology like pagers for communication with field executives
- ☆ Regular and timely payment to contracted farmers through computerised receipts and transparent system
- ☆ Maintenance of perfect logistics system and global marketing standards.

Mahindra Shubhlabh Services

One important aspect of this business model is to provide one stop shop to the farmers for all his needs. The main provisions of the Shubhlabh model are as follows:

- Arrange all agri-inputs such as seeds, fertilizers, and pesticides and so on to farmer
- Rent out farm machinery like tractors, transplanters and other special machinery that helps to reduce the cost to the farmer
- Provides commercial agricultural extension by bi-weekly visits to the farms
- Offer crop spraying, harvesting and post harvesting services
- Provide commodity trading in final produce of the farmers.

In order to increase its reach to remote off villages, it adopted a hub and spoke model. Hub and the spokes, are operated with the help of franchises (Singh).

ITC e-Choupal

ITC started its ambitious e-Chaupal project with an intention of enhancing the global competitiveness of Indian agriculture and raising the standard of living in Indian villages. It intends to leverage information technology to reduce aggregate cost of its supply chain. and to extract value through a near disinter-mediation of the supply chain. It is a well-known fact that the sheer number of intermediaries in food and agricultural supply chain are too many making chain uncompetitive as well as these intermediaries block market

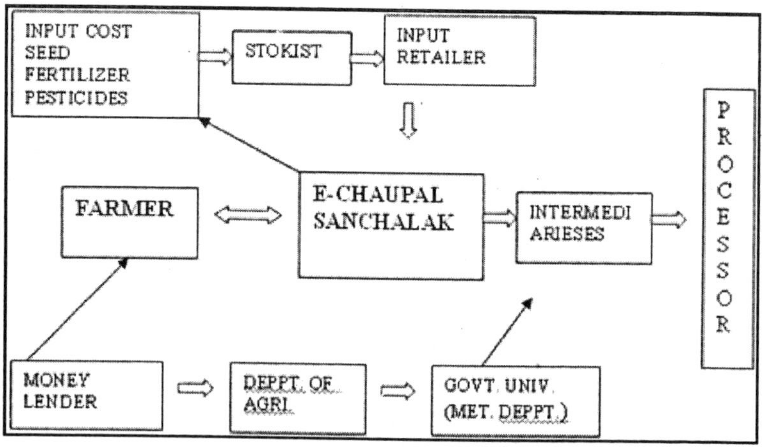

Figure 10.1: Process Diagram of e-Choupal

information making transaction cost unfavourable to the Indian farmer. With this e-initiative ITC hopes to disinter-mediate the supply chain through virtual integration.

Across various villages in interior Madhya Pradesh, Karnataka, Uttar Pradesh and Andhra Pradesh ITC's e-Chaupal's holding Internet-enabled Pentium desktops and printers display the itcibd.com portal. These Internet kiosks are manned by a lead farmer of the village, called the Sanchlaks. The Sanchalak is trained to operate the computer. These Sanchalaks, with the help of Internet kiosks are suppose to perform three distinct activities:

- ☆ Information and knowledge dissemination: These kiosks display real-time data on market price prevailing in the Mandis across States. They also carry information on weather and have a knowledge bank of best scientific practices.
- ☆ Virtual aggregation of demand and supply: By aggregating both buyers and sellers ITC intends to reduce the aggregate cost by providing a kind of commodity exchange which disassociates intermediaries from intermediation of information flow making the chain more competitive.
- ☆ Allowing retailing of agri-inputs as well as other products and services (Singh).

The e-Chaupals provide ITC with the opportunity to directly purchase soya, rice and other crop from the farmers. This has, no doubt, provided the farmers with alternative route to Mandi through online access and transaction across remote locations. This has reduced transaction cost pre- and post-Chaupal experiment. Farmers incur transaction cost, which arose due to trolley freight to Mandi, labour cost, cost of labour and handling cost. Process incurs commission to agents, cost of gunny bags, and loading cost of labour freight and transit loss cost. Both farmer and process transaction cost works against the interest of farmers and the company. With the help of e-Chaupal, ITC has been able to reduce this transaction cost drastically claiming a win–win situation for both farmers as well as itself. The coverage of e-Chaupal is currently around 3,50,000 farmers growing soyabean, coffee, wheat, rice, pulses and shrimp in around 3,50,000 villages through 650 kiosks across four States (ITC) (Vivek talwar).

Tata Kisan Kendra (TKK): Information and Communication Technology (ICT)

TKK is the agency that took the first large scale initiative of using ICT in an advanced manner. GIS mapping was the main standout point in this ICT initiative, GIS or the geographic information systems, arc computerized systems that record, store, analyze and produce maps and geographic products based on information obtained from the different sources. The TKK's precision-farming concept uses GIS to manage and analyze data collected from different sources by various means, sophisticated and simple. The information thus collected includes census data, revenue data, socio-economic surveys, satellite imagery, soil-mapping data and market studies. The satellite mapping helps the vendor organization and the farmers to achieve the objectives such as:

- Speed for the conducting the ground surveillance than that done by the airplane and also the comprehensiveness of the surveillance
- Accuracy attained through satellite mapping is more than the traditional processes
- Flexibility in adapting to the changing ownership patterns, climate and soil changes
- Remote-sensing ability is the latest advancement in satellite mapping

The Tata Kisan Kendra (TKK) network has collected census data for the districts in which they operate. This information is combined with the spatial data generated by the GIS facility and correlated with socio-economic information such as the name of the owner of a plot of land, the crop grown on it, the number of members in the family, the family's level of education, its annual income, and so on. Both raw and processed data is fed into the GIS, which then becomes the basis for providing quality decision support for the agronomy services offered by the TKKs. The agronomist at the Kendra uses analyzed information on topography, soils, climate, hydrology, cropping systems and crop suitability to advise farmers on which crops to grow, crop management, market trends, what kind of fertilizers to use and how much, etc. The goal is to maximize the yield from a farmer's land holding, and thereby improve his socioeconomic standing.

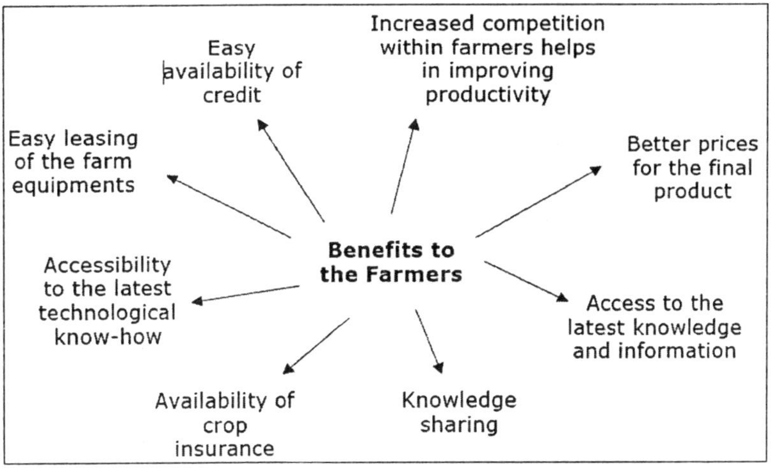

Figure 10.2: Benefits to Farmers through TKK

Benefits to the Farmers

The farmers from the states of Uttar Pradesh, Punjab and Haryana have benefited in multiple ways. TKK has been pivotal in providing value-added services to these farmers, which has helped in uplifting these farmers and improving their quality of living. The benefits derived by the farmers are shown in the figure below.

Food Retail Chains

For a total population of a billion and a middle class population of over 400 million people, organised food retailing is still in its nascent stage in this country. At the moment, India has one of the most fragmented produce-supply chains on the planet. 30 percent of all fresh produce is lost or gets spoilt before it reaches the market. On an average, after getting plucked from the field, the fresh produce passes through six or seven middlemen before a consumer can buy it; resulting in tortuous journeys, big markups and poor quality damaging the products at the end.

Therefore, one can say that the most rewarding effort lies in replacing the existing supply system with efficient network of international quality of supply chain but adapting it rightly to Indian conditions. The food retailing basket mostly comprises of fast-moving, short life cycle fresh products in offerings which demands a highly modified and a bit complicated supply chain process. Working with

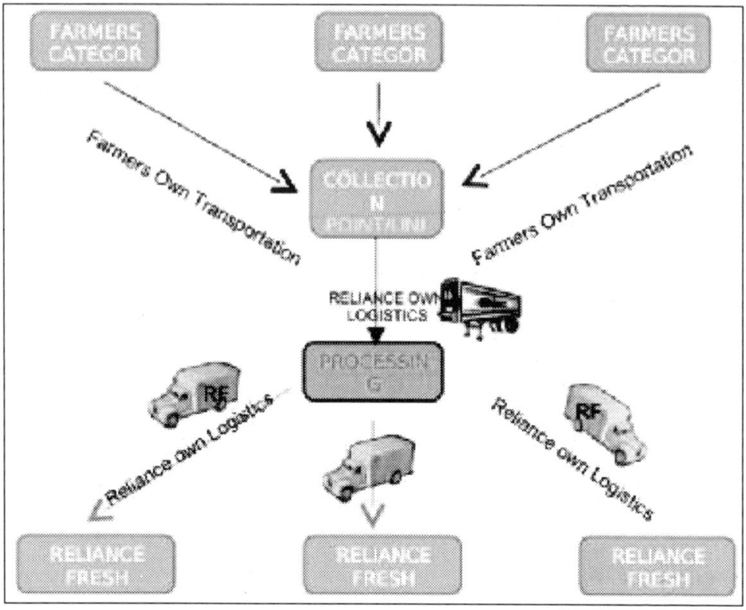

Figure 10.3: Process of Food Movement in Case of Reliance Fresh (Verma, 2009)

the suppliers and getting them in sync with the fast paced process pose a challenge for the organisations. Technology adds in synchronizing and balancing the system at the lowest cost and resulting in a high customer service level. Supply chain planning helps dramatically increase forecast accuracy, streamline product introductions, assess promotions and create plans attuned to the market; and supply chain execution provides transportation, warehousing and inventory management to ensure cost effective order fulfillment and on-time deliveries (Sethi).

Other than this the involvement of middlemen is negligent which helps in increased returns to the farmer. Installation of cold storages and temperature controlled logistics systems has reduced the food wastage by a huge margin.

Conclusion

Agri-initiatives taken by Indian corporate will play an important role in dissemination of right information as well as knowledge,

Provide total farm solution and act as buyer of agri-produce as well as provide the resource for producing these agri-produces. As suggested by MR Banga, the chairman of Hindustan lever limited these firms have to strive hard to create a win-win situation both for themselves as well as the farmer. A well thought out collaborative model could help firms share facility and infrastructure cost on one hand and increase complemantarity in their marketing efforts enhancing customer satisfaction through a partnered customer relationship management approach.

The Three firms can use their resources and can very well form a collaborative agri-service centre. The proposed model has collaboration and partnership as the basis. This partnership culminates into formation of farmer service centre. Farmer service centre would be run as a private enterprise between the food processor and a number of other input providers such as bank, agrochemical/seed/fertilizer, farm equipment manufacturers, and so, on. Either the agri-input provider or food processor can take the lead in establishing this model. The benefit of this model is very significant. Agri-input would be made available to the farmer directly to the farmer at cheaper rates. Credit and insurance would be available to the farmer. The farmer service centre would provide extension services. The food processor would access the farm producer directly. Specialized grain-handling equipment, transport and vertical storage would be installed reducing both costs spillage losses to pests. Such a model will drive down the cost of agricultural produce. The farmer's efficiencies would result in increased production and increased off take, and increase his incomes, despite lower prices.

References

Agriwatch. (2012). markets, prices and food security.

ITC. (n.d.). Retrieved september 4th, 2012, from e Choupal : http://www.itcibd.com/pf.asp

Kumar, S. (n.d.). india development blog. Retrieved august 2012, from http://www.indiadevelopmentblog.com/2008/08/challenges-facing-indian-agriculture.html

Sethi, S. (n.d.). Indian Retail. Retrieved sept 2012, from Indianretailing.com: http://www.indiaretailing.com/food-retailers-kirana.asp

Singh, D. R. Farms + corporate new farm supply chain initiatives in indian agriculture. Chennai: GLIM.

Verma, M. S. (2009). Reliance fresh: Acase study.

Vivek talwar, N. M. (n.d.). ICT Platform for Enhancing Agricultural Productivity: the case of tata kisan kendra. 15.

Chapter 11

Animate Energy in Mountain Agriculture: Women's Critical Role in Food Production in the Central Himalayas

☆ *Vir Singh*

Most of the rural population in the Himalayan mountains is engaged in naturally sustainable but marginal agriculture. Women have primary roles in building up agriculture-based livelihood systems, providing much of the labour required for agricultural activities. A high degree of sexual division of labour is visible in Central Himalayas as also virtually in all the countries of the Hindu Kush-Himalayan region.

No Alternative to Animate Energy

Mountain agriculture cannot afford to use mechanical energy for agricultural operations. Animate energy is the only feasible source with no viable alternative. Bullocks and humans are the exclusive source of animate energy to carry out all agricultural operations. Among the humans; women are the major source of power to keep the agriculture going. In other words, cattle bullocks and women are the two main sources of motive power for mountain agriculture.

Experiences show that there is a direct relation between the level of energy use, either human, animal or fossil (mechanical), and the level of production per unit of land. In fossil energy-driven systems, the relatively high energy use explains the relatively high productivity in the transformed Green Revolution areas. However, there are organic, integrated systems in which virtually no fossil energy is used, which, in terms of overall production, are at least as productive as modern systems, but have less negative impact on the environment and may be socially more acceptable (Durno *et al.*, 1992). That the source of energy is not important for the level of production is also demonstrated by comparative research in the Philippines (Kuether and Duff 1981), where it was found that the same yield of rice could be obtained in mechanical, transitional and traditional farms. Basing policies on comparing energy balances only, therefore, can lead to wrong decisions if these data are not combined with information on, *e.g.*, production, availability, cost, impact on environment, gender and the community as a whole (Reijntjes 1992).

Agricultural transformation and mechanization often go hand in hand. But, in this respect too, mountains are the exception. Almost complete transformation in some favourable pockets of the mountains, it has been experienced, has not invited mechanization of any degree. In transitional areas, *e.g.*, the Shivalik and Foot-hill range where handful farmers occasionally use hired tractor for land preparation, a very limited use of fossil fuel energy is visible, and it is because of the availability of even land which is easily accessible and well-linked to the plains (Singh 1998, Singh and Partap 2002, 2005, Singh and Gautam 2004).

Energy systems used for agricultural work in the mountains exist as an integrated system. Farmer-manual tools system can exist independently; and, to a great extent, so can the farmer-machine system. But the farmer-animal power system can never exist independently. When, through the use of an implement, an agricultural operation absorbs some amount of animal energy, it would simultaneously absorb some amount of human energy. So both systems (animal power being dominant) are inseparably integrated. Use of a mix of energy technologies in crop production is referred to as integrated energy system. We can call this energy system for agricultural work as 'animate energy system' since the energy is produced by the living system.

The fossil-fuel energy, on the contrary, may be referred to as inanimate energy. The former is renewable, the latter non-renewable. In this text, unless specified, the word 'energy' has been referred to the form of energy which is used for agricultural work, *e.g.* tillage, weeding, puddling, threshing etc.

Animate energy based system is obviously the most suited to mountain agriculture. Why does animal power seem to be the best source for developing sustainable agriculture in the mountains and why is it superior to fossil fuel powered machines? A number of sound reasons can be given for this. Arguments in favour of the draught animals have been derived from earlier studies (Gill 1981, Bhalla and Chadha 1982, Nair 1982, Ramaswamy 1983, Bodet 1987, Singh and Naik 1987 and Reijntjes 1992, Singh and Partap, 2002, Singh and Tulachan 2001, Singh and Gautam 2004, Singh and Partap 2005) and have been looked at from the mountain perspective. The following points have been derived after Singh (1998):

- ☆ The sources of energy already exist in the region. Animate energy does not have to be manufactured or bought at a high cost.
- ☆ The use of animate energy considerably increases a farmer's work force. It enables the farmer to diversify the crop planted, to increase the cultivated area of the farm, to carry out agricultural work in time.
- ☆ Machine-based energy system causes the production activity to concentrate on a limited number of crops, thus reducing the diversity of the production system. The animate energy system does the other way round what is preferred in mountain agro-ecosystems.
- ☆ Animal-drawn plough and other implements are cheaper and more affordable than a large tractor-drawn plough/ power tiller. Animal-drawn implements can be made in the village itself and are more suitable for the small, often fragmented and scattered, farms found in the mountains.
- ☆ Use of bullocks does not entail any investment in expensive and non-renewable fuel. Another enormous advantage of the ruminants used as draught animals is that they can be

fed residues and by-products available on farm, producing in return not only energy but food (milk from the female cattle), methane (biogas) for lighting and cooking, manure to fertilize the fields, and many other products obtainable after their death without competing with people for food.

- ☆ The use of bullocks enables the farmers to integrate livestock with crop production and permits the exploitation of the very large potential of cattle kept on settled, subsistence farms.
- ☆ Mechanization causes direct labour displacement in land preparation. If it does not also contribute directly to increasing cropping intensities and yields, or a switch to more labour-intensive crops, there will be a net loss of employment opportunity in areas, *e.g.*, the mountains, where alternative sources of income are extremely meagre.
- ☆ Fossil energy to be used in the machines is a finite resource and its use has a considerable negative impact on the environment and most farmers in the mountains cannot afford fossil energy-based technology.
- ☆ Where animals are used as draught power, it is possible for farmers to cultivate more land or they make time free for other activities.

The above-listed arguments clearly reveal that animate energy system excels the mechanical energy. In the mountain areas, owing to specific resource base characteristics altogether different from those of the plains, improvement in bullock power system efficiency and its sustainable use is an imperative to improve the lot of women folk.

Woman Work Hours

Use of human energy is inevitably linked with all agricultural operations carried out by draught animals, *i.e.*, ploughing, levelling, puddling, weeding and threshing. Other operations – hand-weeding, irrigation, manure transport and application, breaking of clods, sowing and transplantation, fertilizer and pesticide application, harvesting and hand-threshing – use only human energy. Many of these operations use only women power. Here bullocks means a pair of bullocks while man and woman denote only single individual performing work together with a pair of bullocks or alone.

Among the four areas studied, the transformed middle mountain villages require maximum bullock and human hours followed by the Shivalik villages. Total bullock hours requirement by traditional Middle Himalayan villages is nearly twice of the Greater Himalayan villages (Table 11.1).

Woman work hours devoted to all agricultural operations per hactare of cropland over a period of one year have been compared with those of man and bullock hours. The information is based on the investigation of 12 villages situated in four different agro-ecological zones, three villages in each zone. There are four peculiar agro-ecological zones prevailing in the region, namely, the Shivalik hills, middle mountains under traditional agriculture, middle mountains under transformed agriculture, and Greater Himalayas. These four types of agro-ecological zones are distinguishable from each other, geo-physically, ecologically, and socio-economically.

From Table 11.1 (all values expressed in terms of one ha cropland over a period of one year), it is clear that a woman devotes far much more time to agricultural activities than bullocks and a man. A woman in the Shivalik hills spends 757 more hours than a pair of bullock and a man together do. In the middle mountains under traditional agriculture, a woman spends 645 more hours than a pair of bullocks and a man together do. In middle mountains under transformed agriculture two bullocks and a man devote 1671 less hours than a woman. In the Greater Himalayas, agriculture uses 890 more hours of work by a woman than by two bullocks and a man.

In Shivalik agriculture, a woman devotes 2.79 times more hours of work than a pair of bullocks and 2.08 times more than a man. In traditional middle mountain agriculture, a woman spends 2.5 times more hours of work than a pair of bullocks and 3.04 times more than a man. Transformed middle mountain agriculture consumes as much as 3.25 times greater woman work hours than a pair of bullocks and 2.38 times more work hours than a man. The Greater Himalayan agriculture consumes 4.41 times more hours of a woman's work in comparison to a pair of bullocks and 2.91 times more than a man for all the operations required for the cultivation of single ha of land over a period of one year.

On the basis of per day work load on a woman farmer, it may be observed that she devotes as many as 17 hours exclusively to

Table 11.1: Working Hours of a Woman Devoted to Various Operations for Crop Cultivation per Hectare of Cropland in Different Agroecological Zones of Central Himalayas in a Year

Agricultural Operation	*Source of Animate Energy*	*Shiivaliik Hills*	*Middle Mountains: Traditional*	*Middle Mountains: Transformed*	*Greater Himalayas*
Ploughing	Bullocks	1000	486	1296	351
	Man	1000	486	1485	378
	Woman	00	00	00	00
Levelling	Bullocks	225	18	95	45
	Man	225	18	95	81
	Woman	00	00	00	00
Puddling	Bullocks	60	30	63	00
	Man	90	15	63	00
	Woman	90	15	126	00
Weeding	Bullocks	80	108	81	00
	Man	80	108	81	00
	Woman	496	192	1262	200
Irrigation	Bullocks	00	00	00	00
	Man	100	50	100	00
	Woman	32	16	50	00
Manure Transport and Application	Bullocks	00	00	00	00
	Man	00	00	00	00
	Woman	1000	475	1175	400
Clod Breaking	Bullocks	00	00	00	00
	Man	00	00	00	00
	Woman	180	100	278	100
Sowing/ Transplantation	Bullocks	00	00	00	00
	Man	100	19	106	80
	Woman	644	70	700	100
Fertlizer and Pesticide Application	Bullocks	00	00	00	00
	Man	300	00	300	00
	Woman	25	00	50	00
Harvestinng	Bullocks	00	00	00	00
	Man	80	00	280	100
	Woman	1600	960	1700	800
Threshing	Bullocks	330	275	355	75
	Man	300	70	70	75
	Woman	660	500	800	475
Total	Bullocks	1695	917	1890	471
	Man	2275	766	2580	714
	Woman	4727	2328	6141	2075

agriculture-related work in the villages under transformed agriculture. In transitional hill agriculture (the Shivalik Hills), she works for as many as 13 hours a day. Traditional middle mountain agriculture requires a woman to devote only little over six hours a day, while in primitive-type Greater Himalayan agriculture she does agriculture-related work at the rate of less than six hours a day.

We thus can infer that it is the transformed agriculture that imposes the most burden of work on women folk. The transitional agriculture is at number two in this regards. Traditional agriculture puts comparatively less burden on women farmers. The Greater Himalayan agriculture requires minimum work input by a woman farmer.

Power Output during Different Agricultural Operations

Work done for certain length of time by different sources of power for agriculture can be converted into actual power invested in mountain agriculture. Experiments on draught animal power (DAP) output during ploughing, levelling, weeding, and threshing operations have been conducted at different sites in 12 villages under all agro-ecological conditions by Singh (1998). Data for various operations has been derived from these experiments (Table 11.2). For threshing operation, energy estimate of 0.25 kW (Singh and Naik 1987) was used.

Table 11.2: Bullock Draught Power Output during Different Agricultural Operations

Operations	*Average Speed (km/h)*	*Tractive Effort (kgf)*[1]	*Power (kW)*[2]
Ploughing	2.4	78	0.52
Levelling	2.7	48	0.36
Puddling*	1.6	95	0.42
Weeding and Earthing up*	2.6	47	0.34

Source: Singh (1998)

Figures are based on eight hours' operation (seven hours' ploughing and one hour's levelling) by a pair of bullocks.

Each bullock weighed 250 kg.

1: 1 kgf = 9.806 Newton; 2: 1 kW = 1.34 hp

* Estimates based on Singh and Naik (1987).

Measuring the energy content of human labour which is one of the major sources of motive power in rural energy systems, is infinitely more complex, both conceptually and empirically. In particular, relation to human labour complexities arise because of varying views as to whether human labour is a factor of production that is substitutable by energy, or a form of energy that is substitutable by other forms of energy (Ramani *et al.*, 1995).

However, for the ease of analysis of a production system and/or ecosystem functioning inevitably depicting energy flow pattern, considering human labour in terms of energy, becomes urgent particularly when a concrete strategy is to be evolved. Considerable variation in the criteria of converting human labour into energy content exists in the past studies. Energy figures used by Revelle (1976), Gopalan *et al.* (1979) and Bhatia and Sharma (1990) appear to be towards higher side. In our analysis we have used human energy input value sponsored by ICAR (1978), *i.e.* 0.1 hp or 0.075 kW per adult per hour, for it appears appropriate when we compare human weight with that of a local bullock. Singh (1998) has also used the same criterion.

Energy Contribution to Crop Cultivation

Table 11.3 presents data on the magnitude of power that actually invests into the cultivation of all crops through various operations. All figures are based on per ha of cropland per year. In order to generate data on actual DAP contribution to the cultivation of individual crops per ha per year, the total hours devoted to an operation for the cultivation of a crop were multiplied by the DAP output (kW) for respective operations shown in Table 11.2. For threshing operation, energy estimate of 0.25 kW (Singh and Naik 1987) was used. One man-hour has been considered equal to 0.075 kWh (Ram 1982; Singh and Naik 1987).

The total DAP for raising all major crops is the lowest (217 kWh) for the Greater Himalayas and the highest (851 kWh) for the transformed middle mountains. Most of the DAP is expended through ploughing operation in all the agro-ecological zones of the Himalayas. Overall amount of power input in agriculture by a woman is lower than by a pair of bullocks. However, if power of only one bullock is considered, power input values of a woman and that of a bullock are quite close in the Shivalik and traditional middle

Table 11.3: Power Contribution to Agriculture (per ha per year)

Agricultural Operation	*Source of Animate Energy*	*Shiivaliik Hills*	*Middle Mountains: Traditional*	*Middle Mountains: Transformed*	*Greater Himalayas*
Ploughing	Bullocks	520.00	252.72	673.92	182.52
	Man	75.00	36.45	111.38	28.35
	Woman	00	00	00	00
Levelling	Bullocks	81.00	6.48	34.20	16.20
	Man	16.88	1.35	7.13	6.08
	Woman	00	00	00	00
Puddling	Bullocks	25.20	12.60	26.46	00
	Man	6.75	1.13	4.73	00
	Woman	6.75	1.13	9.45	00
Weeding	Bullocks	27.20	43.52	27.54	00
	Man	6.00	8.10	6.08	00
	Woman	37.20	14.40	94.65	15.00
Iirrigation	Bullocks	00	00	00	00
	Man	7.50	3.75	7.50	00
	Woman	2.40	1.20	3.75	00

Contd...

Table 11.3–Contd...

Agricultural Operation	*Source of Animate Energy*	*Shiivaliik Hills*	*Middle Mountains: Traditional*	*Middle Mountains: Transformed*	*Greater Himalayas*
Manure Transport and Application	Bullocks	00	00	00	00
	Man	00	00	00	00
	Woman	75.00	35.63	88.13	30.00
Clod Breaking	Bullocks	00	00	00	00
	Man	00	00	00	00
	Woman	13.50	7.50	16.35	7.50
Sowing/Transplantation	Bullocks	00	00	00	00
	Man	7.50	1.43	7.95	6.00
	Woman	48.30	5.25	52.50	7.50
Fertlizer and Pesticide Application	Bullocks	00	00	00	00
	Man	22.50	00	22.50	00
	Woman	1.88	00	3.75	00
Harvestinng	Bullocks	00	00	00	00
	Man	6.00	00	21.00	7.50
	Woman	120.00	72.00	127.50	60.00
Threshing	Bullocks	82.50	56.75	88.75	18.75
	Man	22.50	5.25	5.25	5.63
	Woman	49.50	37.50	60.00	35.63
Total	Bullocks	735.90	372.07	850.87	217.47
	Man	170.63	57.46	193.52	53.56
	Woman	354.53	174.61	456.08	155.63

mountain zones. But, in the transformed middle mountains and the Greater Himalayan zone, power input by a woman is more than by a bullock.

The amount of human energy expended in mountain agriculture varies in the same fashion, being minimum in the Greater Himalayas and highest in the transformed areas of the middle Himalayas. Energy invested by a woman is two to three times more than by a man per ha per annum. Weeding, manure transport and application, sowing and transplantation, harvesting, and threshing operations consume much of woman energy.

This analysis presents only the crop production related activities a woman is devoted to. A woman also does most of the animal husbandry related activities. All other household chores are also to be accomplished by her. If she is supposed to devote only an hour per day, or 365 hours per annum, to non-cropping activities, she would be putting 27.37 kWh additional energy to get these tasks accomplished. Though this value is towards lower side, but if added to her total energy output figures, one would certainly be led to appreciate that a woman, on the whole, surpasses the other two other animate sources of energy. This energy of a woman is so precious and critical for the land-related economy of mountain areas.

It is clearly revealed that the transformed agriculture – where a woman devotes more time and expends more energy – aggravates drudgery on woman. Green revolution-type transformation not only invites ecological, environmental, and socio-cultural crises, but also renders the production system unsustainable. An augmentation of draught animal power system would help mitigate woman's problems. For instance, improved animal harness, efficient implements and tools, increasing DAP supplies through more use of animals, and the likes would reduce work burden on a woman significantly. However, our conventional animal husbandry policy calls for large-scale crossbreeding of cattle. Crossbred bullocks have proved less efficient for ploughing and other agricultural operations. If the crossbreeding programme assumes success to a significant level, drudgery of woman would further aggravate.

References

Bhalla, G.S. and Chadha, G.K. 1982. Green Revolution and Small Peasant : A Study of Income Distribution in Punjab Agriculture. *Econ. Pol. Weekly*, May 15-22, 1982.

Bhatia, R and Sharma, R. 1990. Energy and agriculture: a review. In Desai, A V (ed.) *Patterns of Energy Use in Developing Countries.* New Delhi: Wiley Eastern India, 205-251.

Bodet, P. 1987. "Animal Energy : An Introductory Review". *World Animal Review,* 63: 2 - 6.

Durno, J.; Moeliono, I. and Prasertcharoensuk, R. 1992. *Sustainable Agriculture for Lowlands : Resource Book.* Bangkok : South-East Asian Sustainable Agriculture Network.

Gill, G.J. 1981. Choice of Cultivation Techniques in Bangladesh. In Jackson *et al.* (eds.) *Maximum Livestock Production from Minimum Land.* Mymen Singh, Bangladesh : Bangladesh Agricultural University.

Gopalan, C.B., Ramasastri, V. and Balasubramanium, S.C. 1979. *Nutritive Value of Indian Foods.* Hyderabad: NIN.

ICAR. 1978. *Report on Energy Requirements of Intensive Agricultural Production 1977-78.* Pantnagar: GBP University of Agriculture and Technology.

Kuether, D.O. and Duff, J.B. 1981. *Energy Requirement for Alternative Rice Production Systems in the Tropics.* IRRI Research Paper Series 59. Manila : IRRI.

Nair, K.N. 1982. Animals and Tractors in Agrarian Economies: An Analysis of Some Issues Concerning Cultivation Techniques in Agriculture. Paper presented at Seminar on *Maximum Livestock Production from Minimum Land* at Dacca, Bangladesh, 15-17 February, 1981.

Ram, R A. 1982. Use of bullock power in farming system. *Proceedings and Seminar Papers.* Bangalore: IIM.

Ramani, K.V., Reddy, A.K.N. and Islam, M.N. (eds.). 1995. *Rural Energy Planning: A Government-Enabled Market-Based Approach.* Kuala Lumpur, Malaysia: APDC and GTZ, 252-253.

Ramaswamy, N.S. 1983. Draught Animal Power in the Developing Countries with Specific Reference to Asia. *Asian Livestock,* May and June 1983.

Reijntjes, C.; Haverkort, B.; and Waters-Bayer. 1992. *Farming for Future: An Introduction to Low-External-Input and Sustainable Agriculture.* Leusden: Macmillan and ILEIA.

Revelle, R. 1976. Energy use in rural India. *Science* 192: 969-975.

Singh, V. 1998. *Draught Animal Power in Mountain Agriculture: A Study of Perspectives and Issues in Central Himalayas, India*. Mountain Farming Systems Discussion Paper No. 98/1. Kathmandu: ICIMOD.

Singh, V. and Gautam, P.L. (eds.). 2004. *Livestock Production Systems for Sustainable Food Security and Livelihoods in Mountain Areas*. Pantnagar: GB Pant University of Agriculture and Technology. pp. 413.

Singh, V. and Naik, D.G. 1987. Animal Draught Power in the Mid-altitude Himalayan Villages. In Pangtey, Y.P.S. and Joshi, S.C. (eds) *Western Himalaya: Environment, Problems and Development*, 755-770. Nainital: Gyanodaya Prakashan.

Singh, V. and Partap, T. 2002. Draught Animal Power in Mountain Agriculture: Management Scenarios in the Indian Central Himalayas. *Indian Journal of Animal Sciences* 72 (11): 1022-1033.

Singh, V. and Partap, T. 2005. Draught Animal Power Management in Mountain Agriculture: Scenarios of Central Himalayas, India. In Rowlinson, P.; Wachirapakorn, C.; Pakdee, P.; and Wanapat, M. (eds.) *Integrating Livestock-Crop Systems to Meet the Challenges of Globalisation*, Vol. 2. London: British Society of Animal Science.

Singh, V. and Tulachan, P.M. 2001. Gender Contribution to Smallholder Dairy Production in Uttaranchal. *ENVIS Bulletin: Himalayan Ecology and Development*, 9 (2): 38-39.

Chapter 12

Utility of Mass Media in Agriculture Extension

☆ *Mukesh Kumar*

Mass Media has been defined as "means of communication designed to reach and influence very large number of people" (Encyclopaedia Britannicca, 1980). Defleur and Ball-Rokeach (1996) defines mass communication as a technology which helps a message to be transmitted among a large number of people at the same time. Thus, it includes newspapers, magazines, television, radio, cinema and the now internet also. It has also to be noted specially that the nature of any society's communication process is necessarily linked to virtually every aspect of its daily life. Various theories have been floated about the study of mass communications. The study of mass communications should throw significant light on-

1. The impact of the society on a medium,
2. The various processes involved in the working of mass communication systems, and
3. The influence of medium on society.

The society has to function in the context of social reality and one of the significant tools that the society has at its command to achieve this is language. From another point of view, language is the medium used by the society to exchange or explain the understandings and standpoints of one section of the society to its other sections.

Mass Media is an important component of strategy recognized as such in the midterm appraisal of 10th Plan for revitalization of agricultural extension system. It aims to contribute to the lives of the local community by creation of content by the people and for the people of that community. It will focus on issues relating to education, health, environment, agriculture, rural and community development. It is a powerful communication medium, particularly in India where, in the absence of regular and stable electric supply in rural and far flung areas. People have to depend on radio to meet their needs of information, education and entertainment. Community radio serves to bring small communities together, focuses on the common man's day-to-say concerns and helps in realizing local aspirations.

Whether it is realized or not the agriculture sector remains as one of the pertinent sectors in many countries and its significant role in uplifting the economy of a nation cannot be argued. Agriculture sectors ability in uplifting the community socio-economic status and reducing the poverty problems in India and other countries cannot be argued (Amekawa, 2010; Md. Salleh Hassan *et al.*, 2010). India has doubled its effort to ensure the success and sustainability of agriculture sector. Mass media and agriculture sector are pertinent to each other. Mass media especially television, radio, printed media and internet have disseminated a number of agriculture programs and information (Gorg, 2001; Bauman, 2006). Printed media has its own strength to disseminate valuable information. Almost 60-70 per cent people from the rural area directly and indirectly engage in agriculture in India. Agriculture is a relatively conservative sector of Indian economy; despite Green Revolution agriculture farmers are least equipped with tools for knowledge and information access to operate efficiency in a dynamic global environment. Indian farmers have marginal holdings. In the area of globalization it is very important to Indian farmers to produce higher production within minimum cost. It is possible to the farmers by providing the techniques and ideas related to farming through various medias like T.V. Channels, radio agricultural exhibition, magazines etc. (Bauman, 2006; Opara, 2008). Shetkari a Maharastrian magazine is one of them which plays very important role (Thiam *et al.*, 2001).

Agricultural Journalism

Agriculture is vital to India, as it produces 23 per cent of GDP and employs 66 per cent of the workforce. Over the years, India's agricultural productivity has improved to the point that the country is now both self-sufficient and a net exporter of a variety of food grains. However, most rural Indian farmers have remained quite poor, due to remnants of an archaic agricultural system based on small landholdings, scarcity-era regulations and inefficient market structures.

Agricultural journalism is of recent origin in India. It came into existence just six decades ago. It is now gaining importance, particularly after the establishment of agricultural universities in India, technical information needs to be provided to the farmers at the right time and in the right way, so that the productivity can be increased. In the view of increase in literacy level, print media has acquired a greater role in dissemination of information on improved agricultural practices to the farming community and also to inform the public in general. The pattern of the collection of news has now been changed. The role and risk of the reporters is increasing day by day as they cover each and every aspect of life and show live broadcast of important events on various channels of television.

Types and Utility of Mass Media

Media is one of the most important pillars of democracy. It serves the nation in two forms *i.e.* print media and electronic media. Print media includes the newspapers and newsletters published by private and public sectors.

Print Media

Among the several mass media, newspaper and farm magazines are commonly used. They have a vital role to play in the communication of agricultural information among the literate farmers. Increasing rate of literacy in the country offers new promises and prospects for utilizing print medium as a means of mass communication. The print media has widened the scope of communication. It is cheap and people can afford to buy and read them at their convenience. It is a permanent medium in that the message are imprinted permanently with high storage value which makes them suitable for reference and research. India has farm magazines in every state, published mostly in local languages. Agricultural department also encourages the publication of farm magazines particularly through farmers association.

Farm Magazines

In India, several magazines are dedicated to farmers and agriculture. For example, Kheti, Farm Food, Successful Farm Food, Shetkari etc. Shetkari magazine is famous since 1965. Shetkari is the print media that is focused to provide improved methods and techniques of cultivation. Peasants in western Maharashtra especially the literate, youth and commercial cultivator are utilizing latest agricultural ideas for agricultural development. Agricultural development means economic growth along with maintaining the fertility of the soil. Purpose of Shetkari magazine is to guide the farmers about their farming tools, of use better seeds for increasing production within minimum period. Method for good cultivation, management of irrigation, mixed cropping system, Business of fisheries, self-employment schemes, based industries and pastoral management.

Newspapers

Newspapers regularly publish the expert views of agricultural scientists in various languages. Through which the farmers become aware about the schedule of the sowing the seeds, irrigation pattern, demand of the fertilizers and harvesting schedule. They also know about the diseases and their control methods. The farmers get the information of high yielding new species or variety only with the help of media. One of the biggest obstacle before the print media is that most of the Indian farmers are illiterate they cannot read the newspapers. As such only the literate farmers are benefitted from the news published in newspapers.

Electronic Media

The electronic media render its services through radio, television and mobile phones. It is very quick and effective way of delivering the information at national and international levels. The responsibility of media has increased with the increase of the literacy.

Figure 12.1: Cover Pages of some Farm Magazines

(a) (b)

Figure 12.2: (a) Newspaper Stall in Chennai, (b) English Newspaper 'Daily Mail'

The reporters of electronic media are trained in such a way that they bring the report of various social, cultural, political or scientific events before the public within seconds. Up-to-date knowledge of

Figure 12.3: Photographs of Electronic Media (Radio, Television and Mobile Phone)

Government policies and scientific achievements is now available to the common man only because of the electronic media. The media matters a lot because they have a key role not only in agricultural and rural development but in governance, democracy and transparency. Radio, television and mobile phones have been acclaimed to be the most effective media for diffusing the scientific knowledge to the masses.

Electronic media has emerged as a powerful tool in this direction. Radio came forward as a source of inspiration in this direction. Even the illiterate farmers are taking benefit from the radio and television programs related to their crops. There are a number of programs on radio which are dedicated to the farmers. They are broadcasted in local language so that the farmers could understand and follow the information related to the agriculture. These programs have been very popular as they provide the information related to the crops being sown in the current season. Some programs are developed and made interested by the addition of songs or dramas of local language especially for the farmers. The farmers hear these programs regularly. They also share their agriculture related problems with the experts.

Radio for Agricultural Development

Mass media plays an important role in the development of agriculture sector. Agriculture has always been a highly knowledge-intensive sector requiring continuous information flow. Farmers' quest for authentic, credible and usable information both from established systems and traditional practices is ever increasing in this fluctuating global environment, to operate efficiently and compete economically. The rapid changes happening around with globalization, uncontrolled urbanization, uncertainty in climate change, discerning consumer segment and continued farm crisis emphasize the importance of timely, appropriate and need based information and knowledge to meet myriad developmental challenges.

Effective extension, education and communication services are probably some of the key strategies for sustaining agricultural growth, strengthening food security and combating hunger and malnutrition. However, diverse socio-cultural backgrounds, linguistic barriers, geographical remoteness and differential incentives make the task of information dissemination challenging.

Agricultural extension is the vehicle or system for delivering useful information to farmers and assisting those farmers to develop requisite knowledge, skills and attitudes to make use of this information or technology effectively. In recent times advances in Information and Communication Technologies (ICTs) are revolutionizing agriculture extension by offering various technological options such as television, internet, mobile, telephony etc.

Since independence, India has implemented many extension programs for agriculture and rural development. Agriculture being a state subject, there is a long list of multi-sectors as well as single sector extension models and approaches that were tried, one after another and often in overlapping manner, in the public domain. Despite being well-intentioned and comprehensively designed, these efforts have been often criticized for their poor performance as they all fell well short of set objectives.

Among the three main categories of mass communication tools for agricultural extension such as radio, television and print media, the importance of radio for agricultural extension cannot be denied. Radio is a powerful communication tool. India's post-independence experiments with ICT use in agricultural development started with radio. A network of All India Radio (AIR) stations were established across the country that broadcast agricultural programmes in regional languages. AIR (now Prasar Bharathi) has been playing a significant role since many years – bringing new technological information on agriculture and other allied subjects to the farmers. With the recent liberalization of the broadcasting licensing policy, Community Radio has received a new impetus in India. This form of participatory communication has proved to be very successful as a tool for social and economic development at grass root level. The local community needs which are often neglected by the mainstream media could be adequately addressed by community radio. Even farmer to farmer extension can be easily made possible through adequate capacity building as the HAM radio experience underway in Tamil Nadu and Andhra Pradesh shows. Experience with rural radio has shown the potential for agricultural extension to benefit from both the reach and the relevance that local broadcasting can achieve through participatory communication approaches. Extension workers use radio for communicating information on new methods and techniques, giving timely information about the control of crop pests and diseases, weather, market news, etc. For this purpose, talks, group discussions, folksongs, dialogues and dramas are usually organized.

Radio initiatives as part of broader communication for development strategies have been used by various international agencies like UNESCO, UNICEF and FAO of the United Nations since 1960's. The FAO developed the Strategic Extension Campaign (SEC) methodology in many countries of Africa, Asia and Latin America in order to support the local extension workers. For example the campaign in Malaysia, in collaboration with FAO's Inter Country Programme on Integrated Pest Management in Rice, radio was used to discourage the use of a particular chemical, Zinc Phosphide, in preference to a safer alternative. The follow up evaluation showed impressive results as number of farmers dropping use of Zinc Phosphide fell by 52 per cent. Various services like market information, market standards, certification, post-harvest technologies etc. besides production specific knowledge are critical for farmers. In this era of globalization, radio can prove to a cost-effective and reliable ICT with manifold advantages.

There is an interesting combination of approaches in the use of rural radio for agriculture extension. They are locally focused, using indigenous knowledge to build on local cultural and agro-ecological diversity, blending with technology and scientific innovation. Also a two way communication of sharing farmers experience can be an interesting adaptation. Historically agriculture extension has often failed to communicate technical information to farmers in a way that has enabled it to be adopted locally. Thus the combinations of approaches strike an effective balance between indigenous and scientific approaches to agricultural development.

The experience of agricultural extension at Simli Radio has shown that the most popular programmes are those that can provide farmers with a direct income-earning opportunity. This frequently involves discussion and training on topics that help to combine growing traditional crops with a supplementary activity that does not require high levels of investment or risk in terms of ceasing existing activities. Specific examples of popular programmes have been on bee-keeping, rearing grass-cutters and giant snail production especially for sale to customers in the south of the country. These additional extension programmes are most popular during the dry season when farmers have the time to consider alternative strategies. During the cropping season specific advice is referred on the full range of crops being grown locally, timed to coincide with the various stages of land preparation, planting, weeding, water management, harvesting and marketing. However, using radio for agriculture extension is just one dimension, as rural radio can serve multiple roles of extending socio-economic development in rural areas such as health, nutrition, sanitation etc.

Prasar Bharti has started Prashnottri Karyakram in which the farmers are able to ask the problems through letters. A team of experts at radio station summarize the questions asked by the farmers and invite the experts from various Universities or scientists of IARI, CPRI etc., and also to the leading farmers to answer these problems. This program has earned a great reputation among the farmers all over the country and they have been benefitted from the views expressed by the agricultural experts. At the end of news weather forecast at Radio and Doordarshan is also beneficial to the farmers. The farmers can plan their work according to the weather conditions. Media also warns the coastal farmers and fishermen not to go deep into the sea or seashores. In this way it saves them from the danger of the cruelty of the weather.

Television for Agricultural Development

In a country like India, where literacy level is low, the choice of communication media is of vital importance. In this regard the televisions are significant, as they transfer modern agricultural technology to literate and illiterate farmers alike even in interior areas, within short time.

In India farm and home broadcast with agricultural thrust were introduced in 1966, to enlighten farmers on the use of various technologies to boost agricultural development. With the main stream of Indian population engaged actively in agriculture, television could serve as a suitable medium of dissemination of farm information and latest technical know – how. The farmers can easily understand the operations, technology and instruction through television. The culture of the media is changing to be a vehicle of development and not an instrument of the State.

Doordarshan is most powerful means of electronic media. It shows the pictures of the actual position of farming, difficulties of the farmers, natural calamities and more over the solutions of these problems. Media forwards the policies of the Government among the people so that they may get benefit from them. Time to time, Government declare several policies like loan for seeds and fertilizers, subsidy on agricultural machines like tractor, cultivator, threshing machine, tube well, solar system etc., the information of these policies also reach to the farmers through the media only. Television encourages the farmers by bringing the success stories of some farmers before the others. It works like a bridge between the farmers and the Government machinery. If the farmers are in some difficulty, the media brings it to the knowledge of the Government officials so that a solution may come. Doordarshan plays an important role in organizing 'Kisan Melas' etc. at Government organizations like IARI. Here the farmers come in direct contact of the agricultural scientists and are free to clarify their doubts.

Electronic media is an integral part of the society and plays a vital role in the development of the farmers and also the nation. The scientists at Doordarshan suggest many ways to enhance the economic condition of the farmers. There are several co-agricultural professions like organic farming, aromatic farming, sericulture, vermicomposting, fishery, poultry, piggery, honey industry; dairy etc. which can be efficiently run with agriculture at low costs and the farmers can be benefitted from them. Farmers are free to satisfy their queries through Doordarshan on toll free 'Kisan Call Centers'.

Use of Mobile Phones for Agricultural Development

Mobile phones are rapidly spreading all over the world. The global mobile penetration rate was estimated at about 76 per 100 inhabitants in 2010 (ITU, 2011). Poor developing countries are increasingly part of this widespread use of mobile phones and mobile phones are also making quick inroads to rural areas where most of the poor live. This rapidly spread of mobile phone owners new possibilities for poor rural and agricultural households in developing countries as they allow users to overcome important barriers of physical distance and improve access to information and services.

Mobile phones are increasingly used in rural areas in Africa and Asia to disseminate daily prices of agricultural commodities.

Figure 12.4: Indian Farmer Using Mobile Phone to get Weather and Market Data

Better and timely price information may improve the welfare for small farmers in different ways. First, better information may lead farmers to make better allocation of production factors. When the farmers receive clear production incentives, they can better seize market opportunities through the adjustment of production plans. Second, information can improve the bargaining position of the small farmers and improve competition between traders. Thirdly, given the provision of alternative nearby markets, farmers can use the information to switch between end markets. And, the farmers can use the information to make choices around the timing of marketing. Consequently, erratic price variations should be reduced as arbitrage over time and space becomes easier and more widespread.

At present, only 10 to 15 per cent of the farmers are benefitting from the mobile phone services and about 24 per cent of farmers are aware of it. The economic benefit of these services, however, has been estimated by India's National Council of Applied Economic Research (NCAER) to be Rs.50,000 per year—approximately US$10 billion. If the country's entire farming community were to tap this resource, that amount would more than quadruple, to Rs. 211,000 crores. Farmers can also receive market data through their mobile phones. Dr. Raj S. Paroda, Executive Secretary of the Asia-Pacific Association of Agricultural Research Institutions (APAARI), explains that farmers previously had difficulty accessing market information, putting them in a weak position.

The coverage of different subject matter by radio, television, newspaper and farm magazine are almost similar with regard to agriculture, horticulture, animal husbandry, agricultural marketing, agricultural engineering and cooperatives (Purushothaman *et al.*, 2003). Greater exposure of new agricultural technologies to the farmers is likely to enhance awareness about the latest recommendations and to lead to farmers putting these recommendations into practice in a precise manner (Muhammad and Garforth, 1995). It is an important fact that the amount of detailed information transmitted by mass media is limited, they can serve an important and valuable function in stimulating farmers' interest in new ideas. Once stimulated or made aware through mass media, farmers may seek additional information from neighbors, friends, extension workers or progressive farmers in the area.

Computer and Internet

Computers are among the most important discoveries of 21st century. Our Prime Minister Late Shri Rajiv Gandhi had advocated for new scientific approaches in this century. According to him- "Development is not about factories, dams and roads. Development is about people. The goal is material, cultural and spiritual fulfillment for the people. The human factor is of supreme value in development."

Figure 12.5: Farmers Enjoying Internet Facility at e-Choupals (*Source*: ITC Limited)

The e-Choupal, India's largest rural ICT initiative, leverages information technology and the Internet to improve efficiency in the rural Indian agricultural sector, promoting greater information exchange and the creation of an alternative market structure. Although, rural India suffers from a weak ICT infrastructure and poor literacy profile, the greater access and exchange of market and farming information provided by this initiative alleviates rural isolation and poverty by creating market transparency. This in turn improves the rural Indian farmers' productivity and incomes.

In mature agricultural economies such as the United States, farmers benefit greatly from easy access to market information and vertical market integration. However, the agriculture landscape in India is characterized by fragmented farms, weak infrastructure and the involvement of numerous intermediaries. In this system, crops are sold by rural farmers with small holdings to traders, who act as purchasing agents for corporate buyers at a local, government-mandated marketplace called a mandi. Due to the lack of market information, rural Indian farmers have only an approximate idea of price trends and have to accept whatever the price offered them by the traders on the day that they bring their crops to the mandi. As a result, traders are well positioned to exploit both farmers and buyers through practices that sustain system-wide inefficiencies.

Typically poor and often illiterate, rural Indian farmers generally have very limited access to information and education regarding improved farming techniques, that could enhance their yield. Farmers also typically do not have ready access to quality inputs, like sowing seeds, herbicides and pesticides, or to critical information such as accurate weather forecasts that could help them improve the quality of their crops. Such inefficiencies drastically increased transaction costs and slashed potential profits for the rural Indian farmers.

Under the e-Choupal (which means "village square" or "gathering place" in Hindi) project, Internet centers are set up in rural Indian farming villages to provide farmers of soybeans, wheat, coffee, and shrimp with easy access to real-time information and the Internet. These real-time prices are collated from the mandi via an arrangement with ITC Limited and are provided on ITC Limited's e-Choupal portal. The real-

Figure 12.6: Farmers Accessing Internet to Gather Information Related to Various Crops (*Source*: ITC Limited)

time market prices for wholesale products enable poor Indian farmers to better negotiate prices, and thus get the most out of their crops. The e-Choupal portal also provides the rural agricultural communities with information in their respective local languages on weather forecasts, education on improved farm practices and risk management, and as well as knowledge and purchases of better quality farm inputs. Through the Internet, farmers can even share best practices and consult with an agronomist by e-mail to seek assistance for problems associated with their crops. This ready access to localized, relevant information and resources greatly helps poor, rural Indian farmers to improve the quality of their crops and thus realize a better price for their efforts.

The e-Choupal project integrates the Internet centers (e-Choupals) into the livelihood of the rural Indian communities, using "click-and-mortar" principles, combining Internet and real-world intermediaries, to bridge the gap of real-time information access to otherwise poor, illiterate farmers. Much of the project depends on a local representative. ITC Limited, the initiator of the project, selects a respected farmer from the village and trains him to host and facilitate the e-Choupal project. This trained farmer, called sanchalak (which means "lead farmer"), hosts the computer (with Internet connection via phone lines or VSAT) in his house, thus taking care of security and maintenance of the computer system. The sanchalak, who has to take a public oath of service to the entire community, also serves as an intermediary for illiterate farmers to gain access to the requisite information for their farming needs. Each e-Choupal typically serves an average of about 600 farmers in 10 surrounding villages within about a 5km radius. The access to the e-Choupals remains free for the farmers, while the sanchalak gains a small commission from ITC Limited for transactions via the e-Choupals.

Media is therefore an integrated part of modern life in the form of entertainment, knowledge and social welfare. It imparts scientific, social and cultural knowledge in a wide section of the society in fraction of seconds.

References

Ali M (1994). An inquisition of the constraints hampering agricultural extension work: A case study of Faisalabad tehsil.

M.Sc. Thesis, Department of Rural Sociology, University of Agriculture, Faisalabad–Pakistan.

Amekawa Y, Sseguya H, Onzere S and Carranza I (2010). Delineating the multifunctional role of agroecological practices: Toward sustainable livelihoods for smallholder farmers in developing countries. J. Sustain. Agric, 34(2): 202-228.

Bauman A, Smith BJ, Maibach EW and Reger-Nash B (2006). Evaluation of mass media campaign for physical activity. J. Eval. Program Plann., 29(3): 312-322.

Behrens JH and Evans JF (1984). Using mass media for extension teaching. In: Swanson, B.E. (ed.), Agricultural Extension: A Reference Manual, pp. 144-155. FAO, Rome, Italy.

Defleur and Ball – Rockeach (1975). Theories of Mass Communication. David McKay.

Encyclopaedia Brittannicca. London, 1980.

Gorg, H. and E. Strobl. (2001). Multinational companies and productivity spillovers: A meta-analysis. Royal Economic Society 111 (475): F723–F739.

Hanif S (1992). Comparative effectiveness of various sources of information for cane growers in Crescent Sugar Mills' Zone Area. M.Sc. (Hons.) Thesis, Department of Agriculture Extension, University of Agriculture, Faisalabad–Pakistan.

Md. Salleh Hassan, Hayrol Azril Mohamed Shaffril, Muhamad Sham Shahkat Ali and Nor Sabila Ramli (2010). Agriculture agency, mass media and farmers: A combination for creating knowledgeable agriculture community. Afri J Agril Res 5(24): 3500-3513.

Muhammad, S and C Garfoth (1995). Farmer's information exposure and its impact on their adoption behaviour. Pakistan J Agr Sci 32: 262–65.

Opara, U.N. (2008). Agricultural information sources used by farmers in Imo State, Nigeria. J. Inf. Dev. 24(4): 289-295.

Purushothaman C, Kavaskar M, Reddy YA and Kanagasabapathi K (2003). Role of mass media in agriculture. In: Paper presented in International Conference on 'Communication for

Development in the Information Age: Extending the Benefits of Technology for All' held at the Department of Extension Education, Institute of Agricultural Sciences, Banaras Hindu University, Varanasi, (India).

Thiam, A., B. E. Bravo-Ureta, and T. E. Rivas. (2001). Technical efficiency in developing country agriculture: A meta-analysis. Agril Econo 25 (2–3): 235–243.

Chapter 13

Sustainable Agriculture: A Pathway for Poverty Alleviation

☆ *Raj Kumar Patel, Manish Kumar Singh, Kamala Kant and Neelima Patel*

Sustainable agriculture has emerged as an alterna-tive agricultural system that addresses many of the constraints faced by resource-poor farmers and at the same time ensures environmental sus-tainability. It refers to the capacity of agriculture over time to contribute to overall welfare by pro-viding sufficient food and other goods and serv-ices in ways that are economically efficient and profitable, socially responsible, and environmen-tally sound. This system involves a combination of inter-related soil, crop and livestock production practices in conjunction with the discontinua-tion or the reduced use of external inputs that are potentially harmful to the environment and/or the health of farmers and consumers. Instead, it emphasizes the use of techniques of food pro-duction that integrate and are adapted to local natural processes such as nutrient cycling, biologi-cal nitrogen fixing, soil regeneration and natural enemies of pests composting, water and soil conservation, and crop diversification. Using local resources to make initial soil and land improvements can get farmers on a virtuous cycle where rising incomes relieve the constraints to adoption of more resource-intensive sustainable practices.

The ultimate goal of sustainable agriculture is to develop farming systems that are productive and profitable, conserve the natural resource base, protect the environment, and enhance health and safety, and to do so over the long-term. The means of achieving this is low input methods and skilled management, which seek to optimize the management and use of internal production inputs (*i.e.*, on-farm resources) in ways that provide acceptable levels of sustainable crop yields and livestock production and result in economically profitable returns. This approach emphasizes such cultural and management practices as crop rotations, recycling of animal manures, and conservation tillage to control soil erosion and nutrient losses and to maintain or enhance soil productivity.

Definition of Sustainable Agriculture

At the 1992 earth summit in Rio de Janeiro, the UN Food and Agriculture Organization (FAO) defined "sustainable agriculture and rural development" as follows:

"Sustainable development is the management and conservation of the natural resource base and the orientation of technological and institutional change in such a manner as to ensure the attainment and continued satisfaction of human needs for present and future generations. Such sustainable development (in the agriculture, forestry, and fisheries sector) conserves land, water, plant and animal genetic resources, is environmentally non-degrading, technically appropriate, economically viable and socially acceptable".

In 1995 FAO went on to define sustainable agriculture and rural development more specifically as a process that meets the following criteria:

- "Ensures that the basic nutritional requirements of present and future generations, qualitatively and quantitatively, are met while providing a number of other agricultural products.
- Provides durable employment, sufficient income, and descent living and working conditions for all those engaged in agricultural production.

- ☆ Maintains and, where possible, enhances the productive capacity of the natural resource base as a whole, and the regenerative capacity of renewable resources, without disrupting the functioning of basic ecological cycles and natural balances, destroying the socio-cultural attributes of rural communities, or causing contamination of the environment, and
- ☆ Reduces the vulnerability of the agricultural sector to adverse natural and socio-economic factors and other risks, and strengthens self-reliance".

Why Sustainable Agriculture?

We can compare three broad types of farming: traditional production systems, conventional modern agriculture (such as Green Revolution technologies), and sustainable agriculture. We can compare them across three dimensions: ecological, economic and social.

Ecological Sustainability

Sustainable agriculture has major advantages over both traditional and conventional practices. It has capability of maintaining soil fertility, increases water holding capacity of soil, increases biodiversity, reduces pollution due to pesticides, reduces chances of landscape, flooding and soil erosion, reduces green house gas production by reducing use of artificial fertilizer and hence helpful in reducing climate changes also.

Economic Sustainability

Agriculture cannot be sustainable unless it is economically viable over the long term. Conventional agriculture poses greater long term economic risks than sustainable alternatives. In modern agricultural practices there is increased risk of loss due to market fluctuation, increased debt in small and marginal farmers due to increased input-output cost ratio, reduced employment opportunities due to mechanization.

Social Sustainability

Social sustainability will cause inclusive development of rural people, reduces the feeling of social injustice among those who feel neglected and excluded from development opportunities. Local acceptance will increase as it practices are more likely based on social customs, traditions, norms, and taboos. Sustainable agriculture is base on indigenous knowledge with locally adopted farm practices with involvement of farm women and hence along with development, it will cause women empowerment. As women participate in farm practices she also get share in farm returns which is less practical in mechanized farming.

Approaches to Sustainable Agriculture

Approach to sustainable agriculture is to achieve environmentally sound, economically profitable ethically acceptable and socially responsible form of land husbandry. The discussion below illustrates some of these approaches.

Organic Agriculture

Organic agriculture was developed as a holistic, ecosystem-based approach, conceived as an alternative to what proponents see as the ecologically unsound practices of conventional agriculture. It is necessary to distinguish between certified organic agriculture, and agriculture which is practiced in an organic way but without certification.

Traditional Organic Practices

Many traditional agricultural practices around the world refrain from using chemical fertilizers and pesticides. They do this for various reasons: by tradition, because farmers cannot afford agrochemicals, they cannot buy them locally, or they do not know how to use them. This traditional form of organic agriculture is not necessarily sustainable, even if it has been adapted to local conditions over many generations. Population growth, declining prices, insecure land tenure and water-use rights, along with many other factors, have often led to overuse, loss of diversity, soil degradation and other environmental problems. In many instances, traditional forms of agriculture can no longer produce enough income and a secure livelihood. Hence then urgent need for more sustainable approaches. There are numerous modern attempts to update these traditional forms of land use. Some of them are described below.

Site-Appropriate Agriculture or Eco-Farming

This tries to cut down on costly inputs and minimize negative environmental impacts by making intelligent use of existing ecological fac-tors. It developed as an alternative to the increasingly intensive use of irrigation and fertilizers, and tries to free farmers from constraining factors in the local natural environment.

Low-External-Input Agriculture

This also aims to practise sustainable agriculture with minimal use of external inputs, but does not completely exclude the use of pesticides or synthetic fertilizers.

Integrated Pest Management

This approach reduces the use of synthetic pesticides by integrating a range of ways to control pests and disease pathogens, from crop rotations to determining damage thresholds before applying plant protection products.

Integrated Nutrient Management

This approach makes a special effort to minimize fertilizer inputs.

Watershed Management

The rehabilitation of degraded watershed areas has become a high priority. Watershed management aims to adapt land management practices in ecologically vulnerable hill and mountain regions to the natural carrying capacity by means of systematic management. Unlike the other methods mentioned above, it is not an agricultural produc-tion system. Rather, it is a process that plans and regulates the use of land, water and other resources within a watershed area, in ways that sustain these resources. It involves not just technologies, but also devising policies and usage guidelines. It emphasizes adapting technical solutions to the socio-economic circumstances of users, respecting the (often conflicting) needs of different resources users and attempting to reconcile their interests.

Conservation Agriculture and Minimum Tillage

This aims to conserve the soil structure and improve the water storage capacity of the soil. Introduced on a large farm level it is often combined with weed management through pesticides. Because it eliminates ploughing, con-servation agriculture needs less labour, so is a viable option for areas with labour shortages. By using crop rotation and intercropping, it reduces risk through diversification.

The Components of Sustainable Agriculture

Economic Profitability

The agricultural sector has potential to create economic growth in rural areas. It generates job opportunities in adding value (as in the food processing industry), in bringing agricultural products to the consumer (market linkages), and in providing support (infrastructure, information, quality control and training). Simultaneously reducing machinery, chemi-cal fertilizer and pesticide costs (for farmers who can afford these inputs), depending on the specific characteristics of the production system.

ATTRA lists the following indicators that a farm is achieving economic sustainability:

- ☆ The family savings or net worth is consistently going up.
- ☆ The family debt is consistently going down.
- ☆ The farm enterprise is consistently profitable from year to year.
- ☆ Purchase of off-farm feed and fertilizer is decreasing.
- ☆ Reliance on government payments is decreasing.

Environmental Stewardship

Typically this is achieved through pro-tecting, recycling, replacing and/or maintaining the natural resource base such as land (soil), water, biodiversity and wildlife that contribute towards conservation of natural capital. Synthetic fertiliz-ers can be used to supplement natural inputs, as needed. Under sustainable agriculture, synthetic chemicals known to harm soil organisms, soil structure and biodiversity are avoided or reduced to minimum use.

ATTRA lists the following indicators that a farm is achieving environmental sustainability:

- ☆ There is no bare ground.
- ☆ Clean water flows in the farm's ditches and streams.
- ☆ Wildlife is abundant.
- ☆ Fish are prolific in streams that flow through the farm.
- ☆ The farm landscape is diverse in vegetation.

Social Responsibility

Social sustainability relates to the quality of life of those who work and live on the farm, as well as those in the surrounding communities. It includes ensuring equitable revenue or returns to different stakeholders of the agricultural production chain.

ATTRA lists the following indicators that a farm is achieving social sustainability:

- ☆ The farm supports other businesses and families in community.
- ☆ The number of rural families is going up or holding steady.
- ☆ Young people take over their parents' farms and continue farming.
- ☆ College graduates return to the community after graduation.

Sustainable Agriculture and Poverty

There are strong, direct relationships between agricultural productivity, hunger, and poverty. Most poverty is concentrated in rural areas, especially amongst small scale farmers and landless families. Hunger is not simply a function of how much food is produced. Differences in purchasing power and access to land and resources are among the major causes of underdevelopment in rural areas. Agriculture can be sustainable when it not only produces a lot of high-quality food, but also generates income for poor people. That means rural development: improving transport, development of market facilities and linkages, improving (access to) information, participation of the rural poor in decision making, providing access to credit, and so on.

FAO has formulated the following priority areas:

- ☆ Improve agricultural productivity in poor rural communities
- ☆ Develop and conserve natural resources
- ☆ Expand rural infrastructure and market access
- ☆ Strengthen capacity for knowledge generation.

Main Constraints to the Adoption of Sustainable Agriculture Practices

Given evidence indicating that sustain-able agriculture practices can in fact create multiple benefits, including reduction in production costs, environmental benefits and at the same time increased food production; it is crucial to understand what drives or constrains resource-poor farmers from adopting such technologies. Innovation Brief, (2009) pointed out following constraints

Heterogeneity in Agro-Climatic Environments

Implies that no single approach can be applied all over the world in a uniform manner. Different techniques and systems are applied, and adapted, in different agro-ecological conditions, giving dif-ferent results. For example:

Local or regional biophysical factors such as land quality and plot characteristics have been found to be key determinants of adoption of soil conservation technologies. Similarly, the same technologies may not fit all households equally because of different endowments in resources and imperfect or non-existing markets such as credit markets.

Biomass Availability

The adoption of sustainable agricultural practices by resource-poor farmers depends on the amount and availability of biomass (*e.g.*, crop residues, animal dung). This is because benefits of most sustainable agriculture practices (*e.g.*, erosion control, moisture conservation, soil fertility enhancement, carbon sequestration) are directly related to the amount of biomass used as soil amendments. Although resource-poor farmers might be aware of soil and environmental degradation caused by not using biomass as soil amendment, they may still choose to divert scarce biomass to use either as cooking fuels or as fodder for the cat-tle because they do not have alternatives.

Economic Incentives in Determining the Economic Viability of Sustainable Agriculture

The profitability (both in the short and long term) of sustainable agriculture practices will affect their broader diffusion. The adoption and economic returns of a technology are a function of several factors such as prices, consumer demand for food type, physical infrastructure, market access and development, agro-ecology, and household characteristics (*e.g.* rich versus poor and male versus female headed households).

Final Demand

Also drives adoption of technolo-gies. Greater knowledge and improved channels of communication are leading consumers to demand food increasingly produced through organic methods in many developed countries. At the same time, consumers are increasingly demanding that their food be produced using techniques that conserve natural resources, limit environmental pressures and pay greater attention to rural viabil-ity and animal welfare.

Access to Information

Is crucial in creating awareness and attitudes towards technology adoption. Inadequate information on availability, net benefits of adoption, and technical details of implementation of sustainable practices are barri-ers to adoption.

Institutions

Institutions are important in facilitating the promotion and adoption of sustainable agriculture practices. Applied research, extension services, and NGO networks could typically serve as a vehicle for the development, implementation, and adaptation of these practices. Participatory approaches that take into account local social capital in implementing technologies have been identified as one of the key factors influencing adoption of sustainable agriculture practices.

Lack of Proper Extension Services

It has been identified as constraining adoption of produc-tivity-enhancing technologies. Lack of skills of extension workers, particularly on sustainable agriculture practices, has been recognized as a key shortcoming of many extension delivery systems. Given limited governmental resources and the fiscal pressure on existing extension services, it is important to recognize the value of encouraging farmer-to-farmer extension through proper train-ing of selected farmers. Informal networks among farmers have always been powerful channels for exchanging information and spreading knowledge.

Political Constraints

At the national and inter-national level the policy environment may be more or less conducive to the widespread adop-tion of sustainable agricultural practices. Factor affecting the design of agricultural policies is the degree of awareness of policy-makers of the benefits of sustainable agricultural practices, and sustainable agriculture by discouraging the use of external inputs such as chemical fertilizers and chemicals for weed management and pest control, might face resistance from agro-chemicals indus-tries and other traditional factors in intensive agri-cultural supply chains.

Conclusion

Sustainable agriculture meets economic, environmental, and social objectives simultaneously; because these three objectives always overlap, they are managed together. Economic sustainability requires selecting profitable enterprises and doing comprehensive financial planning. Social sustainability involves keeping money circulating in the local economy, and maintaining or enhancing the quality of life of the farm family. Environmental sustainability involves keeping the four ecosystem processes (effective energy flow, water and mineral cycles, and viable ecosystem dynamics) in good condition. Managing economics, society, and environment simultaneously depends on clear goal-setting, effective decision making, and monitoring to stay on track toward the goal. Wise decisions allow us to extract our living from the land as the interest, while preserving the social, water, and soil capital.

References

Applying the Principles of Sustainable Farming ATTRA (2003). Information available at https://attra.ncat.org/attra-pub/summaries/summary.php?pub=295.

FAO (1992). Information available at: www.fao.org/docrep/W7541E/w7541e04.htm.

FAO (1995). Information available at: www.fao.org/wssd/Sard/index-en.htm.

Chapter 14

Expert System: An Effective Tool for Knowledge Management in Agriculture

☆ *Manmeet Kaur, Neelam Bhardwaj and Kiran Arya*

The agriculture sector plays an important role in the overall development of Indian economy. Agriculture contributes about 14.8 per cent of Gross Domestic Product (GDP) and accounts for half of employed labour force. In any agricultural production system, accumulation and integration of related knowledge and information from many diverse sources play an important role. Agriculture specialists utilizes personal experiences and mass media sources to provide information to stakeholders required for decision making to improve agricultural production. Agricultural specialists' assistance is not always available when the need arises for their help. In order to alleviate this problem, various tools, technologies and applications of information technologies have emerged as efficient and effective measures for up-gradation of the whole agricultural field, ranging from scientific studies to farmers help. Integration of expert system as a powerful tool for the stakeholders of agricultural production has extensive potential.

Need of Expert System in Agriculture

The extension worker: farmer ratio is very wide in India *i.e.*1: 1000 and reaching the farmer at the grass root level is very difficult. Thus, the use of information technology for providing technical information to the farmers on specific crops and agro-climatic conditions can be boost for agricultural development. Development of expert system is one such innovation which can provide need based information to the farmers. Expert system in a way addresses many problems and constraints like information unavailability and information dissemination problems.

Information Unavailability

Information may not be available in any form of media. It is only available from human experts, extensionists and/or experienced growers. In addition, the information transfer from specialists and scientists to extensionist and farmers represents a bottle neck for the development of agriculture at the national level. The current era is witnessing a vast development in all fields of agriculture. Therefore, there is a need to transfer the information of experts in certain domain to farmers, especially that the number of experts in new technologies is lesser than their demand. In order to make a viable information dissemination system there is need to look into various information transfer problems.

Information Dissemination Problems

- *Static Information*: Examining the information stored and available in the agriculture domain revealed that this information is static and may not respond to the growers need. All extension documentations give general recommendations because there are many factors if taken into consideration but there are variations in agro-climatic condition and cropping pattern. Therefore, the generalize information can not suitable for stakeholders of varied needs.
- *Specialties Integration*: Most of the extension documents handle problems related to certain specialty: plant pathology, entomology, nutrition, or any other specialty.

In real situations the problem may be due to more than one cause, and may need the integration of the knowledge behind the information included in the different extension documents and books.

- *Combination of More Than One Information Source*: Images may need sometimes an expert to combine other factors to reach an accurate diagnosis, and even if a diagnosis is reached, the treatment of the diagnosed disorder should be provided through extension document.
- *Updating*: Updating the document information is a difficult task. Changes in chemicals, their doses, and their effect on the environment should be considered. Updating this information in documents and distribute them takes long time. The same arguments can be made for audio tapes that are another form of extension documents but in voice instead of written words. Video tapes are more stable than other media as the information provided through the tape describes usually well established agricultural operations. However, if the tape includes information as what is commonly included in documents and audio tapes, this information should be updated.

Suitability and Feasibility of Expert Systems

The problems already raised can to large extent be solved using expert systems to generate the information to the growers by using its knowledge base and reasoning mechanism acquired from human experts and other sources. The expert system generates the advice based on its knowledge base and its reasoning mechanism that are actually behind all developed extension documents, and more. Consequently, when a user enters the data of his/her plantation to the system, the appropriate advice is generated. There are no limitations on the number of generated recommendations. Therefore expert system overcomes the problem of static information provided in extension documents. The knowledge acquisition process for building an expert system facilitates the integration of knowledge and experiences of different specialties. For example, an agricultural diagnostic expert system requires the integration of specialists in nutrition, plant pathology, entomology, breeding, and production. Therefore, when a problem occurs, the system can help the user in identifying the cause of the problem in a much more efficient way than consulting a document that handles a specific problem.

Expert systems can be integrated with other information sources such as images bases and/or textual bases to make use of these sources. For example, images can be used for describing symptoms as it is very difficult and very confusing to describe them in words. Images can also be used for confirming the diagnosis of the cause of a certain disorder. It can also be integrated with textual data bases that may be the extension documents related to the specialty and/or commodity handled by an expert system. This textual data base can be used for explanation purposes of basic terms and operations. It can also be used to confirm the reached conclusion in some situations.

In order to develop an expert system the knowledge has to be extracted from domain expert. This knowledge is then converted into a computer program. Knowledge Engineer performs the task of extracting the knowledge from the domain expert. Rule based expert systems are the most commonly known type of knowledge based systems. The knowledge is represented in the form of IF-THEN rules. Figure 14.1 shows different modules for a rule-based expert system. Expert systems have been developed and applied to many fields. There are many objectives of expert system but in general terms the objective is to generate expert advice for use by a decision-maker.

Expert Systems are Used to Aid

- ☆ Single point decisions. *e.g.* Planning
- ☆ Designing. *e.g.* Design of an irrigation system

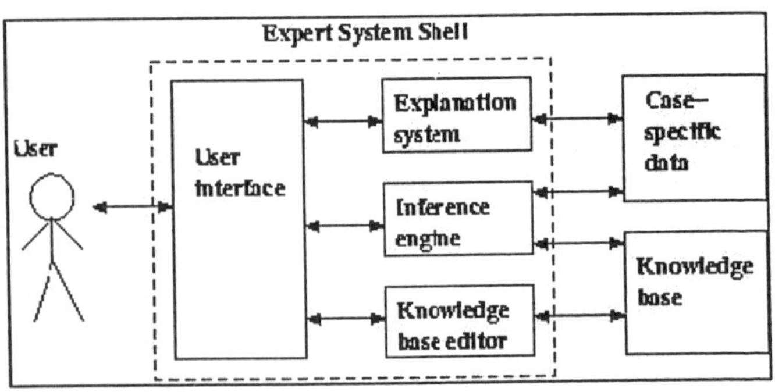

Figure 14.1: Expert System Architecture

- ☆ Selection. *e.g.* The most suitable Crop variety or market outlet
- ☆ Diagnosis or identification. *e.g.* Of a livestock disorder
- ☆ Interpretation. *e.g.* Of a set of financial accounts
- ☆ Prediction. *e.g.* of extreme events such as thunderstorms and frost;
- ☆ A sequence of tactical decisions throughout a production cycle. *e.g.* plant protection and nutrition decisions, livestock feeding.

Further, an Expert System for a Particular Decision Problem can be Used

- ☆ As a stand – alone advisory system for the specific knowledge domain perhaps with monitoring by a human expert
- ☆ To provide decision – support for a high-level human expert
- ☆ To allow a high-level expert to be replaced by a subordinate expert aided by the expert system
- ☆ As a delivery system for extension information
- ☆ To provide management education for decision makers
- ☆ For dissemination of up-to-date scientific information in a readily accessible and easily understood form, to agricultural researchers and advisers

The Logic Flow

The brief logic flow of the expert system is as follows:

- ☆ The part of the plant where symptoms have been the observed is given by the extension officer
- ☆ The basic symptoms are given as input;
- ☆ Considering these symptoms the user is expected to give further information based on other visual symptoms
- ☆ At this step the disease and pest are identified
- ☆ The user is then given the option to either stop or further diagnose and other disease/pest or get preventive or curative measures on these.

All these operations are done using a "mouse", which helps a new user to get acquainted with the system faster and operate it easily. In this system, computer, graphics, digitized pictures and text are being used following a "Decision Tree", logic.

Characteristics of Agricultural Expert System

- ✰ It simulates human reasoning about a problem domain, rather than simulating the domain itself.
- ✰ It performs reasoning over representations of human knowledge
- ✰ It solves problems by heuristic or approximate methods.

Different Expert Systems in Agriculture

On the basis of review from secondary sources certain types of expert systems are identified and elaborated here:

The first software for use by the grape cultivators was prepared by the Indian Institute of Horticultural Research Institute, Bangalore. This spontaneous response made them to undertake similar software for providing guidance to mushroom cultivators, which became extremely popular and a large number of growers using it regularly for getting solutions to their problems. The Institute has launched an effort to give a comprehensive package of practices of about 148 horticulture crops for cultivation in the four Southern states of Kerala, Tamil Nadu, Karnataka and Andhra Pradesh. Center for Informatics Research and Advancement, Kerala has also prepared an Expert System called AGREX to help the Agricultural field personnel give timely and correct advice to the farmers. These Expert Systems find extensive use in the areas of fertilizer application, crop protection, irrigation scheduling, and diagnosis of diseases in paddy and post harvest technology of fruits and vegetables.

POMME (Roach *et al.,* 1985) is an expert system for apple orchid management. POMME advises growers about when and what to spray on their apples to avoid infestations. The system also provides advice regarding treatment of winter injuries, drought control and multiple insect problems.

COMAX (Lemon, 1986) is a crop management expert system for cotton which can predict crop growth and yield in response to external weather variables, soil physical parameters, soil fertility, and pest damage. The expert system is integrated with a computer model, Gossym that simulates the growth of the cotton plant. This was the first integration of an expert system with simulation model for daily use in farm management. In 1987 expert system technology was identified as an appropriate technology to speed up agricultural desert development in Egypt (Rafea and El-Beltagy, 1987). The paper has discussed the importance of applying expert systems in agricultural desert development in Egypt and suggested an integrated structure of an R and D unit to develop and maintain an efficient use of these systems.

CALEX system (Plant, 1989) has been developed for agriculture management. It is domain independent and can be used with any commodity. CALEX consists of three separate modules: an executive, a scheduler, and an expert system shell. The executive serves as the primary interface to the user, to models, and to the disk. The scheduler generates a sequence of management activities by repeatedly activating the expert system. The expert system makes the actual management decisions. Initial development of the system has focused on the development of a package of modules for California cotton and another package for peaches.

In the nineties, several expert systems have also been developed. A sample of these expert systems has also been selected as examples. The selected examples demonstrate trends in the nineties and their accessibility by the reader is also considered. An agroforestry expert system (UNU-AES) was designed to support land-use officials, research scientists, farmers, and other individuals interested in maximizing benefits gained from applying agroforestry management techniques in developing countries (Warkentin *et al.*, 1990). UNU-AES is a first attempt to apply expert systems technology to agroforestry. This system addresses the option for alley cropping, a promising agroforestry technology which has potential applicability when used under defined conditions in the tropics and subtropics. Alley cropping involves the planting of crops in alleys or interspaces between repeatedly hedgerows of fast-growing, preferably leguminous, woody perennials. With the inclusion of more climatic and socio-economic data and improved advisory recommendations, UNU-AES can be expanded to provide advice on alley cropping in more diverse geographical and ecological conditions and eventually address other agro forestry techniques.

In 1991, serious efforts have been started in Egypt to develop crop management expert systems for different crops. A prototype for an expert system for cucumber seedlings productions has been developed. This prototype has six functions: seeds cultivation, media preparation, control environmental growth factors, diagnosis, treatment, and protection. The implementation has used the Hypertext facility included in the EXSYS shell. The overall control was implemented using the language provided by the tool and consequently, the rule base was divided into modules according to the system functions (Rafea *et al.,* 1991). Another expert system for cucumber production management under plastic tunnel (CUPTEX) has been developed to be used by agricultural extension service within the Egyptian Ministry of Agriculture, and by private sector. The main objective of developing such systems is to transfer new technology in agro-management to farmers through packaging this technology using expert systems. This will lead to increasing the production and hence the national income, from one hand, and reducing the production cost from the other hand. CUPTEX is composed of three expert systems for fertigation, plant care, and disorder remediation. The validation of CUPTEX has revealed that it over performs a group of experts in different specialties. Although the direct payoff is not the main objective of the development, experimenting CUPTEX in two research sites has revealed that approximately 26 per cent increase in the production, and 15 per cent decrease in direct cost have been attained. These results show that CUPTEX could pay off approximately 60 per cent of the development cost in four months if it is used to manage the plastic tunnels cultivating cucumber in the five sites in which it was deployed (Rafea *et al.,* 1995). This system is the first deployed agricultural expert system to be selected in the conference of innovative application for artificial intelligence. It is also the first deployed expert system in developing countries not only in agriculture but in other fields as well.

In Italy, an expert system for integrated pest management of apple orchards (Gerevini *et al.,* 1992), POMI, has been developed. Integrated pest management is definable as the reasoned application of agronomic methods products as well as chemicals to allow optimal productive factors, while respecting the farm worker, the environment and the consumer. POMI addresses the first preliminary phase of the complex process of apple orchard integrated control namely the detection of the insect populations in the field and approximate the populations dimensions. The system consists of two parts: classification of user findings, and explanation of these findings using abductive reasoning.

In India, an intelligent front-end for selecting evapotranspiration estimation methods (Mohan and Arumugam, 1995) has been integrated with the methods that calculates the evapotranspiration factor. Evapotranspiration (ET) is an important parameter needed by water managers for the design, operation and management of irrigation systems. Since there are many methods to compute ET, based on climatic data, an inexperienced engineer or hydrologist is perplexed with the selection of an appropriate method. An intelligent front end expert system (ETES) has been developed to select suitable ET estimation methods under South Indian climatic conditions. Ten meteorological stations located in different climatic regions and thirteen ET estimation methods have been considered in this ES. Along with the recommended method, ETES also suggests suitable correction factors for converting the resulting ET values to those of methods that result in accurate estimation.

A picture-based expert system for weed identification (Schulthess *et al.*, 1996) has been developed. Most current expert systems for weed identification are rule-based and using text that contains a large number of botanical terms. In this system the hierarchical classification generic task was used and the text descriptions were replaced with pictures to minimize the use of technical terms. Hypotheses are established or ruled out on the basis of the user's choices among options presented as pictures.

The National Institute of Agricultural Extension Management, popularly known as MANAGE, is an apex national institute set up in 1987 as an autonomous society under the Ministry of Agriculture, Government of India. MANAGE is the Indian response to the challenges of management in a rapidly growing agricultural sector. The MANAGE has developed an expert system to diagnose pests and diseases for rice crop and suggest preventive/curative measures. The rice crop doctor illustrates the use of expert-systems broadly in the area of agriculture and more specifically in the area of rice production through development of a prototype, taking into consideration a few major pests and diseases and some deficiency problems limiting rice yield. This prototype is results of joint effort by the experts from NIIT and computer professionals of MANAGE while the subject matter expert knowledge on rice pathology and entomology, has been obtained from Scientists of Andhra Pradesh Agricultural University (APAU), Directorate of Rice Research (DRR). The following diseases and pests have been included in the system for identification and suggesting preventive and curative measures. The diseases included are rice blast, brown spots, sheath blight, rice tungro virus, false smut fungi, bacterial leaf blight, sheath rot and zinc deficiency disease. The pests included are stem borers, rice gall midge, brown plant hopper, rice leaf folder, green leaf hopper and Gundhi bug.

Conclusion

This paper discussed the use and needs of expert systems in agriculture and also revealed the availability of various expert systems in various countries. The rapid development of internet technology has changed the way of expert system development. It is easy to access the system via internet. The advantages that an expert system can offer better than traditional methods are:

- ☆ Providing the growers with dynamic information related to their actual situations,
- ☆ Taking into consideration different specialties and different sources of information,
- ☆ Shortening the update time of information especially if the expert system is centralized and accessible from different locations,
- ☆ Transferring real experience that is not documented in any form of media by acquiring it from its sources: extensionists, highly experienced growers, and/or researchers.

It is proven that expert systems in agriculture helps a lot in increasing the crop production. But most of the expert systems are in English language. As developing an expert is collaborative effort. Therefore, there is need to strengthen linkages among different stakeholders and users so that the developed expert system is location specific, need based and in local languages.

References

Clancy W.J. (1983) The Epistemology of a Rule Based Expert System; A Framework of Explanation, AI, Vol. 20.

Donald A. (2004) Waterman: A guide to Expert Systems; Perason Education.

Gerevini, A., Perini, A., Ricci, F., Forti, D., Ioratti, C., Mattedi, l.(1992) POMI: An Expert

Gillard, P. (1998) PCAI magazine. Expert System used to disseminate Complex Information in

Agriculture and Horticulture, Knowledge Technology Inc. July/ August.

Lemmon, H. (1986) COMAX: An expert system for cotton crop management. Science 233:29-33.

Michalski, R., Davis, J. Visht, V. and Sinclair, J. (1983) A computer-based advisory system for diagnosing soybean diseases in Illinois. Plant Disease 67:459-463.

Mohan, S., Arumugam, N. (1995) An intelligent front-end for selecting evapotranspiration estimation methods. Computers and electronics in agriculture 12(4): 295-309.

Plant, R. (1989) An integrated expert decision support system for agricultural management. Agricultural Systems 29:49-66

Rafea, A. El-Beltagy, A. (1987). Expert Systems as An Appropriate Technology to Speed Up Agriculture Desert Development in Egypt.Proceedings of the Second International Desert Development Conference, Harwood Academic Publisher. 47-57

Rafea, A., El-Azhari, S., Hassan, E. (1995) Integrating Multimedia With Expert Systems For Crop Production Management. Proceedings of the Second International IFAC Workshop on Artificial Intelligence in Agriculture, Wageningen, The Netherlands.

Rafea, A., Warkentin, M. and Ruth, S. (1991) Knowledge Engineering: Creating Expert Systems for Crop Production Management in Egypt. Chapter 7: 89-104 in Expert Systems in Developing Countries:Practice and Promise, Stephen R. Ruth and Chip

Mann (eds.), Boulder, CO: Westview Press, ISBN0-8133-8397-8.

Roach, J., Virkar, R., Weaver M. and Drake, C. (1985). POMME: A computer-based consultation system for apple orchad management using Prolog. Expert Systems 2(2):56-69

Schulthess,U. et.al. (1996) NEPER-Weed: A Picture-Based Expert System for Weed Identification, Agron. J. 88: 423-427. System for Integrated Pest Management of Apple Orchards, AI Applications, 6(3):

Warkentin, M., Nair, P., Ruth, S. and Sprague, K. (1990) A Knowledge-Based Expert System for Planning and Design of Agroforestry Systems. Agroforestry Systems 11(1): 71-83.

Weis, S.M. and Kulikowasaki,C.A. (1994) A practical guide to designing expert system:, Rowman and Allanheld NJ, USA.

Chapter 15

Adoption and Large Scale Plantation of *Populus deltoides* under Agroforestry in Vaishali District of Bihar

☆ *Aditya Kumar, Rameshwar Das and B.K. Mishra*

In Bihar most of the farmers are marginal or small, who cultivate mainly rice, wheat, maize and pulses. To get more income from less land they utilize agrochemicals in injudicious manner or grow crops in monoculture fashion, which depleted and deteriorated soil health and water resources in the state. The option to achieve more gain without hampering the soil and water health is diversification in crop rotation, but it can be done only in irrigated areas. Agroforestry is one of the land husbandry systems which can be followed for diversification of agricultural systems. It is being promoted and popularized by the Government of India and wood-based industries that, requirements of fuel, fodder and timber for industries can be fulfilled from farms. But for agroforestry the selection of species used in the system is very important, as the species should be fast growing, of short rotation, having high market demand and give more income. Keeping these points in consideration, poplar can be one of the best options. Polar based agroforestry is also considered best to meet the increasing demand of fuel-wood, fodder, timber and to reduce the pressure on forests. Poplar was introduced in India during 1950 from USA and several clones from introduced material were identified suitable for agroforestry in northern India. In northern India it is a most successful agroforestry tree because of its fast growth, straight-growing stem, short rotation, quality wood production and less adverse effect on agricultural crops (Bangarwa, 2008). However, the adoption of poplar based agroforestry is confined to N-W India alone, and it was observed that net income from poplar plantations would be three times greater than agricultural crops alone.

The genus populous belongs to family Salicaceae. It is characterized by unisexual flowers with perinth absent or insignificant and inferior. Its population in natural forest is declining due to many biotic and abiotic factors. Indigenous species of poplar occur in the Himalayan region of Northern India are *P. ciliata, P. gamblei, P. jacquemontii var glauca, P. rotundifolia, P. eupharatica, P. alba* but exotic species *Populus deltoides* is commercially cultivated in India. In India, presently approx 60,000 ha is under poplar plantation and to increase the area under poplar plantation, the only way is to introduce it in nontraditional area for Poplar. It is widely cultivated in Gangetic plains of Uttar Pradesh, Uttarakhand, Punjab, Himachal Pradesh and Haryana while the soil and climatic conditions of northern India is suitable for its cultivation.

Keeping these points in consideration Institute of Forest Productivity (IFP), Ranchi under the aegis of Indian Council of Forestry Research and Education (ICFRE), Dehradun implemented poplar based Agroforestry component of *Samudai Adharit Samanvit Van Prabandhan Evam Sanrakshan Yojana (SASVPSY)* in Vaishali and nearby districts of Bihar. The project was conceived by ICFRE for promotion of economically viable Poplar based agroforestry model in North Bihar districts having vast tract of Gangetic plains. Poplar has been selected as leading species to be introduced in the project. There was target of planting of 76 lakh seedlings (ETP) of poplar raised and introduced on farmers field spread over 1, 250 villages covering 35,000 farmers in all the 16 administrative blocks of Vaishali district and adjacent blocks of nearby districts. The effort also developed forest nursery based entrepreneurs among farmers for raising Kisan nursery and capacity building of farmer's skill in forest nurseries, plantation techniques for different species, apart from exposure study tours to different poplar growing regions of the country. Establishment of Model nursery, Demonstration centers, Clonal garden and Hedge garden were also some of the key activities.

Keeping all these points in consideration Institute of Forest productivity (IFP), Ranchi implemented Poplar based Agroforestry system in Vaishali and nearby districts of Bihar with following objectives:

1. To motivate farmers to adopt polar based agroforestry in the farm lands.
2. To expand area under polar based agroforestry in non-traditional areas of Bihar through afforestation program.
3. To encourage for expansion and improvement of homestead forestry, farm forestry, village woodlots, private woodlots through adequate extension and appropriate incentives with emphasis on Poplar and other important species.
4. To study the impacts of poplar based agroforestry on rural livelihood.

Methodology and Results

As environmental conditions, soil and geographic location of Vaishali district are almost similar to that of traditional poplar growing areas, the Vaishali and adjacent districts were selected for this project implantation. It has been found that in these districts plantation of horticultural trees like mango, litchi, guava and banana are very common. However, forestry trees plantations were meagre and mainly found species was Semal. The climatic condition and soil in these areas were found very suitable for agroforestry and particularly for poplar based agroforestry, but the adoption of any new system depends on user's awareness, attitude, risk bearing ability etc. so, it was needed to motivate and create awareness among the farmers.

To achieve objectives of the project following methodologies/ activities were adopted:

Motivation and Awareness Programme

The farmers of Vaishali were ignorant about the agroforestry and trees planted mostly on homestead land and wastelands. They traditionally managed *Delbergia sisoo* plantations, but due to problem of its drying in recent years, they lack interest towards tree planting. For personal use they also raised bamboos. The tree planting or agroforestry was limited to big farmers only so, to achieve the target of huge plantation in limited period, multi-prolonged strategies were adopted to motivate the farmers.

Village Meetings

Initially, village meetings were conducted in which farmers were explained about the benefits of agroforestry by resource persons from Forest Research Institute, Dehradun, Forest Training Academy, Haldwani and other Universities. Posters and pamphlets were distributed among the farmers. Efforts were made to sensitize them about choice of species and benefits of opting Poplar.

Involvement of NGOs

Four NGOs namely "Pratigya Samjik Seva Sansthan, Hajipur, Vaishali", "Mahila Utthan Samiti, Samastipur", "Narayani Seva Sansthan, Hajipur, Vaishali", and "Voluntary Action for Research Development and Networking (VARDAN), New Delhi" were engaged. Each NGO was given its area of jurisdiction for making farmers aware. Street drama and door to door meetings were conducted by NGOs. Essay competition, slogan writings, painting competitions were organized amongst school children for mass awareness.

Engagement of Extension Workers

Large numbers of extension workers were engaged for making personal contacts with each and every household, a door to door campaign was launched in villages. Due to its massive awareness campaign, Poplar plantations could spread over 1, 250 villages covering 35,000 farmers in all the 16 administrative blocks of Vaishali district and adjacent blocks of nearby districts.

Socio-economic Survey

Baseline survey was conducted to prepare socio-economic and environmental profile of the area with structured questionnaire with appropriate statistical design. Structured questionnaires were prepared with the help of scientists of Institute of Social Science, Patna.

Training

To provide trainings to such a large number of farmers having wide coverage was a difficult task. Initially trainings were provided to trainers. Trainers constituted NGOs, extension workers, contractual workers of project, State Forest Department personnel etc. For the villagers, initially meetings were conducted at Jadua where farmers were invited from nook and corner of the district. They were given both class-room and field trainings. Continuous persuasion to the farmers for training was given at village level. The attempts were made to cover maximum villages. Selected farmers were taken to traditional Poplar growing regions of Haldwani (Uttarakhand), Yamunanagar and Dehradun on Kisan Study Tours. At Forest Training Academy (FTA), Haldwani they were provided class room training. In addition, the farmers also interacted with local successful Poplar growers involved in agroforestry.

Choice of Tree Species and its Propagation

The choice of species required suitability to the site, economic viability for the farmers and above all acceptability to the farmers. This task was achieved by educating and continuously motivating them. Earlier, there were apprehensions about the performance of Poplar in Vaishali district, but continuous motivation, training and study tours to farmers resulted in acceptance of poplar as species of choice alongwith other agroforestry species *viz.* mahogany, teak, semal etc.

Supply of Quality Planting Material

Raising quality planting material was essential to get maximum productivity and economic return. Several efforts were taken to ensure availability and utilisation of quality planting stocks *viz.*

Kisan Nursery

In 2007-08 due to heavy rain and flood in Bihar there was problem of water logging in the area, while in 2009-10 and 2010-11 districts experienced severe draught which affected growth and survival of plants. Due to unfavourable weather condition, the survival rate of quality planting material was low, which remarkably increased in subsequent years. The successful farmers were identified for development of nursery based entrepreneurship skills for future sustenance of planting programme.

Farmers were motivated to raise kisan nursery for which they were suitably trained and assisted with appropriate guidelines at each and every stage of nursery rising. The nursery planting materials were provided by the institute and quality ETPs grown by farmers were buy-backed (@ Rs 5.00/ETP). Initially 50,000 ETPs were procured from WIMCO Seedling Ltd, Rudrapur (UK) during 2006-07. Subsequently, during 2007-08 eight (8.0) lakh ETPs were procured from Tanda, Pipal Parao, and South Gadgadia nursery of Central Tarai Division, Haldwani.

From 2006-07 to 2010-2012, a total of 78.49 lac quality ETPs were produced by 600 farmers from 700 ha land (Table 15.1). The total payment distributed to farmers was Rs 39.6 million against raising of kisan nurseries. Some of the farmers even got more than Rs. 9-10 lakh from their 5-8 ha of Kisan nurseries.

Table 15.1: Details of Plants Raised in Kisan Nurseries

Year	*No. of Plants Raised (in Lakh)*
2007-08	1.22
2008-09	31.19
2009-10	25.73
2010-11	14.80
2011-12	5.55
Total	**78.49**

Poplar nursery takes 10-11 months before being ready for uprooting and planting. To get additional income, some farmer inter-cropped Poplar nursery with agriculture crops like garlic, vegetables, mentha, marigold, pulses etc. as most of these agricultural crops were raised during month of January to May.

Establishment of Demonstration Plot

The demonstration field of ICFRE at Goraul has been established where different agroforestry models have been demonstrated. The centre is being used for training of the farmers. Similar demonstration plots have also been established in farmer's field.

Extension of Planting Techniques

Farmers were supplied quality planting materials available mainly from Kisan nurseries. They were assisted in layout of plantations, intercropping of suitable crops; inter cropping of suitable crop combinations, silviculture of Poplar for better productivity and other technical know-how. The farmers were distributed 1990 augurs (tool for pit digging) to facilitate a large number of plantation in limited period of time. Initially due to flood and drought the survival percentage was low. But with passage of years performance improved and farmers became conscious and started taking interest in poplar.

Buyers-Sellers Meet

Since Vaishali was a newer area for Poplar based agroforestry, it was needed to create trust and confidence among farmers regarding assured market of their products. Keeping this in mind a buyers-sellers meet was organised which facilitate interaction among Poplar growers in the area and owner of plywood industries. In the meeting plywood industrialist from Yamunanagar, Haldwani, Roorhkee, Calcutta and local industrialist participated. They were also taken to farmer's field to access marketability and quality. The industry people expressed satisfaction and even granted agreement to purchase trees from the farmers. State government has also agreed to exclude Poplar and other agroforestry from the purview of transit pass.

The project activities helped in economic upliftment of the locals in various ways. *viz.*:

Employment Generation

The project generated 8.21 lacs man-days in last four years. This will go up with various silvicultural operations *e.g.* pruning, harvesting etc.

Availability of Firewood

Poplar requires pruning from the 2nd year of plantation in order to get quality timber. Lops and tops can be used as firewood.

Table 15.2: Year-wise and Species-wise Distribution of Plants Under Agroforestry is as Follows

Financial Year	*Poplar*	*Teak*	*Mahogany*	*Gamhar*	*Semal*	*Kadamb*	*Jamun*	*Bamboo*	*Others*	*Total*
2006-07	0.05	0.00	0.00	0.00	0.00	0.00	0.00	0.00	0.00	0.05
2007-08	1.22	0.28	0.00	0.03	0.00	0.00	0.00	0.00	0.00	1.53
2008-09	23.82	1.60	0.65	0.66	0.13	0.20	0.01	0.06	0.72	27.85
2009-10	21.94	3.90	0.14	0.27	1.00	0.28	0.37	0.00	1.64	29.54
2010-11	14.55	0.13	0.001	0.001	0.03	0.31	0.04	0.00	0.12	15.182
2011-12	3.87	1.38	0.58	0.00	0.25	0.34	0.03	0.00	0.67	7.12
Total	65.45	7.29	1.371	0.961	1.41	1.13	0.45	0.06	3.15	81.27

Income from Kisan Nursery

Kisan nursery has provided livelihood support to farmers. Some of the farmers received more than 8.00 Lakh during last 5 years. One of farmer, Shri Suneel Rai got more than Rs 8.00 Lakh against his investment of less than Rs.90,000 for raising kisan nursery in 5 acre land. Apart from poplar nursery raising, he also intercropped the same with tori and obtained additional 5.0 quintal of tori from 1.5 Acre plot in return. Success of raising kisan nursery and its profitability motivated more than 200 farmers to develop entrepreneurship skill in nursery rising. Their technical and entrepreneurship skill would help in extending poplar in other districts of Bihar.

Development of Rural Wood-Lot

65.45 lakh Poplar and 15.82 lakhs non poplar species have been distributed to the farmers. From the growth data it is expected that each plant will have yield of 5-6 quintals in a rotation period of 8 years. Even by taking lowest estimate of survival (50 per cent), it is expected to provide yield of 18, 79, 300 MT of timber.

Landscape Improvement

Due to large scale plantation landscape has improved. The agroforestry has been adopted both at the nursery and plantation level. In the nursery poplar has been intercropped with garlic, vegetables, *Mentha* spp. etc. The plantation has been done along bund, row and in some cases in block. The silvi-horticulture model has been raised with mango and banana. In block plantation mostly Rabi crops were grown, where normal crop composition of area was being practiced. At some places, farmers have raised poplar with paddy also.

Carbon Sequestration

Poplar is a fast growing species having huge carbon sequestration potential. Poplar sequestrates carbon 93.1ton/ha compared to 51, 79, 38.8 and 38 ton carbon/ha in case of eucalyptus, teak, mango and litchi grown under agroforestry system (Gerra, 2006). During the last five years the anticipated carbon sequestration from project plantation is shown in Table 15.6.

Table 15.4: Growth Pattern of Poplar in Vaishali

Year of Planting	*Average Girth (in inch)*	*Average Height (in ft)*
Jan, 2007	24.0	48.9
Jan, 2008	17.9	36.0
Jan, 2009	14.5	27.4
Jan, 2010	9.9	22.5
Jan, 2011	5.8	17.0

Table 15.5: Expected Yield of Poplar in Vaishali

Planting year	*No of Poplar planted*	*Harvesting year*	*Expected yield (MT)*
Jan 2007	0.05 Lac	2013-14	1,000
Jan 2008	1.22 Lac	2014-15	24,400
Jan 2009	23.82 Lac	2015-16	4,76,400
Jan 2010	21.92 Lac	2016-17	4,38,400
Jan 2011	14.55 Lac	2017-18	3,10,000
Jan 2012	3.87 Lac	2018-19	77,400
Total	**65.45 lac**		**13,27,600**

Note: the estimate was based on following considerations

i) Survival as present assessment.

ii) Assuming 6-7 year rotation.

iii) Moderate growth of 4.0 quintal timber per tree.

Above per tree yield calculation is based on average per tree timber 0.40 MT and fire wood 0.15 MT. The entire output comes to 13.27 Lac MT Timber and 6.13 Lac MT Firewood. The expected value will be around Rs.1210.25 crore from Poplar plantations only, at the prevailing market rate of timber Rs. 7500.00/MT and Rs. 3500.00/MT firewood.

Conclusion

The acceptability of poplar by farming community and its cultivation along with agricultural crops is most important breakthrough. The success story of poplar based agroforestry created interest and awareness among farmers which resulted in adoption of Agroforestry is spreading like forest fire. Farmers are interested in taking this calculated risk for getting 3-4 fold increased revenue

Table 15.6. Estimated Carbon Sequestrated by Plantation Under the Project

Sl.No.	*Activity*	*Species*	*Land Area (Ha)*	*Rate (t/Ha)*	*Sequestration (MT)*
1.	Nursery	Poplar	700	8	5600
		Teak, Semal, Arjun, Jamun	5	NA	NA
2.	Plantation	Poplar	7500	12.74	95,550
		Other Species	3500	1.75	6125
	Total				**1,07,275**

return from the same piece of land. Poplar is replacing Semal the traditional industrial wood raw material of the area aggressively. The initial strategy of "Push" the Poplar has gradually turns into "Pull" (demand) driven stage. Approach of farmers towards tree farming has gone a sea change and they are trying to stick to irrigation and pruning and other tending activities in the tree crops. The large scale plantation has tremendously improved the landscape of this region. It has opened new arena for socioeconomic development of farmers who are traditionally dependent on vagaries of monsoon. The project has provided additional income to the farmers from kisan nursery, wage to landless laborers in addition to providing raw material to wood based industries. It is expected from the growth data that each plant will have yield of 4-6 quintal having rotation of 6-7 years. Even by lower estimate of average survival it expected to provide yield of 13, 27,600 MT of timber which will develop a huge rural wood-lot. This wood lot will provided forestry based raw material to industries which will further lead to employment generation. Based on the prevailing market rate of timber and firewood the expected yield from Poplar plantations will be around Rs. 1210.25 crores. It is anticipated that carbon sequestration from project plantation is around 107275 MT. The project activities has already bringing socio-economic changes in the area in a very short period by eliciting community participation, by providing research and technological inputs by ICFRE and is being seen as a future industrial development based on generation of raw material for wood based industries.

References

Bangarwa Kulvir S (2008). Production potential, market fluctuations and present status of extotics poplar in India. In abs of 23rd Session of the International Poplar Commission, jointly hosted by FAO and by the Beijing Forestry University, the State Forest Administration of China and the Chinese Academy of Forestry; Beijing, China, 27-30 October 2008.

Chaturvedi, A.N. and Rawat, B.S. (1994) Poplar Tree improvement programme. *Indian Forester*. 120 (1):14-20.

Dhiman, R.C. (2010) Growing poplar in Bihar. Ply Gazette, August 2010, page 87-91

Jha K.K.and Chhindwal, C.B. (1992) Nursery testing for development of poplar Planting in Tarai, *Indian Jour. Forestry* 15(4):285-297.

Jha, K.K., Gupta, C.; Verma, R.S. and Chhindwal, C.B. (1993) Performance of Exotic Poplar in Tarai. *Indian Forester*. 119 (2):97-111.

Kaul, R.N. and Sharma, K.K. (1982) Status report on Popalr. *Proc. workshop on Poplars*, Haldwani, January 23-24, FRI Dehradun. 21-53.

Khan, M.A.; Rajkhowa, W.A. and Ghei, V.A. (1961). Trials with poplar. *Proc tenth silvicultural conference*, FRI Dehradun. 691-703.

Kumar, Dinesh; Singh, N.B. Rawat, Srivastava G.S.S and Mohan Dhananjay (1999) Improvement of Populus deltoids Bartr. Ex Marsh. In India. Present status. *Indian Forester* 125 (3) 245-263.

Land, S.B.Jr. (1996) Consultant Paper:forest management/tree improvement of poplars in India, July 1996. Forestry Research, Education and Extension project, ICFRE, Winrock international, 46p.

Seth, S.K. (1969) Poplar trials in Uttar Pradesh. U.P. Forest bulletin No.34, Forest Department, Uttar Pradesh,106p.

Chapter 16

Adoption of Tribal and Non-Tribal Farmers about Coriander Production Technology

☆ *D.K. Meena, L.S. Bareth, B.S. Badhala and H.L. Jat*

Coriander is an important dominant and highly valued spice grown in India. It is the first probably the first spices to be used by men as common flavouring substance. The stem, leaves and grains have a pleasant aroma. The entire plant used in preparing "Chatany" whereas, leaves are used for flavouring curries, sauce and soups. The dry grains are extensively used in preparation of curry powder, pickling spices and seasoning.

Coriander seed have aromatic odour and tests of coriander fruits is due to an essential oil, which is made up of hydrocarbon and oxygenated compounds. Beside the essential oil, the seed contains 16.1 per cent fatty oil, 14.1 per cent protein, 21.6 per cent carbohydrate, 32.6 per cent fibers, 11.2 per cent moisture and 4.4 per cent mineral matters (Sharma and Sharma, 2004).

Methodology

The present study was conducted in Khanpur Panchayat Samiti of Jhalawar district, which was selected purposely. Similarly, from Khanpur Panchayat Samiti, five Gram Panchayats were selected on the basis of having highest area and production of coriander among all the Gram Panchayats of Khanpur Panchayat Samiti. From the selected Gram Panchayats five villages were selected on the basis of area as well as having tribal population. From each village 32 coriander growers (16 tribal and 16 non-tribals) were selected randomly.

Findings

Distribution of Respondents According to the Extent of Adoption

The data have been reported in Table 16.1 that if we look the table as coriander growers irrespective of tribal or non-tribal coriander growers, the data revealed that 11.88 per cent respondents were high adopters, 37.50 per cent respondents were low level adopters and 50.62 per cent respondents were in the category of medium adopters of coriander production technology in the study area.

Table 16.1: Distribution of Coriander Growers According to their Extent of Adoption

Sl.No.	*Extent of Adoption*	*Tribal (n=80)*		*Non-Tribal (n=80)*		*Overall (n=160)*	
		F	*%*	*F*	*%*	*F*	*%*
1.	Low (below 42 score)	37	46.25	23	28.75	60	37.50
2.	Medium (42 - 75)	38	47.50	43	53.75	81	50.62
3.	High (above 75 score)	5	6.25	14	17.50	19	11.88

F: Frequency; %: Percentage

In case of tribal coriander growers, all most equal number of them fallen in low and medium adoption group. Only 6.15 per cent tribal respondents were found in high level adoption group regarding coriander production technology. Further, in case of non-tribal respondents, majority of them 53.75 per cent had medium level of adoption followed by low adoption group. Only 17.50 per cent non-tribal farmers fall in high level of adoption group.

The Extent of Adoption of Coriander Production Technology among Tribal and Non-Tribal Respondents

If we look the data of Table 16.2 Irrespective tribal and non-tribal coriander growers, it is observed that respondents had very good adoption level regarding field preparation and time of sowing with 71.88 and 71.67 MPS, respectively. They had good amount of adoption level of regarding practices like harvesting, threshing and storage, fertilizer application, irrigation management, seed rate and spacing and weed management with 69.13, 64.69, 58.13, 55.78 and 51.88 MPS, respectively. In rest of practices, they possessed low adoption level ranging from 30 to 40 MPS.

Table 16.2: Extent of Adoption of Coriander Production Technology among Tribal and Non-tribal Respondents

Sl.No.	*Package of Practices*	*Tribal (n=80)*		*Non-Tribal (n=80)*		*Overall (n=160)*	
		MPS	*Rank*	*MPS*	*Rank*	*MPS*	*Rank*
1.	Field preparation	63.33	3	80.42	1	71.88	1
2.	High yielding varieties	24.90	10	33.75	9	29.32	10
3.	Seed treatment	36.25	8	45.63	8	40.94	8
4.	Time of sowing	67.50	1	75.83	2	71.67	2
5.	Seed rate and spacing	46.04	6	65.52	5	55.78	6
6.	Fertilizer application	55.83	4	73.54	4	64.69	4
7.	Irrigation management	52.50	5	63.75	6	58.13	5
8.	Weed management	43.75	7	60.00	7	51.88	7
9.	Plant protection measures	30.17	9	33.17	10	31.67	9
10.	Harvesting, threshing and storage	64.50	2	73.75	3	69.13	3
	Pooled	48.48		60.54		54.51	

r_s = Rank correlation,

** = Significant at 1 per cent level

r_s = 0.93**

t = 7.75

r_s= Rank correlation; **Significant at 1 per cent level of significant

Table 16.2 shows that tribal coriander growing respondents possessed very good adoption level regarding time of sowing harvesting, threshing and storage and field preparation with the 67.50, 64.50 and 63.33 MPS, respectively. They possessed good adoption level regarding fertilizer application, irrigation management, seed rate and spacing and weed management with 55.83, 52.50, 46.04 and 43.75 MPS, respectively. They had least adoption level regarding plant protection measures and high yielding varieties. The non-tribal coriander growers had very good adoption level regarding practices like field preparation, time of sowing, harvesting, threshing and storage and fertilizer application with 80.42, 75.83, 73.75 and 73.54 MPS, respectively. Respondents had good adoption level regarding seed rate and spacing, irrigation management, weed management and seed treatment. They had least adoption level of high yielding varieties and plant protection measures.

The overall extent of adoption level for coriander production technology by the tribal, non-tribal and pooled coriander growers were 48.48, 60.54 and 54.51 MPS, respectively.

To see the relationship in ranking assignment between tribal and non-tribal coriander growers rank order correlation test applied as under. The value of calculated rank order correlation (r_s) was 0.93 which is positive and highly significant, leading to conclusion that there is rank correlation with extent of adoption of improved coriander production technology by the tribal and non-tribal farmers, though there were difference in magnitude of MPS of tribal and non-tribal coriander growers.

Practice Wise Comparison of Extent of Adoption between Tribal and Non-Tribal Respondents about Coriander Production Technology

It is clear from the data in Table 16.3 show that calculated 'Z' value was higher than the table value at 5 and 1 per cent level of significance in seven package of practices of coriander production technology. In remaining three package of practice *i.e.* time of sowing, irrigation management and plant protection measures, there was non-significant difference. This call for rejection of null hypothesis and acceptance of alternative hypothesis leading to conclusion that there is significant difference in level of adoption between tribal and non-tribal respondents regarding above seven practices of coriander production technology recommended in the study area.

Table 16.3: Practice-wise Comparison of Extent of Adoption between Tribal and Non-Tribal Farmers with Regard to Different Package of Practices of Coriander Production Technology

Sl.No.	*Package of Practices*	*Tribal (n=80)*		*Non-Tribal (n=80)*		*'Z' Value*
		Mean	*S.D.*	*Mean*	*S.D.*	
1.	Field preparation	5.70	2.10	7.24	2.00	4.75**
2.	High yielding varieties	2.99	0.49	4.05	1.65	5.52**
3.	Seed treatment	2.18	1.34	2.74	1.44	2.56*
4.	Time of sowing	2.03	0.81	2.28	0.85	1.91 NS
5.	Seed rate and spacing	5.53	1.99	7.86	2.31	6.86**
6.	Fertilizer application	6.70	2.94	8.83	2.27	5.12**
7.	Irrigation management	1.58	1.50	1.91	1.44	1.45 NS
8.	Weed management	2.63	1.98	3.60	2.14	2.99**
9.	Plant protection measures	13.58	7.59	14.93	8.05	1.09 NS
10.	Harvesting, threshing and storage	9.68	3.29	11.06	2.54	2.99**
	Pooled	**5.26**		**6.45**		**3.52****

NS: Non-Significant.

* Significant at 5 per cent level of significance.

** Significant at 1 per cent level of significance.

The overall calculated 'Z' value was also greater than that of its table value. This indicates that there was significant difference between the overall adoptions of coriander production technology between tribal and non-tribal respondents.

Conclusion

1. Majority of coriander growers were in medium adoption group followed by low and high adoption group, respectively. More number of non-tribal farmers fell in high adoption group as compare to tribal farmers.
2. Both type of coriander growers *i.e.* tribal as well as non-tribal adopted more the practices like field preparation, time of sowing and harvesting threshing and storage. Minimum adoption was found in practice of plant protection measures and high yielding varieties.

3. There was correlation between ranks given to adoption of various package of practices of coriander cultivation by the tribal and non-tribal. There was significant difference in the extent of adoption of coriander production technology between tribal and non-tribal respondents in seven out of the ten package of practice of coriander cultivation.

Recommendations

1. Coriander growers possessed less adoption regarding high yielding varieties and plant protection measures for improving the adoption of farmers the training on these aspects may be organized where in farmers of the area could participate actively.
2. Farmers faced constraint with regard grading and standardization. To overcome this problem training programmes should be arranged for coriander growers by different agencies.
3. Government should be fix the minimum support price of the coriander in advance of the sowing time of crop.

References

Jaitawat, G.S., Sisodia, S.S. and Bhimawat, B.S. (2007). "Adoption of improved fennel cultivation technology". *Indian Research of Journal Extension Education*, Vol. VII (2 and 3): 52-54.

Kumar, S., Khajuria, R and Chouhan, M. S. (2003). "Adoption and perceived training needs for turmeric growers in Udaipur district of Rajasthan". Rural India, Vol. III and IV : 156 – 158.

Nagar, S.N. (2006). "Knowledge and adoption of recommended coriander cultivation technology among the farmers of Atru tehsil in Baran district of Rajasthan". M.Sc.(Ag.) thesis (unpub.) MPUAT, campus - Udaipur.

Vijay, O. P. and Malhotra, S. K. (2001)."Present status, production constraints, future strategies and trust area of research in seed spice in India". *Indian Journal of Arecanut, Spices and Medicinal plants*. Vol. III : 111 – 115.

Chapter 17

Adoption of Pulses Production Technology in Arid Region of Rajasthan

☆ *B.S. Badhala, L.S. Bareth and Hanuman Lal*

Pulses are the main source of protein particularly for vegetarian. The per capita availability of pulses declining fast from 56 gm per day in 1968 to 32 gram per day as on 2007 against the minimum requirement of 70 g per day as prescribed by ICMR (Anonymous, 2007).Apart from protein source, pulse crop, being legume, fit well in diverse type of cropping system on account of their wide adaptability under variable agro-climatic conditions and relatively lower input demand, matching socio-economic status of larger section of Indian farmers.

Mothbean is mainly used in the Bikaneri Bhujia, papad and namkeen industry which is an important source of earning the foreign currency and provides the year long employment to the large number of people. This makes mothbean an important economic crop of Bikaner district.

The pulses sector has also come out as a net foreign exchange earner thus pulses have great potentiality in foreign trades also. Bikaner district stands first rank in term of area and production of mothbean in the state. In this district, the mothbean crop is grown in an area of 274661* ha with an annual production of over 42684 tonnes (Anonymous, 2006-07). The result of demonstrations had remained the effective medium of extension in India since 1952 when the Community Development Programme was started, since then the concept of result demonstrations had gone many changes including its theory, principles, aim and objectives. The latest concept in this series is "Front Line Demonstration" the new concept of field demonstration evolved by the ICAR with the inception of the technology mission on oilseed and pulses crops during mid eighties.

Methodology

The present study was conducted in purposely selected Bikaner district. Four Panchyat Samities *viz.*, Bikaner, Nokha, Kolayat and Dungargarh were selected. 17 villages and 80 beneficiary respondents where the FLDs conducted by KVK, Bikaner were included in the study sample. Likewise 17 another villages and 80 non-beneficiary respondents on whose farm's FLD were not conducted within the distance 5 to 15 km were also selected randomly and included in the study as control group. Thus the total study sample comprised of 160 respondents (80 beneficiary and 80 non-beneficiary). Data were collected by personal interview method. To arrive at specific inferences, various statistical measures *viz.*, chi-square test, 'z' test, 't' test and spearman's rank correlation tests were used. The data collected were classified, tabulated and inferences were drawn after subjecting the data to appropriate statistical analysis which led to the following major findings.

Findings

The front line demonstration conducted on mothbean crop by the K.V.K., Bikaner is supposed to have imparted adoption of mothbean production technology to the farmers on his farm, where the FLDs were conducted. In this section, efforts were made to assess the knowledge level of beneficiaries as well as non-beneficiaries regarding improved mothbean production practices.

Table 17.1: Distribution of Respondents According to their Extent of Adoption (N=160)

Sl.No.	*Extent of Adoption*	*Beneficiary (n=80)*		*Non-beneficiary (n=80)*		*Pooled (N=160)*	
		F	*%*	*F*	*%*	*F*	*%*
1.	Low (below 23 score)	30	37.50	52	65.00	82	51.25
2.	Medium (23 to 29 score)	30	37.50	26	32.50	56	35.00
3.	High (above 29 score)	20	25.00	02	2.50	22	13.75
	Overall	80	100	80	100	160	100

F: Frequency; %: Percentage

The table as whole irrespective of of beneficiary or non-beneficiary, the date revealed that 22 (13.75 per cent) farmers were high adopters, 56 (35.00 per cent) farmers were medium level adopters

Table 17.2: Extent of Adoption of Mothbean Production Technology among Beneficiary and Non-Beneficiary Respondents (N=160)

Sl.No.	*Package of Practices*	*Beneficiary (n=80)*		*Non-beneficiary (n=80)*		*Pooled (n=160)*	
		MPS	*Rank*	*MPS*	*Rank*	*MPS*	*Rank*
1	High yielding varieties	81.67	2	56.87	2	69.27	2
2	Field preparation	70.00	3	45.00	4	57.50	4
3	Seed treatment	67.50	5	33.75	9	50.62	7
4	Time of sowing	84.38	1	68.75	1	76.56	1
5	Seed rate and spacing	69.69	4	44.37	5	57.03	5
6	Fertilizer application	44.25	9	41.37	6	42.75	9
7	Irrigation management	66.25	6	50.00	3	58.12	3
8	Weed management	56.87	8	38.37	8	47.62	8
9	Plant protection measures	28.50	10	11.50	10	20.00	10
10	Harvesting, threshing and storage	61.43	7	40.53	7	50.98	6
	Overall	63.05		43.04		53.04	

$r_s = 0.78^*$

$t = 3.55$

r_s = Rank correlation; *Significant at 5 per cent level.

and 82 (51.25 per cent) farmers were in the category of low adopters of mothbean production technology in the study area. The Table 17.2 shows that beneficiary respondents possessed very good adoption level (above 75 per cent) regarding time of sowing and high yielding varieties. Similarity they had good adoption level (above 50 per cent) regarding field preparation, seed rate and spacing, seed treatment, irrigation management, harvesting threshing and storage and weed management. The beneficiary respondents adopted the practices like fertilizer application and plant protection measures to very lesser extent of adoption.

The overall extent of adoption level for mothbean production technology by the beneficiary and non- beneficiary farmers were 63.05 and 43.04 MPS, respectively.

The calculated value of rank order correlation (r_s) was 0.78 which is positive and significant, leading to conclusion that there is correlation with extent of adoption of improved mothbean production technology by the beneficiary and non-beneficiary

Table 17.3: Comparison of Extent of Adoption between Beneficiary and Non-Beneficiary Farmers with Regard to different Package of Practices of Mothbean Production Technology

Sl.No.	*Package of Practices*	*Beneficiary (n=80)*		*Non-beneficiary (n=80)*		*'Z' Value*
		Mean ±	*S.D.*	*Mean ±*	*S.D.*	
1.	High yielding varieties	4.90	1.83	3.41	1.35	5.86*
2.	Field preparation	2.10	1.14	1.35	0.92	4.58*
3.	Seed treatment	1.35	0.94	0.68	0.47	5.76*
4.	Time of sowing	1.69	0.78	1.38	0.71	2.64*
5.	Seed rate and spacing	2.79	0.98	1.78	0.92	6.72*
6.	Fertilizer application	2.21	1.07	1.65	0.63	4.05*
7.	Irrigation management	1.33	0.86	1.00	0.59	2.78*
8.	Weed management	1.14	0.95	0.78	0.65	2.82*
9.	Plant protection measures	1.43	1.05	0.58	0.54	6.45*
10.	Harvesting, threshing and storage	4.30	1.86	2.81	0.25	5.94*
	Overall	2.32		1.54		4.76*

* Significant at 5 per cent level of significance.

farmers, though there were difference in magnitude of MPS of beneficiary and non-beneficiary respondents.

It is clear from the data in Table 17.3 that calculated 'z' value was greater than its tabulated value at 5 per cent level of significance for all the 10 practices of mothbean production technology studied. This calls for rejection of null hypothesis, leading to conclusion that there existed significant difference in level of adoption between beneficiary and non- beneficiary respondents regarding all the 10 practices of mothbean production technology recommended in the study area.

The overall calculated 'z' value was also greater than that of its tabulated value. These indicate that there was a significant difference between the overall adoption of mothbean production technology between beneficiary and non- beneficiary respondents.

Thus, this is proved evidently that the adoption of mothbean production technology was more among beneficiary farmers compared to non-beneficiary farmers. The significant difference between beneficiary and non- beneficiary farmers about adoption of mothbean production technology in the study was not unexpected. It may be due to the fact that beneficiary farmers being in continuous touch with the K.V.K. personals might have acquired sufficient skills pertaining to mothbean production technology. Thus they are more likely to practice the learnt skills in their fields.

The findings are in conformity with that of, Singh (2000), Ashiwal (2006) and Singh and Chouhan (2008) who in their studies have reported significant adoption difference between beneficiary and non- beneficiary farmers.

Conclusion

1. Majority of mothbean growers were in medium adoption group followed by low and high adoption group, respectively. More number of beneficiary farmers fell in medium adoption group as compare to non- beneficiary farmers.
2. Both type of mothbean growers adopted, high yielding variety, seed rate and spacing and time of sowing. Minimum adoption was found in fertilizer application and plant protection measures of improved mothbean production technology.

3. There was correlation between ranks given to adoption of various package of practices of mothbean cultivation by the beneficiary and non- beneficiary.
4. There was significant difference in the extent of adoption of mothbean production technology between beneficiary and non-beneficiary respondents.

Recommendations

1. In view of the findings, it is suggested that subject matter specialist of K.V.K., should visit the field more frequently and assure that the adoption of all the practices (as a package) at the farmers' field.
2. Village extension worker is the ultimate link in the chain for transfer of technology to farmers' field. It is also an essential ingredient of the system that establishes a personal contact and rapport with the farmers. So, it is suggested that village extension worker must live at headquarter for easy, accessibility to the farmers.

References

Anonymous. (2006-07). "Vital Agriculture Statistics", Deptt. of Agricultural, Pant Krishi Bhawan, Jaipur.

Ashiwal, B.L. (2006). "Impact of Front Line Demonstration on adoption of improved mustard production technology among the farmers of Laxmangarh Panchayat Samiti of Sikar district of Rajasthan". M.Sc. (Ag.) thesis (unpub.) Rajasthan Agricultural University, Bikaner, campus-Jobner.

Singh, B. and Chouhan, T.R. (2008). "3rd National Symposium on enhancing productivity nutritional security and export potential through arid legumes" 28-30 June, 2008 : 127.

Singh, N. (2000). "Impact of Front Line Demonstration on adoption of mustard production technology by the farmers of Bharatpur district". M.Sc. (Ag.) thesis (unpub.), MPUAT, Udaipur campus-Udaipur.

Chapter 18

Extent of Adoption of Soil and Water Conservation Practices by the Farmers in Watershed Development Project Area

B.M. Thombre, I.M. Tamboli and J.V. Mande

In India hardly 35 per cent of the total cultivated area is under irrigation. With all efforts we can bring only 50 per cent of the total cultivated area under irrigation and the rest of 50 per cent of the total cultivated area will be permanently under the mercy of rain. In order to increase the production, productivity in dry land area and to narrow down the economic status between irrigated farmer and rainfed farmer, watershed concept has been evolved. In order to achieve an overall improvement in dry land areas, all the aforesaid components were brought under one umbrella that itself is called as watershed management.

Watershed management is an integrated scientific management of natural resources aimed at the optimal use of land, water, plant, man, animal and environment on watershed basis for optimizing production of food, fodder, fuel, fiber and fruits to meet the increasing demand of human and animal population on sustained basis. Watershed development is a vital strategy of agricultural and overall rural development in rural areas.

India's ever increasing population is exerting tremendous pressure on agriculture. Deforestation and natural calamities are some of the evils which have led to direct consequences like poor yields, erratic rainfall and famine. To meet the requirement of our increasing population, soil and water conservation and management technology holds the key. So present study with following objective was undertaken.

Objectives

1. To know the personal characteristics of the farmers in watershed development project area.
2. To find out level of adoption of soil and water conservation practices by the farmers
3. To study relationship of independent variables with adoption of soil and water conservation practices by the farmers

Methodology

The present study was carried out in Bindusara watershed development project designed by Government of Maharashtra. Bindusara watershed having storage capacity about 7.106 cubic mm and operational area about 1288 ha. This project operated in Beed district and covered nearby villages under irrigation. For the purpose of the study, five villages were randomly selected from Bindusara watershed area namely, Pali, Karjani (Mothi), Karchundi, Karjani (Chhoti) and Kolwadi. From these five selected villages, 20 farmers from each village were selected randomly to comprise a sample of 100 respondents for the study. Ex-post facto research design with one shot case study method was adopted for the study. The data were collected with the help of predesigned interview schedule by personal interviews of farmer. The qualitative data were quantified in view of the objectives. Correlation coefficient was worked out to describe the relationship of personal characteristics with adoption of soil and water conservation practices by the farmers. Multiple regression analysis was employed to find out the association between personal characteristics of farmers and their adoption of soil and water conservation practices.

Findings

Personal Characteristics of the Farmers in Watershed Development Project Area

As regard with the personal characteristics of the farmers it was observed from Table 18.1, that, 59.00 per cent of the farmers were having medium and 28.00 per cent farmers had high level of

Table 18.1: Distribution of the Respondents According to their Personal Characteristics (n = 100)

Sl.No.	*Category*	*Frequency*	*Percentage*
1.	**Farming experience**		
	a) Low	**13**	**13.00**
	b) Medium	59	59.00
	c) High	28	28.00
2.	**Education**		
	a) Illiterate	02	02.00
	b) Primary school	10	10.00
	c) Middle school	42	42.00
	d) Higher school	40	40.00
	e) College and higher education	06	06.00
3.	**Family type**		
	a) Nuclear	54	54.00
	b) Joint	46	46.00
4.	**Family size**		
	a) Small	20	20.00
	b) Medium	50	50.00
	c) Large	30	30.00
5.	**Land holding**		
	a) Marginal	12	12.00
	b) Small	44	44.00
	c) Semi-medium	42	42.00
	d) Medium	02	02.00

Contd...

Table 18.1–Contd...

Sl.No.	Category	Frequency	Percentage
6.	**Annual income**		
	a) Low	09	09.00
	b) Medium	81	81.00
	c) High	10	10.00
7.	**Use of sources of information**		
	A) Individual contact method		
	a) Low	24	24.00
	b) Medium	34	34.00
	c) High	42	42.00
	B) Group contact method		
	a) Low	13	13.00
	b) Medium	33	33.00
	c) High	54	54.00
	C) Mass contact method		
	a) Low	16	16.00
	b) Medium	49	49.00
	c) High	35	35.00
8.	**Social participation**		
	a) Low	16	16.00
	b) Medium	69	69.00
	c) High	15	15.00
9.	**Extension contact**		
	a) Low	10	10.00
	b) Medium	49	49.00
	c) High	41	41.00

farm experience while, 42.00 per cent of farmers had middle school level of education, 54.00 per cent farmers belongs to nuclear family type, 50.00 per cent farmers had medium family size and 44.00 per cent of the farmers were possessing small land holding. Further, it could be concluded that majority (81.00 per cent) of the farmers were from medium annual income category. It was also observed that the use of sources of information by individual contact method majority

(42.00 per cent) of the farmers were having high level, by group contact 54.00 per cent of the farmers had high level and with the help of mass contact method majority (49.00 per cent) of the farmers had medium level of use of sources of information. About 69.00 per cent of the farmers had medium level of social participation and 49.00 per cent of the farmers had medium level of extension contact.

Level of Adoption of Soil and Water Conservation Practices by the Farmers

Table 18.2: Distribution of the Respondents According to their Level of Adoption of Soil and Water Conservation Practices (n = 100)

Sl.No.	*Adoption Level*	*Frequency*	*Percentage*
1.	Low	21	21.00
2.	Medium	61	61.00
3.	High	18	18.00
	Total	100	100.00

It is vivid from Table 18.2 that, 61.00 per cent of the farmers were in the medium level of adoption of soil and water conservation practices while, 21.00 per cent and 18.00 per cent of them had low and high level of adoption, respectively. The people should be motivated by arranging trips to the area/village where soil and water conservation is successfully implemented. Sufficient loans from banks for soil and water conservation practices should be provided to the farmers. Similar results were found by Dhapke K.A. (2004)

Relationship of Independent Variables with Adoption of Soil and Water Conservation Practices by the Farmers

A perusal of data in Table 18.3 vividly present the fact that the independent variables namely farming experience, education, family type, family size, land holding, annual income, use of sources of information, social participation and extension contact were positive and highly significant relationship with the level of adoption of soil and water conservation practices.

The regression analysis in Table 18.3 show that the nine independent variables namely, farming experience, education,

Table 18.3: Correlation and Multiple Regressions Co-efficient of Independent Variables with Adoption of Soil and Water Conservation Practices by the Farmers

Sl.No.	Independent Variables	Correlation Coefficient ('r')	Regression Coefficient ('Bi')	Standard Error (SE)	Calculated 't' Value
1.	Farming experience	0.644**	-8.945	4.142	-2.159
2.	Education	0.865**	2.878	3.720	7.738**
3.	Family type	0.687**	1.591	1.343	1.184^{NS}
4.	Family size	0.751**	-1.057	2.519	-4.196
5.	Land holding	0.681**	-8.876	7.843	-1.131
6.	Annual income	0.681**	-1.693	1.481	-1.143
7.	Use of sources of information	0.775**	1.374	9.725	1.413^{NS}
8.	Social participation	0.770**	2.778	5.217	5.325**
9.	Extension contact	0.785**	2.505	1.191	2.102*

* Significant at 0.05 per cent level of probability; NS: Non-significant.

** Significant at 0.01 per cent level of probability R^2 = 0.825, F-value = 4.709.

family type, family size, land holding, annual income, social participation, use of sources of information, extension contact accounted for 82.50 per cent of total variation in the dependent variable adoption. Data shows that education and social participation had exhibited highly significant, extension contact had significant, family type and use of sources of information had non-significant and farming experience, while family size, land holding, annual income had negatively significant impact on adoption of soil and water conservation practices.

Conclusions

1. It was noticed that, majority of the respondents with 9 to 14 years of farming experience, were educated up to primary as well as higher school, majority of them having nuclear family type, medium in family size, majority farmers in small land holding, medium annual income, high use of sources of information, medium social participation, medium extension contact, medium level of knowledge about soil and water conservation practices and medium level of adoption of soil and water conservation practices.
2. Majority of the farmers had medium level of adoption of soil and water conservation practices. The extension agency should organize special training programmes for the farmers.
3. Independent variables namely farming experience, education, family type, family size, land holding, annual income, and use of sources of information, social participation and extension contact were positive and highly significant relationship with the level of adoption of soil and water conservation practices.
4. It was elucidated from the data that education and social participation had exhibited positive and highly significant contribution. Extension contact had significant, family type and use of sources of information had non-significant and farming experience, while family size, land holding, annual income had negatively significant impact on adoption of soil and water conservation practices.

References

Dhapke K.A., 2004. A study on soil and water conservation practices adopted by the farmers in rain water harvesting project. *Asian J. of Extn Edu.* 23(2) :186-190.

Kadam J.R., Patil, V.G. and Hardikar D.P. (2001) Knowledge and adoption of soil and water conservation practices in watershed development project. *Maharashtra J.Ext. Edu,* 20: 138-140.

Thakare L.S., Deshmukh A.N. and Tripathi A.O., 2010. Adoption of soil and water conservation practices by farmers. *Agriculture Update,* 5(2 and 3):470-472.

Chapter 19

Agroforestry and Livestock in the Development of Sustainable Mountain Agriculture

☆ *Akanksha Rastogi, Bipin Kumar, J.C. Badola and Mohan Singh*

Mountains of the world are now a global development agenda. Mountain ecosystems, however, are in a perilous state due to rapid depletion of natural resources and accentuating agricultural unsustainability – the two major global concerns. This situation could be impacted significantly through agroforestry practices. The state of forest degradation is manifested into agricultural unsustainability and a large number of other negative ecological and socioeconomic changes. Excessive soil erosion, catastrophic landslides, disturbances in local hydrological cycle, and paucity of fuel wood, fodder, timber, etc. are but a few examples indicative of an inadequate/dwindling forest cover in the mountains. The state of unsustainability of agriculture mountain areas are facing is evident from a large number of emerging negative indicators, such as reduced flows of forest/agroforestry products, decreased production of foodgrains, decreased flow of water in rain-fed rivers, reduced animal production, increasing hunger gap, reduced level of contentment, increasing desperation, spurt in out-migration, etc. Agroforestry offers an enormous scope to address the vicious problems of the mountains (Singh, 2005).

Agroforestry, indeed, is an age-old practice mountain farmers have been depending upon for their livelihoods. Green Revolution type agriculture, largely based on monocultures of few varieties of fewer food grain crops, has undermined the scope of agroforestry in recent decades. It is why the agricultural systems in the plains depict a tree-less gloomy scenario, truly not indicative of long-term sustainability. In the mountain areas too irrigated cropping systems are virtually devoid of trees, but the rain-fed cropping systems essentially involve agroforestry practices. Moreover, the hill agriculture, unlike that of the plains, is in organic linkages with the forests. The whole of mountain agriculture, thus, in a sense, is a unique example of agroforestry.

Nature-subsidised solar-powered agriculture overwhelmingly practiced in the mountains receives organic inputs from within the farming systems, contrary to the so-called Green Revolution agriculture, which depends heavily on the inputs from outside the system. Mountain agriculture, in order to receive optimum nutrient supply from within the farming system, must be dominated by forest component that functions as a natural fertilizer factory for agriculture and infuses sustainability into the whole system.

Under some specific circumstances, when human demands are radically transformed or delinked from local resources and managed through external subsidization, it is conceivable to sustain human welfare without sustainable resource use. To realize sustainable resource use aimed at sustainable development of agrarian economy in the mountains – which is a precondition for sustaining human welfare in the inherently resource-rich Himalayas – regeneration of natural forests, and farmland planning involving trees and other perennial woody species, should be fundamental part of our area perspective-based strategy (Singh, 2005).

Livestock – Agroforestry Linkages

Livestock acquire special importance in mountain farming systems both on ecological and socio-economical grounds. They are an integral part of farming system and a lively 'bridge' connecting two types of land, *viz.*, the uncultivated forestland and the cultivated land. This linkage is crucial for the ecological and economical sustainability of the system. Forests, especially the natural ones, are the rich repository of the nutrients, which become a subsidy for cultivated land. These nutrients are transferred to the cultivated land via the agency of livestock.

The nutrient transfer takes place in two ways. Forest biomass – tree leaves and ground flora – are fed to the livestock. The biomass is also used as bedding materials in the livestock shed. Both, dung and bedding material are converted into manure, which is transferred to the cultivated land. The livestock also recycle the nutrients in the cultivated land. Crop residues are fed to the animals and thus the nutrients in them are recycled into the cropland.

The biomass transfer and cyclic flow pattern of nutrients mediated by livestock infuse vitality in the production system and livestock themselves fulfill their requirements for maintenance and production (milk, draught power, etc.). This dynamic relationship among forest ecosystems, livestock and agro-ecosystems is vital for sustainability of mountain agriculture (Singh and Gautam, 2004).

Depletion of Forest Resources and their Consequences

Much of the forest cover in the Himalayas has already disappeared. Consequences of such deforestation leading to possible extinction of plants and animals, and environmental implications contributing to a decline in food production, are now well discussed and recognized throughout the world. Paucity of fuel wood, fodder and minor timber – symptomatic of such a poor state of forests – is to immediately affect the livelihoods of the local residents.

Destruction of forest resources has added to extra burden on women. As women put more time into gathering firewood, fodder and other forest products, they have less time for working in the fields. Shortages also contribute to a decline in nutritional status of children through the reduced time of mother for cooking and food preparation and childcare.

Although forests have been left on considerably small geographical area, they still continue to be the largest single component in the farming system having tremendous bearing on agriculture. Over the last half a century or so, several alarming negative trends in food production systems in the hills have emerged. For instance, according to a study of the author, soil erosion rate on sloping lands has increased (20-30 per cent), part of agricultural land has been abandoned due to decline in fertility (3-11 per cent), appearance of stones/rocks on cultivated land has increased (130-200 per cent), forest area has decreased (15-85 per cent), pasture/grazing area has declined (25-90 per cent), food grain production and self sufficiency have reduced (30-60 per cent), rate of manure application has decreased (75 per cent), productivity of different crops has gone down (33-75 per cent), livestock holding size has reduced (63-70 per cent), livestock productivity for milk has decreased (50-67 per cent), and fetching time of fuel wood, fodder and bedding material has increased (50-80 per cent). These persistent negative changes are clearly visible in the mountains of the Indian Central Himalayas. Also referred to as the indicators of unsustainability, these negative changes are rooted in the depletion of forest resources in the area (Singh, 1998).

Due to deterioration of forest, in general, and agriculture in particular, the people are facing increased difficulties in maintaining their livelihoods. In response to this, the people are now guided by short-term considerations, which, in turn, lead to further degradation. An increased search for short-term solutions indicates people's increased degree of desperation.

Since most of the problems, as visible in the form of unsustainability indicators, have emerged due to depletion of forest resources, many of them can, therefore, be rectified by restoring forest cover and depending on agroforestry practices in the mountains.

Contributions to Sustainability

Agroforestry system's contribution may be both direct and indirect, in terms of products and component of an ecosystem. In the form of directly extractable products, agroforestry system provides food, feed, fuel, fibre, fertilizer, timber, etc. In terms of services to the ecosystem, the system's contributions will be in terms of biodiversity, moisture circulation, nutrient cycling, and the make-up and stability of environmental and physical resource bases. These services of agroforestry are system's inputs and contributions to sustainability of an agro-ecosystem.

Direct Economic Benefits

Mountain farmers, in order to reduce risks, tend to grow more plants per unit area using a variety of species, multistory structures and temporal arrangement to facilitate relay fashion of crop harvesting. Trees and shrubs in the agroforestry system also enhance food and nutrition security. There is a large number of species of trees and other woody perennials grown in the agroforestry systems that provide edible fruits, nuts, buds, flowers, seeds, leaves, oils, honey, medicines, etc. According to a study by the author of this article, there are as many as 24 trees and other woody perennials in Garhwal Himalayas that provide these food items to the local populace. In addition, there are 52 species providing foliage fodder to livestock, thus contributing indirectly to food production through animal products. This food production through woody perennials, coupled with that from the annual food grain crops in an agroforestry system, might be a key source to enhance food and nutrition security amongst the mountain farmers.

Fuel wood is the most important source of energy in rural mountain areas throughout the length and width of the Himalayas. Majority of the families depends on fuel wood for cooking food. Alternative energy sources are not easily accessible, or are too expensive. Every woody perennial raised in an agroforestry system is systematically used to extract fuel wood. The use of wood as a source of cooking energy also contributes to manage soil fertility indirectly, for in the absence or paucity of it the animal dung, instead of being used as manure, would be dried to be used as cooking food at the expense of health of the soil.

Conventional agriculture, dominating the plains, demands constant supplies of energy, *e.g.*, fossil fuel for operating machines and transportation of the produce. In the agroforestry systems in the mountains, nevertheless – owing to almost no mechanization – the petroleum fuel is hardly in demand. The need for soil nutrients is met instead by farmyard manure and through nutrient recycling management mediated by livestock in the agroforestry system.

An agroforestry system supplies many other raw materials of vital use in daily life of mountain people. Wood extractable from the trees and other woody perennials is used for manufacturing agricultural tools and implements, for building and supporting of houses, and for furniture, etc. Poles, small logs, branch-wood for roofing or thorny bush wood for fencing is also obtained from the agroforestry systems. *Grewia optiva*, a dominant tree species in the agroforestry systems at lower and mid-altitudes in the Himalayan mountains, is extensively used for extracting fibre, making a large number of families self-sufficient in terms of their fibre requirements for ropes, carpets, etc. Dyes, indigo, gums, medicines, beverages, etc. are the other materials obtainable from agroforestry depending on the specificity of the site. Leaves of some of the trees, *e.g.*, *Melia azederach*, *Juglans regia*, etc. have insecticidal properties and are used by the local farmers in preserving food grains in their stores (Singh, 1998, 2005, Singh and Sharma, 1998).

Vital Ecological Services

Mountains, often left on the periphery of the mainstream plains, are altogether distinguishable from the latter in the sense that only a few, and sometime none, of the characteristics of the former are shared by the latter. From whichever development angle one looks at mountain agriculture, it undoubtedly appears to deserve more research attention and conscious and careful development intervention than it has actually received. The characteristics of marginality, fragility and inaccessibility associated with the mountains impart some degree of restriction on the intensification-focused approach to sustainability. Diversity or niche, the other two highly positive characteristics of the mountains, however, offer considerable scope for resource-use intensification with conservation and, hence, are helpful in consolidating the process of sustainability.

In the fragile mountains, ecological stability of the farming systems should be the foremost criterion for sustainability. Forest – or tree-based farming system – to supply massive amount of nutrients to livestock and cropland and to contribute to hydrological cycle, owing to its contribution to the processes and functions leading to the ecological stability of the mountain farming systems, continues to be an essential feature of the mountain agriculture, though much degradation of forests has already occurred in many areas, and such areas are facing grim consequences.

In farming systems, deep-rooted woody perennials contribute to soil organic matter through shedding of their leaves and roots. This organic matter improves soil structure, fertility and water holding capacity. Deep-rooted trees absorb nutrients from greater depths and deposit them on the surface in organic matter so that they are available to shallow-rooted crops in greater quantities.

As windbreakers, trees also increase moisture availability by reducing wind and, thereby, lowering evapotranspiration rate. Tree canopies can lower the impact of heavy rainfall, reducing runoff and increasing water filtration into the soil. Moreover, the shade provided by trees lowers soil temperatures reducing evaporation and slowing the decomposition of organic matter. Leguminous perennials may provide still further advantages by adding nitrogen to soil.

Diverse and complex agroforestry systems, apart from enhancing the productivity level, impart a great degree of resilience to the food production system ensuring farmers' food and livelihood security.

In addition to maintaining the quality of resource base, the trees contribute to the vitality of the entire agro-ecosystem, which is best ensured when the soil is well managed. Since renewable plant diversity and recycled nutrients in the self-contained mountain farming systems are the basis of soil fertility management, and of natural biological protection of plants, no pollution in the system is caused in that the use of eco-malignant pesticides is avoided. Thus, a forest, or assemblage of trees, provides a base for ecologically sound and environmentally safe agriculture. Farmers' traditional agricultural technologies guarantee a healthy human life. Agroforestry management practices involve the use of an ecosystem's produce as a subsidy for the other component (*e.g.*, forest biomass is used as livestock feed and manure for cropland). Forest/trees thus help strengthen linkages amongst various components of farming system. This contribution is vital for maintaining ecological integrity of the whole system. Forest's role in maintaining biodiversity, natural regeneration, nutrient circulation and recycling, moisture circulation, building and binding of soils, etc. is also vital for infusing sustainability in the whole system.

References

Singh, V. 1998. *Draught Animal Power in Mountain Agriculture: A Study of Perspectives and Issues in Central Himalayas, India*. Kathmandu: International Centre for Integrated Mountain Development (ICIMOD) (ISSN: 1024-7548).

Singh, V. 2005. *Agrobiodiversity, Sustainability and Food Security in the Himalayan Mountains: An Uttaranchal Perspective*. Gorakhpur: Gorakhpur Environmental Action Group, 50 pp.

Singh, V. and Gautam, P.L. (eds.). 2004. *Livestock Production Systems for Sustainable Food Security and Livelihoods in Mountain Areas*. Pantnagar: GB Pant University of Agriculture and Technology. pp. 413.

Singh, V. and Sharma, M.L. 1998. (eds). 1998. Mountain Ecosystems: A Scenario of Unsustainability. New Delhi: Indus.

Chapter 20

Communicational Attributes of the Recommended Cauliflower Growers

☆ *Mukesh Soni, K.K. Shrivastava and Lekh Ram Verma*

Agriculture is the backbone of Indian Economy, about 65 per cent of Indian population depends directly on agriculture and it accounted for 14.2 per cent of the country's Gross Domestic Product (GDP) in 2010-11, followed by 14.6 per cent of the country's Gross Domestic Product (GDP) in 2009-10, Furthermore, the sector provided employment to 58.2 per cent of the work force. During the past five years agriculture sector has witnessed spectacular advances in the production and productivity of food grains, oilseeds, commercial crops, fruits, vegetables, poultry and dairy. India has emerged as the second largest producer of fruits and vegetables in the world in addition to being the largest overseas exporter of cashews and spices.

Indian subcontinent is endowed with salubrious climate which permits growing of vegetables throughout the year. Vegetables play an important role in balanced nutrition as they are rich and cheap source of carbohydrates, vitamins and minerals they occupy an important place in the food basket of India. Vegetables not only provide maximum output but also give more income per unit area of land.

The total geographical area of India is 328.7 million hectares of which 140.3 million hectares is net sown area, while 193.7 million hectares is the gross cropped. Vegetables are being grown in India in 79, 85,000 ha with production of about 13, 37, 38,000 MT. and productivity of 16.7 MT/ha. This is second highest in the world, next only to China (Anonymous 2010). The Vegetables grown in Chhattisgarh state in 3,34,916.92 hectares with the production of 41,49,042.11 MT. and productivity of 12.39 MT/ha Among major vegetable crops, cauliflower occupies maximum of 34,79,000 hectares with a net production of 65,69,000 MT. and productivity of 18.9 MT/ha in India. An area of 18,384.45 hectares comes under cauliflower crop in Chhattisgarh state with the production of 3, 05,974.57 MT. and productivity of 16.64 MT/ha and area of 1,600 hectares comes under cauliflower crop in Surguja district with the production of 24,000 MT. and productivity of 9.5 MT/ha (Anonymous 2011).

Materials and Methods

The present investigation was carried out in Surguja district of Chhattisgarh state in India with object to obtain the communicational behavior in context of agriculture information used by the cauliflower growers. It was confined in two blocks out of seven blocks, namely Ambikapur and Batouli were purposively selected on the basis of stratified random sampling. From each block 8 villages and from each village 30 per cent farmers were randomly selected, hence total 160 cauliflower growers were interviewed personally. Both questionnaires and personal interviews were performed for data collection. Data were analyzing through appropriate statistical methods *viz.* mean, frequency, average, percentage etc.

Source of Information

A set of 24 information sources were identified including personal, group and mass media etc. and each source was given equal wattage and categories were made according to the use of information sources. The respondents were grouped into three categories for use of information sources by using following formula:

Table 20.1: S.O.I. = Mean ($\overline{X}$) ± S.D. (Standard Deviation)

Sl.No.	*Categories*	
1.	Low level of use of information sources	(< $\overline{X}$ - S.D.)
2.	Medium level of use of information sources	(In between $\overline{X}$ ± S.D.)
3.	High level of use of information sources	(> $\overline{X}$ + S.D.)

Contact with Extension Agencies

This was operationally defined as the "frequency with which a respondent comes in contact with extension agencies *i.e.* Krishi Vigyan Kendra, Govt. agriculture department, Kisan Call Centre, Agriculture university head quarter, Non govt. organization and others within a specific period of time". The extent of contact was measured into five categories *viz.*, never, twice or thrice in a year, once in a month and weekly and daily with a score 1, 2, 3, 4, 5 and 6 respectively. The respondents were grouped into three categories of contacts with extension agencies by using following formula:

Table 20.2: C.W.E.A. = Mean ($\overline{X}$) ± S.D. (Standard Deviation)

Sl.No.	*Categories*	
1.	Low level	(< $\overline{X}$ - S.D.)
2.	Medium level	(In between $\overline{X}$ ± S.D.)
3.	High level	(> $\overline{X}$ + S.D.)

Results and Discussion

Use of Information Sources

The findings of table 01 indicate that majority (64.37 per cent) of the respondents utilized medium level of Information Sources, followed by 18.75 per cent of the respondents who utilized high level of information sources, 16.88 per cent of the respondents who utilize low level of information sources. Patel (2005) and Shriwas (2011) also found similar findings in his study.

Table 20.3: Distribution of Respondents According to Overall Use of Information Sources

Sl.No.	Sources of Information	Frequency	Per cent
1.	Low level of use of information sources (upto 14 score)	27	16.88
2.	Medium level of use of Information sources (15 – 25 score)	103	64.37
3.	High level of use of information sources (above 25 score)	30	18.75
	Total	**160**	**100.00**

The frequencies of use of various sources of information for obtaining the information about cauliflower cultivation practices by the respondents are given in Table 20.4. It reveals that amongst the information sources, majority of the respondents (93.75 per cent) used to contact neighbour regularly for seeking information about cauliflower cultivation practices and 86.87 per cent of the respondents contacted with friends, 72.50 per cent of the respondents contacted with RAEOs followed by 56.25 per cent of the respondents who contacted progressive farmers, 50 per cent of the respondents who contacted relatives for regularly getting the information regarding cauliflower cultivation practices. Whereas, 26.25 per cent of the respondents regularly listen radio programmes, 20.63 per cent of the respondents watched T.V., 16.87 per cent of the respondents made contact with village leaders, 14.37 per cent of the respondents made contact in village Panchayat, 12.50 per cent of the respondents obtained information from news paper, 9.37 per cent of the respondents had obtained information from agricultural booklets/ literature, 8.75 per cent of the respondents obtained information by from Kisan Mela and Krishi Seva Kendra, 8.13 per cent of the respondents made contact with the Krishi Vigyan Kendra, 6.87, 6.25, and 5 per cent of the respondents used agriculture/horticulture department, internet, and private agency, respectively for getting information about cauliflower cultivation practices. Other sources like KCC, leaflets/pamphlets, agricultural university, bank workers, NGO workers, training and field visit are used for getting information regarding cauliflower cultivation by the cauliflowers growers.

Table 20.4: Distribution of Respondents According to Use of Information Sources

Sl.No.	*Source of Information*	*Never*	*Occasionally*	*Daily*
1.	Neighbours	03 (01.87)	07 (04.37)	150 (93.76)
2.	Friends	02 (01.26)	19 (11.87)	139 (86.87)
3.	Relatives	10 (06.25)	70 (43.75)	80 (50.00)
4.	Progressive farmers	10 (06.25)	60 (37.50)	90 (56.25)
5.	Village leaders	58 (36.26)	75 (46.87)	27 (16.87)
6.	Private agency	81 (50.63)	71 (44.37	08 (05.00)
7.	Bank workers	141 (88.12)	18 (11.25)	01 (00.63)
8.	NGO workers	81 (50.63)	76 (47.50)	03 (01.87)
9.	Village Panchayat	29 (18.13)	108 (67.50)	23 (14.37)
10.	Agriculture/Horticulture department	57 (35.63)	92 (57.50)	11(06.87)
11.	RAEO	05 (03.13)	39 (24.37)	116 (72.50)
12.	Krishi Seva Kendra	63 (39.37)	83 (51.87)	14 (08.76)
13	Krishi Vigyan Kendra	79 (49.37)	68 (42.50)	13 (8.13)
14.	Radio	79 (49.37)	39 (24.37)	42 (26.26)
15.	TV	73 (45.62)	54 (33.75)	33 (20.63)
16	Internet	137 (85.62)	13 (08.13)	10 (06.25)
17.	Kisan Call Centre	127 (79.37)	28 (17.50)	05 (3.13)
18.	Leaflets/Pamphlet	90 (56.25)	65 (40.62)	05(3.13)
19.	News Paper	92 (57.50)	48 (30.00)	20 (12.50)
20.	Agricultural booklets/ literature	65(40.63)	80 (50.00)	15 (09.37)
21.	Kisan Mela	36 (22.50)	110 (68.75)	14 (08.75)
22.	Agriculture University	77 (48.13)	77 (48.12)	06 (03.75)
23.	Training and field Visit	42 (26.25)	117 (73.12)	01 (00.63)
24.	Others	158 (98.75)	02 (01.25)	00(00.00)

* Frequency based on Multiple Responses.

Majority of the respondents (73.12 per cent) occasionally used training and field visit for seeking information about cauliflower cultivation practices and 68.75 per cent of the respondents occasionally attended Kisan Mela for seeking information, 67.50

per cent of the respondents contacted with village Panchayat followed by 57.50 per cent of the respondents who contacted agricultural/horticultural department, 51.87 per cent of the respondents who occasionally contacted in Krishi Seva Kendra for obtained the information regarding cauliflower cultivation practices. Whereas, 50 per cent of the respondents occasionally used agricultural booklets/literature, 48.13 per cent of the respondents obtained information from agricultural university, 47.50 per cent of the respondents made contact with NGO workers, 46.87 per cent of the respondents made contact with village leaders, 44.37 per cent of the respondents obtained information from private agency, 43.75 per cent of the respondents had obtained information from relatives, 42.50 per cent of the respondents obtained information by from Krishi Vigyan Kendra, 40.62 per cent of the respondents used leaflets/ pamphlet, 33.75 per cent of the respondents occasionally watched T.V., 30 per cent of the respondents read news paper occasionally, 24.37 per cent of the respondents occasionally obtained information from RAEO and radio, 17.50 per cent of the respondents occasionally obtained information from Kisan Call Centre, 11.87 per cent of the respondents obtained information from friends, 11.25 per cent of the respondents obtained information from bank workers, respectively. Other information sources like internet, neighbours, etc. are also used occasionally for seeking information regarding cauliflowers cultivation by the cauliflowers growers.

Similarly majority of the respondents (88.13 per cent) had never contacted bank workers for seeking information about cauliflower cultivation practices and 85.62 per cent of the respondents had never used internet for seeking information, 79.37 per cent of the respondents had never obtained information from kisan call centre, 57.50 per cent of respondents never read news paper, 56.25 per cent of the respondents never use leaflet/pamphlet followed by 50.62 per cent of the respondents who never contacted private agency and NGO workers, 49.37 per cent respondents never obtained information from Krishi Vigyan Kendra and radio, 48.13 per cent of the respondents never obtained information from agricultural university, 45.62 per cent of the respondents never watched T.V. for seeking information, 40.62 per cent of the respondents never used agricultural through booklets/literature, 39.37 per cent of the respondents never obtained information from Krishi Seva Kendra, 36.25 per cent of the respondents had never made contact with village leaders, 35.63 per cent of the respondents had never made contact with agriculture/horticulture department, 26.25 per cent of the respondents not attended trainings and visits, under T and V programme, 22.50 per cent of the respondents never attended Kisan Mela, 18.13 per cent never contacted village Panchayat, 6.25 per cent of the respondents had never made contact with relatives and progressive farmers for seeking information regarding cauliflowers cultivation, respectively. Very few farmers did not made any contact with RAEO, neighbours, friends etc. for seeking information regarding cauliflower cultivation by the cauliflower growers.

It could be concluded that maximum numbers of the respondents (58.34 per cent) used to contact friends regularly for seeking information about cauliflower cultivation practices and 56.67 per cent of the respondents contacted relative. Whereas, 41.67 per cent of the respondents often had contact with neighbors and 94.16 per cent of the respondents never used telephone.

References

Anonymous, 2011. Directorate of Horticulture, C.G.

Gupta, S.P., Amardeep and Vir, K. 2003. Utilization of information sources by the farmers under different production system in Uttaranchal and Uttar Pradesh. *Manage Extn. Res. Rev.*, **4**(2): 70-82.

Patel, B.D. 2005. A study on adoption of recommended chilli cultivation technology in Vadodara district of Gujarat state. M.Sc. (Ag.) Thesis, GAU, Anand.

Shriwas Y. 2011. A study on knowledge and adoption of recommended brinjal production technology among the farmer of Durg district of Chhattisgarh state. Unpublished M. Sc. (Ag.) Thesis, IGKV, Raipur (C.G.).

Lanjewar, O. Y. 2009. Attitude of farmers regarding adoption of recommended cabbage production technology with reference to use of drip irrigation system in Durg and Raipur district of Chhattisgarh. M. Sc. (Ag.) Thesis, IGKV, Raipur (C.G.).

Palaniswamy, K. and Sriram, M. S. 2001. A scale to measure extension participation of farmers. *Ind. J.l of Extn. Edn.*, **19**: 325-328.

Chapter 21

Mobile Telephony: Catalysing Agriculture and Rural Development in India

☆ *Neha Pandey and M.A. Ansari*

Although green revolution of 1960s-70s made the country self reliant in terms of foodgrain production, the benefits of technology didn't percolate down to different sections of the farming community, especially small and marginal farmers. The information asymmetry coupled with resources crunch at farm level were identified as the major reason for that. Besides, the recent stagnation in the foodgrain production points to the technology fatigue as much as the information and resources' asymmetry at the farm level.

In the contemporary information society, knowledge has emerged as one of the critical factor of production in agriculture. The knowledge of the latest and best agriculture technology and package of practices goes a long way in improving the farm productivity as well as efficiency. Telecommunication, especially mobile phones have the potential to provide solution to the existing information asymmetry in various sectors like agriculture. India's agriculture sector suffers from low growth rates and low productivity. Issues in access to information are weak points at every stage of the agri-supply chain. For small farmer-based economy like India, access to information can possibly enable better incomes and productivity to the farmers (Mittal and Tripathi, 2009).

Mobile telephony has emerged as the technology of the choice of the people, be it in the rural or urban area. Cutting across the socio-economic spectrum of the society, mobile are being used for a variety of purposes – for information, education, entertainment. From being a status symbol, the possession of mobile has become a necessity in the contemporary society irrespective of age, income groups or place of residence. Donner (2005) reported that in the early years of the introduction of mobile phones, due to high cost of handsets and call rates, only high income category people were the major users of mobile phones. He also reported that in low income nations like India, Pakistan, Bangladesh, Nigeria and Vietnam, mobile ownership was confined to the privileged middle class and elites in urban as well as rural areas. The next green revolution in India would be preceded by the next generation of technology and infrastructural development. So far Indian agriculture is confronted with some major issues and challenges that continue to hinder the growth of this sector. The challenge for the government and policymakers is to 'regain agricultural dynamism'. The country needs a strong pull-up support to the agricultural sector which should grow at the rate of at least 4 per cent per annum, all the more so since in the past two years the growth in agriculture sector has been on an average 2 per cent only. Share of agriculture in country's GDP has also declined to about 17.1 per cent in 2008-09, which is almost half of that two decades ago. The agriculture sector in India still has about 52.1 per cent of the population dependent on it for livelihood. The infrastructure is crumbling in this sector and the investments as percentage of total investments have been as low as 7 per cent in 2006-07 (Economic Survey, 2008-09).

With the gradual expansion of mobile phone services it has changed the life of people besides the improving their economic and social conditions. Even a poor man can avail this service and get minute and detailed information about his business or services every time. In 2002, the total number of mobile phones in use worldwide exceeded the number of landlines. Current projections suggest that the world will continue to add mobile lines faster than fixed lines;

indeed, the next *billion* new phone users will use primarily mobiles (ITU 2003; Lanvin 2005). Abraham and Jensen,(2007) conducted a study on the increasing penetration of mobile phone networks and handsets in India therefore, presents an opportunity to make useful information available more widely. He has reported that introduction of mobile phones to Kerala fishermen could decrease price dispersion and wastage by facilitating the spread of information which made the markets more efficient by decreasing risk and uncertainty). Mobile phones has been allowed fishermen, particularly marginally more prosperous fishermen, to get timely price information which helps them to decide the best place to land and sell their daily catch. The recent introduction of a number of mobile-enabled information services suggests that it was timely to take a look at their impact on agriculture sector in India. These services deliver a wide range of information to the farmers.

Although there are now over a billion mobile phones in the developing world, these changes in social interactions in the developed world have captured the bulk of the community's attention to date. Though the number of studies focused on mobiles in the developing world is growing steadily, these studies have appeared in relative isolation from each other, separated by regions, and by disciplines. The function of market mechanisms underpinning the stunning spread of a new technology across the planet; those concerned with economic development who sees the mobile as an enabler of broad-based prosperity; and those concerned with describing the social and cultural implications of its use. By focusing on areas where economic constraint is a pressing concern, and by extending analysis to a broader range of cultural and social contexts, these researchers are contributing to a broader, more varied understanding of the implications of mobile and personal communication technologies.

Problem Statement

The next green revolution in India is to be preceded by the next generation of technology and infrastructural development. So far Indian agriculture is confronted with some major issues and challenges that continue to hinder the growth of this sector. The challenge for the government and policymakers is to 'regain agricultural dynamism'. The country needs a strong pull-up support to the agricultural sector which should grow at the rate of at least 4 per cent per annum, all the more so since in the past two years the growth in agriculture sector has been on an average 2 per cent only. Share of agriculture in country's GDP has also declined to about 17.1 per cent in 2008-09, which is almost half of that two decades ago. The agriculture sector in India still has about 52.1 per cent of the population dependent on it for livelihood. The infrastructure is crumbling in this sector and the investments as percentage of total investments have been as low as 7 per cent in 2006- under the situation of recent global food crisis and rising food prices is of striking a balance between the policies of food security and improving the income levels of farmers. Along with this, India's average operational landholding is less than 2 hectares, with a majority of the farmers being small or marginal landholders. Improving the livelihoods of small farmers has been a cornerstone of Indian government policy targets for many years and is imperative for the social and economic development. At the farmers' level, sustainability concerns are being expressed that the input levels have to be continuously increased to maintain yields at the old level. This poses a threat to the economic viability and sustainability of crop production. The states with positive and accelerating total factor productivity (TFP) growth in 1970s and 1980s, have started menstruating stagnant or decelerating rate of growth in TFP since early-1990s (Kumar and Mittal, 2006). Research, extension, literacy and infrastructure have been identified as the most important sources of growth in farm productivity. Development of markets improves input output market interface and it is of crucial importance for the growth in farm productivity. Human resource development is central to the adoption of technology and promotion of sustainable development. In agriculture, education creates conditions that enable farmers to acquire and use knowledge for decision making regarding allocate and technical matters effectively (Mittal and Kumar, 2000; Kumar and Rosegrant, 1994; Evenson *et al.*, 1999; Fan *et al.*, Information-based, decision-making agricultural system (Precision Agriculture) is designed to maximize agricultural production and is often described as the next great evolution in agriculture. The combination of Global Positioning System (GPS) and mobile mapping are supposed to provide farmers with the information for implementation of decision-based Precision Agriculture (Michael, 2008). In the context of India, use of mobile phones as a mode of providing agriculture related information would depend on how far the mobile phone network has been able to link the farmers to market information — timely and accurately. The impact on productivity can be directly measured in terms of increased returns to the farmers with a trickledown effect on the cropping pattern and potential yield of the sowed crop. Information on the price factors — prices of inputs and output, and non-price factors like information about availability of inputs, quality of seeds, modern techniques, etc. would play the primary role in improving farm productivity. The increasing penetration of mobile phone networks and handsets in India therefore presents an opportunity to make useful information available more widely. The key backdrop to this paper is a recent research, which has reported that introduction of mobile phones to Kerala fishermen could decrease price dispersion and wastage by facilitating the spread of information which made the markets more efficient by decreasing risk and uncertainty (Jensen, 2007; Abraham, 2007). Mobile phones allow fishermen, particularly marginally more prosperous fishermen, to get timely price information which helps them to decide the best place to land and sell their daily catch. The recent introduction of a number of mobile-enabled information services suggests that it is timely to take a look at their impact on agriculture sector in India. These services deliver a wide range of information to the farmers. There are many researchable questions to seek answers to such questions as:

- ☆ Are mobile phones in practice being used for agricultural purposes, and if so, how?
- ☆ Have mobile phones helped in driving Improvement in agricultural productivity of farmers and if so, how.
- ☆ Which types of agricultural information are of high value for farmers, what are the constraints to the potential use of mobile phones in improving agricultural productivity?
- ☆ What type of problems do you encounter in the use of mobile phone?, do whom farmer contact and (how frequently) for agricultural information?

The answers to these questions have important implications for mobile phone operators, information service providers, and policymakers. So that investigator conducted present study on "Mobile Telephony: Catalysing Agriculture and Rural Development in India" under the specific objectives. These objectives are:-

Objectives of the Study

- To study the socio- personal characteristics of the mobile user farmers.
- To assess the utilization pattern mobile phone among the farmers.
- To find out the extent of use of mobile for seeking agricultural information by farmers.

Research Methodology

The state of Uttarakhand constituted the locale of the present study. The state of Uttarakhand was selected purposively. *Sampling procedure:* Farmers visiting the *Kisan Mela* organized in the month of March 2011 at the main campus of the Pantvarsity formed the study universe. All the farmers who got themselves registered during the four days of the said kisan mela formed the sampling frame. Normally, about 2-5 thousand farmers registers at the two registration counters put up at the main entrance gates – *Nagla gate* and *Phoolbagh gate* – of the university campus. About 20 percent farmers who registered during the four days of the *Kisan Mela* were included in the study sample. A structure interview schedule was used for data collection. The method of data collection was personal interview. *Research design:* Therefore, descriptive research design was used in the present study.

Results and Discussion

Profile of Mobile Phone Users

The study was conducted to find out the socio-economic profile of the users of the mobile phones for obtaining agricultural information. The results obtained are given in the following table.

It is clear from the above table that more than half of the respondents (77.78percent) belonged to middle age category and 17.22 percent were from old age category. Rest of the respondents was in young age category. Gender-wise breakup of the respondents reveals that a large majority of them were male (98.34 percent) and rest of the respondents was female (1.66 percent). It appears that the society here follows patriarchal system *i.e.* males earn the bread for family and females take care of the household responsibilities. Besides, most of farmers who visited *Kisan Mela* were males; a very

Table 21.1: Distribution of the Respondents on the Basis of Socio-economic Profile

Distribution of the Respondents N= 180

Sl.No.	Variables	Frequency	Percentage
A	Age		
1.	Young (35 years)	9	5.00 per cent
2.	Adult (35-55 years)	140	77.78 per cent
3.	Old (above 55 years)	31	17.22 per cent
B.	Gender		
1.	Male	177	98.34 per cent
2.	Female	3	1.66 per cent
C.	Education		
1.	Illiterate	18	10.00 per cent
2.	Primary	30	16.68 per cent
3.	Middle	23	12.77 per cent
4.	High school	45	25.00 per cent
5.	Intermediate	34	18.88 per cent
6.	Graduate and above	30	16.68 per cent
D.	Respondent Occupation		
1.	Primary Occupation	140	77.77 per cent
2	Secondary Occupation	60	33.33 per cent
E.	Respondent Income		
1.	Low Income (10,000-50,000 per year)	60	33.34 per cent
2.	Medium Income (50,000-1,00000 per year)	80	22.22 per cent
3.	High Income (1,00000-10,00000 per year)	40	44.44 per cent
F.	Type of Farming		
1.	Subsistence Type	70	38.88 per cent
2.	Commercial Type	110	61.12 per cent

small number of females visit the *Kisan Mela*. We need to find out as to why less number of females visits the kisan mela. The educational level of the respondent shows that (25 percent) were educated up to high school level followed by those who were intermediate (18.88 percent), 16.68 percent were primary and graduate level,

12.77percent were middle level. Only 10 percent of respondents were illiterate. As regards occupation of the respondents, 77.77 percent were involved in primary occupation (farming), 33.33 percent had involved in primary as well as secondary occupation. Analysis of income of respondents indicates that 44.44 percent were from high income group, 33.34 percent were from low income group, and only 22.22 percent respondents were from high income group. It is evident from the above table that maximum number (36.13 percent) of respondents was medium farmers whereas 30.55 percent were small farmer, and 16.66 percent were marginal farmer and an equal number were large farmers. As regards the type of farming, majority (61.12 percent) was involved in commercial farming and only 38.88 percent were involved in subsistence farming.

Table 21.2: Distribution of the Respondents on the Basis of Mobile Phone Ownership

Distribution of the Respondents (N= 180)

Sl.No.	Mobile Phone Ownership	Yes	Per cent	No	Per cent
1.	Own a mobile phone	150	83.34	30	16.66

It is evident from the above table that majority of the respondents (83.34 percent) owned mobile phone and only 16.66 percent did not have mobile phone. Further. Distribution of respondents according to the use of mobile is given in Table 21.3.

It is clear that 44.44 percent of the respondents had Nokia mobile and rest number 5.55 percent of the respondents had Spice mobile. Majority of the respondents (50 percent) had purchased a mobile phone at the time of study during the last two years. Further, about 55.55 percent of the respondents were used IDEA mobile service and 27.78 percent of the respondents were used BSNL mobile service. Minimum numbers of the respondents were found to be using Airtel, Vodafone and Uninor.

Feasibility of Mobile Services by the University

Mobile has become the technology of choice for the masses, even in rural areas and across all the socio-economic strata. The farmers are also reportedly using the mobile phones for a variety of purposes. It is yet to be established as to what extent the farmers would be willing to use and pay for the for getting the information

Table 21.3: Distribution of the Respondents on the Basis of Mobile Phone Use

Distribution of the Respondents (N= 180)

Sl.No.	Use of Mobile Phone	Frequency	Percentage
1.	Handsets make		
	(*a*) Sony	15	8.34
	(*b*) Nokia	80	44.44
	(*c*) Samsung	40	22.23
	(*d*) Reliance	35	19.44
	(*e*) Spice	10	5.55
2.	Since when		
	(*a*) 1 year	30	16.67
	(*b*) 2 year	90	50.00
	(*c*) 3 year	20	11.11
	(*d*) 4 year	20	11.11
	(*e*) 5 year	20	11.11
3.	Mobile service used		
	(*a*) BSNL	50	27.78
	(*b*) AIRTEL	15	8.34
	(*c*) IDEA	100	55.55
	(*e*) VODAPHONE	10	5.55
	(*f*) UNINOR	5	2.78

regarding agriculture through mobile (*i.e.* agriculture information through mobile phone). Some of the private companies have already started specialised agriculture service in form of message alerts or voice calls for farmers in different states. This aspect was included in the study to ascertain whether farmers would be willing to use and able to pay for such services if Pantvarsity initiates such service in future. The data obtained is presented in the Table 21.4.

It is clear that majority (83.34 percent) of the respondents expressed that they would be willing to get the information regarding agriculture by the Pantnagar University through mobile phones, but 16.66 percent said that they did not want such services.

Table 21.4(a) Distribution of the Respondents on the Basis of Expected Services through Pantnagar University

Distribution of the Respondents (N= 180)

Sl.No.	*Information through Pantnagar University*	*Yes*	*Per cent*	*No*	*Per cent*
1.	Agriculture information	150	83.34	30	16.66

Table 21.4(b): Distribution of the respondents on the basis of expected services through Farmers

Distribution of the Respondents (N= 180)

Sl.No.	*Expected Services by Farmers*	*Frequency*	*Percentage*
1.	Crop Variety recommended/appropriate	20	11.12
2	Sowing Time	35	19.45
3.	Agronomic Practices	30	16.66
4.	Seed Treatment	30	16.66
5.	Disease Identification and Control Measures	50	27.77
6.	Fertilizer Application: Dose, Method and Time of Application	50	27.77
7.	Harvesting Time	45	25.00
8.	Post- Harvest Operation	40	22.23
9.	Marketing	40	22.23

It is clear that majority (83.34 percent) of the respondents expressed that they would be willing to get the information regarding agriculture by the Pantnagar University through mobile phones, but 16.66 percent said that they did not want such services. Further, as regarding expected service by Pantnagar University, 25 percent respondents told that they would prefer information about harvesting time, 27.77 percent of the respondents about disease identification and an equal number of respondents about control measures, fertilizer application, respectively. Further, 22.23 percent of the respondents mentioned abour post- harvest operations and marketing; and remaining number of the respondents told to get the information about crop variety recommended, sowing time, and agronomic practices and seed treatment through Pantnagar University.

Table 21.5: Distribution of the Respondents on the Basis of Pay for Mobile Phone Services

Distribution of the Respondents (N= 180)

Sl.No.	Pay for Mobile Services	Yes	Per cent	No	Per cent
1.	Less than 100	80	44.44	100	55.56
2.	100-200	45	25.00	135	75.00
3.	200-300	20	11.12	160	88.88

The above table presents findings about the willingness of the farmers about the minimum payment for the agriculture service through mobile phones. It is now clear that 44.44 percent people would be ready to pay rupees less than 100 per month, whereas 25 percent people would be willing to pay rupees 100-200 per month and only 11.12 percent people ready to pay rupees 200-300 per month.

Conclusion

This study, although limited to one state and those farmers who visited Kisn Mela at Pantnagar in March 2011, has implication for contemporary agricultural extension system in the country. Mobile phone can be used to reach the widely scattered and diverse farming community. It can overcome the constraints of time space and scared human resources. On the other hand, farmers are also capable and open to used mobile phones. In addition, mobile phone are also be for agricultural marketing, mobile banking to obtain agriculture credit, etc which are still unexplored. The use of mobile phone technology is still in ancient stage. To enhance the use of mobile phones by the farmers especially belonging to low income groups, there is need to subsidize the cost aspects related to mobile phones. Further there is need to develop a comprehensive information base catering to the specific need s of the farmers regarding agriculture practices. Mobile information must be locale specific. Various information must be provided in local language. Information must be provided in form of voice messages. With these amendments, mobile phone would be able to bridge the information gaps between the research institutions and farmers.

References

Abraham and Jensen, (2007): Getting Prices Right: Mobile Phone Di¤usion, Market Efficiency and Inequality. Francis ANDRIANARISON2bCSAE Conference 2010, Economic Development in Africa. 21st - 23rd March 2010, Oxford.

Andrianarison, F. (2010): Literacy, technology adoption, factor demand and productivity: An econometric analysis. *Indian Journal of Agricultural Economics,* Vol.55(3) p. 90-499.

Dey, B. and Newman, D. (2009): Mobile phones are just more than phones in the hands of FRG farmers.

Donner (2005): Research Approaches to Mobile Use in the Developing World: A Review of Literature. A paper submitted to the International Conference on Mobile Communication and Asian Modernities city university of Hongkong, June, 7-8,2005.

Mariscal, J.and Rivera, E. (2006): Mobile Communication in Mexico in the Latin America Context. Information Technologies and International Development, Vol.3, Winter 2006, p.41-45.

Mittal, S.and Tripathi, G.(2009): Role of Mobile Phone Technology in Improving Small Farm Productivity. Indian Council for Research on International Economic Relations (ICRIER), Lodi Road, New Delhi - 110 003, *Agricultural Economics Research Review,* Vol. 22 (Conference Number) 2009 pp 451-459.

Sarin, A. and Jain, R. (2008): A Survey of Usage of Mobile in Poor Urban Areas. India : The Impact of Mobile Phones, Moving the Debate Forward, The Policy Paper Series, N.9, January 2009, p.34-50.

Chapter 22

Role of Community Radio in Rural Development in India

☆ *Saket Raman and Amita*

Economists defined development as the growth in terms of structural and technological advancement. Typically, in the early stages of development economies have most of their production and labor force in Agriculture. Later, the manufacturing and service sectors become larger. From the macro point of view, development refers to the change from simple forms of organization and production to complex modern ones. Development does not matter only the economic growth but also the social, spiritual and moral enhancement of the entire society or nation.

After independence our growth rate has increased from 3 per cent to 9 per cent, but still we are facing problems like poverty, illiteracy, unemployment etc. That is because of our fast growing population. Our population has multiplied at an alarming level though the available resources more or less remain the same. Besides economic development it is very necessary to facilitate social, ethical as well community based development in order to avoid chaos in the near future. Though our government is taking various steps to facilitate the development process, but we cannot accomplish anything till the condition of a major part of population which resides in villages has not been improved. As, major part of our population still lives in villages, so how could we think of becoming a super power without empowering the rural area of our Nation.

Community radio is a radio service offering a third model of radio broadcasting in addition to commercial and public broadcasting. Community stations serve geographic communities and communities of interest. They broadcast content that is popular and relevant to a local, specific audience but is often overlooked by commercial or mass-media broadcasters. Community radio stations are operated, owned, and influenced by the communities they serve. They are generally non-profit and provide a mechanism for enabling individuals, groups, and communities to tell their own stories, to share experiences and, in a media-rich world, to become creators and contributors of media.

Sociology defines community as a space where a group of interacting people live. Community radio, thus is a type of radio service, that serves a particular community either geographical or communes and are also run by that community. An essential feature of community media is that since it is completely free from the clutches of the market, profit motive in its functioning does not hold water. Community radio derives its genesis from the fundamental principles of democracy necessarily entailing equal and active participation in civic affairs and freedom of speech and expression

In many parts of the world, community radio acts as a vehicle for the community and voluntary sector, civil society, agencies, NGOs and citizens to work in partnership to further community development aims, in addition to broadcasting. There is legally defined community radio (as a distinct broadcasting sector) in many countries, such as France, Argentina, South Africa, Australia and Ireland. Much of the legislation has included phrases such as "social benefit", "social objectives" and "social gain" as part of the definition. Community radio has developed differently in different countries, and the term has somewhat different meanings in the United Kingdom, Ireland, the United States, Canada, and Australia.

Potential of Community Radio

According to a 2005 survey by the media organisation, Charkha, only an abysmal two per cent of media space went to cover issues related to people - like land, forest, water, and so on. It is this trend that Bhan and Rajim are helping to change. Many mainstream journalists are raising the concerns that were first highlighted by them.

In addition, community radio can provide a platform to those individuals and groups, whose voices are often being marginalised by the profit-oriented commercial media enterprises, to express the distinctive needs and socio-political interests. Its colossal potential can be directed towards reflecting and promoting local culture, encouraging participation and democratic process, promoting development and social change, and good governance. Though these works Community radio playing a vital role in Rural development and upliftment in India.

Freedom of speech and expression for a community is the concept of being able to speak openly and freely about matters that concern their lives closely, and influence the decisions making process in their favour. By providing a voice to the neglected and disadvantaged, CR can play a role in preventing governments from shielding themselves from public comment. CR, as an alternative to public and commercial radio, has the potential to revive the plurality of viewpoints that alone can guarantee every community the opportunity to express its concerns without exclusion or discrimination.

Horizontal, non-hierarchical and participatory processes of CR have the ability to strengthen communicative and analytical skills of the people, enhance their engagement in civic life, and build involvement in local democratic governance, thus ensuring membership of communities in the process of social change, while maintaining local identities and language diversity.

At the time of the announcement of CR regulations, officials in the Indian government had enthusiastically predicted that there would be 4000 CR stations in India in two years. If this were to come true in near future, then a vibrant CR sector can be instrumental in subverting the differential access to technologies of self-expression. They can serve as a potent tool of freedom of expression and of deliberations and negotiations among the multiple stakeholders of any social change initiative. The need of the hour for the Indian government, fixated as it is on drawing the 12th plan estimates, is to give a boost to the CR in the country with a view to foster freedom of speech and expression among the underprivileged, and thereby strengthen its claims towards participatory democracy.

Indeed, for those who have traditionally been unacknowledged and silenced, socially and culturally, the opportunity to have one's voice heard can be an imposing experience of self-worth. In the words of the social activist bell hooks, "Moving from silence into speech is for the oppressed, the colonized, the exploited, and those who stand and struggle side by side a gesture of defiance that heals, that makes life and new growth possible. It is that act of speech of "talking back," that is no mere gesture of empty words; that is the expression of our movement from object to subject - the liberated voice."

Community Radio in India

It is enthralling to ascertain that radio was introduced in India not by the government but by a handful of members of the British civilians during the late 1920s and early 1930s who promoted community listening systems on the rural outskirts of Lahore, Delhi, Peshawar, Madras, and Calcutta. One of the most influential champions of rural development and community broadcasting was Frank Brayne. Brayne directed the powerful radio technology towards eliminating social ills of rural life, empowering women, and imparting education on health and hygiene. Unable to sustain under the expansionist policy of the government-controlled All India Radio, by 1937, all the operations were taken over by the government (then British). With their closure went the commitment of broadcasting towards development, participation, and social change.

Though the idea of community broadcasting was short lived, it has set the basis for the future use of radio technology at the community level. The prospect unlocked by the February 1995 landmark judgment of the Supreme Court that the airwaves or frequencies are public property, still seems to be awaiting recognition from the educational institutions, non-governmental organisations, and civil society in Sikkim and other north-eastern States.

The approval of the Community Radio Policy by the Government of India in December 2002 was a follow-up of this judgment. Initially, only the well-established educational institutions, including IITs/IIMs, were eligible to get licenses for setting up community radio stations. The matter has now been reconsidered and today all the non-profit organizations such as the civil society and voluntary organisations can apply for license.

On 16 th November 2006, the government of India notified new community radio guidelines which permit NGOs and other civil society organizations to own and operate community radio stations. About 4000 radio licenses are on offer across India, according to government sources. By 30 November 2008, the ministry of information and broadcasting, Govt. of India, had received 297 applications for community radio licenses, including 141 from NGOs and other civil society organizations, 105 from educational institutions and 51 from agricultural universities and agriculture extension centers. By 30 November 2008, there were 38 operational community radio stations in the county. As on, November 2011, there are 121 functional community radio stations in India.

Under the new community radio policy, any not for profit 'legal body'- except individuals, political parties and their affiliates, criminal and banned organizations, can apply for community radio license. The license entitles them to operate a 100 watt radio station, with a coverage area of approximately 12 km radius. A maximum antenna height of 30 meters is allowed. Community radio stations are expected to produce at least 50 per cent of their programmes locally, as far as possible in the local language or dialect. The stress is on development programming, though there is no explicit ban on entertainment. News programmes are banned on community radio in India. However, the Government recently clarified that certain categories of news are permitted on radio, including sports news, information on trafiic and weather conditions, coverage of cultural events and festivals, academic informations and other mass awareness programmes.

Five minutes of advertising per hour is allowed on community radio. Sponsored programmes are not allowed except when the program is sponsored by the Government.

Popular Community Radio Stations

SARANG 107.8

SARANG Community radio station is run by Aloysius College, Mangalore, a coastal town in the southern part of Karnataka. The local communities of farmers, fisher folks, medical/legal experts, students, workers contribute regularly to this radio. The radio also spreads messages of peace and harmony among people through their programmes. Health and hygiene, agricultural messages, fisherman's issues, road safety, water conservation, rain water harvesting, folk culture and life.

MANDAKINI KI AWAAZ

This community radio station is locate at Pauri in Garhwal region. This radio is supported by a group of people from a small village called BHANAJ. This group aims at creating an open and transparent administrative governance system. The radio mediates between rural masses of the area and the Governing bodies. It is working as a bridge between public and local panchayati raj institutions, in order to create an open platefom where policies, schemes and financial budgets can be made available for public discussion.

UNJAL PANCHHI-KUTCH JI

This station is run and administered by kach women development corporation and is immensely popular among the rural women. This radio station mostly focuces on the issues relating to women and tries to find a solution to each and every problem related to local women. The topic for discussion mostly consists of issues like female foetocide, dowry and women education.

CHALA HO GAON MEIN

The program broadcasted through this community radio is prepared by the people belonging to rural background. The programmes basically cover issues like dowery, violence against women, corruption, social evils etc. This radio really proved to be a landmark in providing common plateform to the residents of palamu district of Jharkhand, from where they can communicate their feelings, thoughts and ideas without any restriction.

Some Icons of Community Radio World

Shilwanti Biranchi of Bhalmanda (Jharkhand), Sudha Rawat, Manvendra Negi and Rajendra Negi of Bhanaj (Uttarakhand), Shantha of Budhikote (Karnataka), Naguveer Prakash of Nagapattinam (TN), Helina Sina and Narsingh of Konark and Koraput respectively (Orissa) have one thing in common. They are all, much-admired community radio (CR) reporters and presenters, who produce amazing programmes, which go on air at the CR stations set up in their region following the announcement of the updated, inclusive policy on Community Radio (CR) by the Government of India (GOI) on 16th November 2006.

All of these CR reporters have a number of other things in common too, which have, in no way, restrained them from carrying out their tasks adroitly. They belong to rural areas or the suburbs; none of them have gone to journalism schools; many have scarcely completed their secondary education; they had negligible exposure to media production before getting involved with radio; and they are members of a disadvantaged cluster (be it on basis of caste, class or gender) even within their own community. Prachi and Dalchand Kushwaha of Orchha (MP), Bharati and Ahmed of Kutch (Gujarat), General Narsamma and Algole Narsamma of Pastapur (AP),

The driving force behind their enthusiasm is an abiding faith that their "own" radio will give them and their community a "voice" that matters most in the struggle for a better life. These superbly motivated CR reporters also aspire to deploy what Jean Burgess calls their "vernacular creativity" to mobilize and empower the communities they belong to. They already have several success stories of local level civic engagement to their credit. The CR policy has been in operation in India for over five years now. The evidence available so far demonstrates that the small number of radio stations operational in the country that belong to non-government and grassroots-based developmental organizations not only endeavour to be effective tools of community development, but also increasingly trying to alleviate what some academic scholars such as Jo Tacchi have termed as "voice poverty."

Conclusion

At present, In India there are a lot of community radio stations are working. In which several radios are realy working with the vision and motive of social upliftment or well-being. In rural areas they are working for rural development and providing information according to the need of rural masses. Community radio stations serve their listeners by offering a variety of content that is not necessarily provided by the larger commercial radio stations. Community radio outlets may carry news and information programming geared toward the local area, particularly immigrants over minority groups that are poorly served by the other major media outlets. More specialized musical shows are also often a feature of many community radio stations. But their focus should be on- Agricultural information, labour problem, scientific agriculture methods, water conservation, rain water harvesting, health and hygiene issues of rural masses, conservation of local culture and traditions, promotion of local arts and artisans, local self governance, legal awareness, human right awareness and eradication of social evils.

Community radio plays pivotal role in making the masses aware about their basic rights and duties. Not only limited to solving problems of ADNA ADMI (Common man) daily life, But also community radio provides him a strong plateform from where he can freely disseminate his ideas and feelings. Besides solving social problems as well as entertaining rural masses, it also acts as an intermediatory between the Government and the local masses. Community radio has played a major role in bridging the communication gap between the government and the locals. It has proved to be one of the best medium of communication at the Grass-root level.

References

http://en.wikipedia.org/wiki/community_radio

http://en.wikipedia.org/wiki/economy_of_india

http://mib.nic.in/writereaddata/html_en_files/crs/CRBGUIDELINES041206.pdf

http://rural.nic.in/

http://www.communityradioindia.org/

http://www.youthkiawaaz.com/2011/02/community-radio-for-rural-development/

www.i4donline.net/july07/1337.pdf

www.thhoeot.org

Chapter 23

Adoption Behaviour of Improved Cultivation Practices for Pigeonpea Growers: A Study of Jaunpur District, U.P.

☆ *Sandeep Kumar, S.K. Kannaujia, A. Kar and T. Singh*

In India pigeon pea is the most important pulse crop which is contributing 90 per cent of the worlds pigeon pea production (Niramjan *et al.*, 1996). Pigeon pea is also one of the most important legumes grown in Uttar Pradesh which has about 10.61 per cent area and 13.87 per cent in terms of production in the country.

Pigeon pea is a major source of 'dal' an important constituent in the food habit of Indian people. Availability of 20-21 per cent protein in pigeon pea in as important source of supplementing the energy rich cereal diet. Additionally, pigeon pea crop improves the soil characteristic and fertility status ensuring better growth to succeeding crop that is considered to be an important asset it is reported that a long duration pigeon pea could fix up to 200 kg N ha-1 it is estimated that pigeon pea has a beneficial effect on subsequent crops equivalent to about 40 kg ha-1. Keeping in this view a study was conducted to find out the adoption behavior of pulse growers in Jaunpur district (U.P.)

Methodology

The study was conducted in four blocks of district Jaunpur of U.P. during 2009-10. These four blocks were having more than 50 per cent area under cultivation and accounted for major amount of production of pigeon pea. Five villages from each block were selected randomly for the study. From each village 25 formers, which cultivating pigeon pea from last 10 years, were selected randomly. Thus total sample size was 500 pigeon pea cultivating formers. The objective of the study adoption of improved cultivation practices of pigeon pea was considered as dependent variable. Socio - personal – economic variables such as age, education, caste, family size, occupation, social participation, land holding and annual income; and communication variables like extension contact and mass media exposure and psychological variables like risk orientation, attitude towards pigeon pea production technology were as independent variables.

The adoption of recommended cultivation practices of pigeon pea by the formers, and the scale developed by Sengupta (1967) was used to measure the adoption behavior of the pigeon pea formers is respect of the recommended practices included in the package of practices in pigeon pea cultivation were used for measuring this adoption. Against each of the practice, there were two columns representing adoption and not adoption with weight age of 1 and 0, respectively. The minimum and maximum score a respondent could get on this scale were 15 and 0, respectively.

Result and Analysis

The data of Table 23.1 shows that 67 per cent of the pigeon pea growers belonged medium level adoption behavior, 18 per cent belonged low level adoption. Sometimes formers got a very low production of pigeon pea and they could not even recover their own cost of cultivation because of the lower adoption of various improved vegetable production technology. The adaption behaviors of recommended practices were also study by Ingle (1999) and Suman (2011).

Table 23.1: Adoption Behaviour of the Pigeon Pea Formers and their Distribution (N-500)

Adoption Behaviour	*No.*	*Per cent*
Low (< 20.50 per cent)	90	18.00
Medium (20.50 To 65.50 per cent)	335	67.00
High (> 65.50 per cent)	75	15.00
Total	500	100.00

Adoption of improved pigeon pea production technology is presented in Table 23.2. Total fifteen practices were taken for the present study and adoption was seen for each practices. It was obtained that maximum level of the pigeon pea growers were adopting time of sowing (85 per cent) followed by proper method of harvesting (68 per cent). A medium level of adoption was found for land preparation and time of harvesting (61 per cent), improved

Table 23.2: Adoption of Improved Practices of Pigeon Pea Production Technology by Recommended Package and Practices

Sl.N.	*Practices*	*Adoption (per cent)*	*Non Adaption (per cent)*
1.	Land preparation	61	39
2.	Improved varieties	52	48
3.	Time of sowing	85	15
4.	Method of sowing	23	77
5.	Seed treatment	6	94
6.	Seed rate	32	68
7.	Spacing	24	76
8.	Quantity of fertilizer	13	87
9.	Time of fertilizer application	5	95
10.	Irrigation	6	94
11.	Intercultural operation	42	58
12.	Disease management	4	96
13.	Insect pest management	9	91
14.	Time of harvesting	61	39
15.	Proper method of harvesting	68	32

varieties (52 per cent), intercultural operation (42 per cent) and seed rate (32 per cent).The practices like spacing (24 per cent), method of sowing (23 per cent), quality of fertilizer (13 per cent), insect pest management (9 per cent), seed treatment and irrigation (6 per cent), time of fertilizer application (5 per cent) and disease management (4 per cent) was seen lower level of adoption compared to other practices.

The correlation analysis of the selected dependent and independentvariables of the pigeon pea growers was studied by using multiple correlation co-efficient (Table 23.3). The results given in Table 23.3 revealed that the adoption of pigeon pea cultivation technology was obtained to be positively and significantly correlated with their education knowledge about improved pulse cultivation practices and attitude towards pulse cultivation at one per cent level of significance. Land holding and annual incomes from pulses were found to have positive and significant correlation at five per cent level of significance. The variable age was found to have negative and significant correlation with adoption behavior and 15 per cent

Table 23.3: Relation between Adoption of Recommended Practices of Pigeon Pea Cultivation and Selected Variables of Pigeon Pea Formers (N=100)

Sl.N.	Variables	'r' Value
1.	Age	- 0.771**
2.	Education	0.753**
3.	Caste	0.042
4.	Family size	0.034
5.	Occupation	0.159
6.	Social participation	0.174
7.	Land holding	0.201*
8.	Annual income from pulses	0.278*
9.	Risk orientation	0.121
10.	Knowledge about improved pulse cultivation practices	0.731**
11.	Attitude towards pulse Cultivation	0.478**
12.	Extension contact	0.067
13.	Mass media exposure	0.012

* and ** indicate significance of value at P=0.05 and 0.01, respectively.

of them had high level of adoption behavior. It reveals that majority of the respondent (85 per cent) were seem to possess low to medium adoption behavior. About eighty five percent of the pigeon pea growers had low or medium adoption of pigeon pea cultivation practices. It means medium adopters were more energetic, knowledgeable, dynamic and having more interest in adopting improved technologies. The rest of the variables, namely, caste, family size, occupation, social participation, risk orientation, extension contact and mass - media exposure of the pigeon pea growers were found to be positive but non-significantly correlated with the adoption of pigeon pea cultivation technology.

Education was found highly significantly correlated with the adoption of pigeon pea growers. It means that more educated pigeon pea growers had greater adoption of cultivation technology. Similarly in the case of knowledge of pulse production technology and attitude towards pulse cultivation as these also had positive correlation with adoption. It implies that pulse growers having more land holding adopted more recommended package of practices for pigeon pea as compared to those having less land holding.

References

Ingle, P.O. (1999). Knowledge and adoption of formers about saybean cultivation practices *PKV Res. J.*, 23(1):59-60.

Niranjan, S.K.D.F.F., Bantielam, M.C.S., Joshi, P.K. and Saxena, K.B. (1996). Evaluating hybrid technology for pigeon pea. *Assessing Joint Research Impacts, ICRISAT*, pp: 131-140.

Sengupta, T. (1967), A simple adoption scale for selection of formers for high yielding varieties programme on rice *Indian J. Exrension Education*, 3(2): 107-115.

Suman, R.S. (2011). Adoption behaviour of the commercial vegetable growers in kullu district of Himanchal Pradesh. *Agric update*, 6(2):31-33.

Chapter 24

Communication Behaviour of Rural Women towards Traditional Health Care Management of Common Infant Diseases

☆ *Sharada, Indira Bishnoi and Ram Jiyawan*

"The lack of progress to combat under nutrition is damaging children and nations," said Unicef's Executive Director Ann M Veneman. A healthy, well-nourished pregnancy is an essential first step in safeguarding a child's future. Child is not only an important structural and functional component of society country but also a human system. Early child hood is a very critical period for child's physical, mental and socio- psychological development. About 40 percent of total child's population comes under 0-5 year age group. India has maximum child population in the world and as well as maximum infant mortality rate that occurs under 0-4 year age group. The highest mortality rate observed in Uttar Pradesh (10.7 per cent) followed by Orissa (10.3 percent) and Bihar and Karnataka. The

World Health Organization (WHO) has categorically remarked that child health care should be ensure every child where ever possible lives and grow up in a family unit with love and security in healthy surroundings receive adequate nourishment healthy supervision and efficient medical attention and sought the element of healthy living. A positive health status depends as a state of complete physical, mental, social wellbeing and not merely the absence of diseases or infirmity (WHO, 1984).

We can often trace the origin of popular concept of health back to the thinking of early Greek philosophers such as Hippocrates whose doctrine of universal- sympathy or harmony viewed health as state of balance or equilibrium between the internal and external environment of an individual. National policy of children was adopted in 1974 has emphasized the need to accord priority to children in the country's development efforts. The policy statement focuses on preventive and promotional aspects of child health and nutrition for expectant and nursing mothers.

Ninety five in every 1000 children born in India do not see their fifth birthday; 70 in every 1000 children born in India do not see their first birthday; 23 per cent of India's children are underweight at birth; 74 per cent of India's children below the age of 3 months are anemic; acute respiratory infections are leading causes of child mortality (30 per cent) followed by diarrhea (20 per cent) in India; amongst married women in India today, 75 per cent were under age at the time of their marriages; more that 50 per cent of India's children are malnourished. This background explores the levels of health, nutrition, education and social security of children, and government policy and action on child rights. Children are suffering as a result of social sector cutbacks/policies and programmes and development initiatives that deprive communities and families of access to and control over land, forest and water resources they have traditionally depended on. The negative fallout is visible: children are being deprived of even the scarce social benefits once available; they are displaced by forced and economic migration, increasing the number of children subsisting on the streets; more and more children are being trafficked within and across borders; and rising numbers of children are engaged in part- or full-time labour. According to World Health Organization Traditional medicine is the sum total of the knowledge, skills, and practices based on the theories, beliefs, and experiences indigenous to different cultures, whether explicable or not, used in the maintenance of health as well as in the prevention, diagnosis, improvement or treatment of physical and mental illness.

Child Status: Ground Realities

Children are important assets of a nation, therefore reduction in infant and child mortality is likely the most important objective of the Millennium Development Goals (MDG). Infant and child mortality rates reflect a country's level of socio-economic development and quality of life and are used for monitoring and evaluating population, health programs and policies. It is an outcome rather than a cause and hence directly measures results of the distribution and use of resources Haines (1995).

According to the United Nations estimates, 10 million infant deaths occur annually in the world. India accounts for a quarter of those. Thus any study of Indian infant mortality has global significance. India has experienced an impressive decline in infant mortality since the 1970s. From 130-140 deaths per 1,000 live births in the early 1970's, mortality levels have declined to as low as 60 deaths per 1,000 live births in 2000. This represents an annual rate of decline of around 2.6 percent.

However the absolute levels of infant and child mortality are still too high (about 68 infant and 95 child deaths per 1,000 live births in 1998-99). According to the Registrar General of India, the IMR for the country as a whole is 57 infant deaths for every 1,000 live births in the year 2006. The National Population Policy 2000 aims at achieving IMR of 30 by the year 2010, Government of India (2000). The MDG is to reduce infant and child mortality by two-thirds between 1990 and 2015. In the case of India this would imply a reduction of the IMR to 27 and of the less than five year mortality rate to 32 by 2015, The World Bank (2004). IMR has declined both in the urban and rural areas. The latest data from the sample registration system shows that the infant mortality rates for the urban and rural regions are 40 and 64, respectively, for every 1,000 live births in the year 2004, Government of India (2006).While there has been a significant decline in IMR in India over the last three decades, it's performance with respect to other countries in Southeast Asia is not that impressive. Countries such as Indonesia, Sri Lanka, and Bangladesh have managed to reduce their IMR levels by between 3-5 per cent annually.

IMR Estimates 2009: Highlights

- ☆ IMR measures number of infant (< 1 year) deaths per 1000 live births.
- ☆ Every 6th death in the country pertains to an infant
- ☆ IMR in India has registered a 3 points decline to 50 from 53 in 2008
- ☆ Maximum IMR in Madhya Pradesh (67) and minimum IMR in Kerala (12)
- ☆ Neo-Natal Mortality Rate (<29 days) and Post Neo-Natal Mortality Rate (1 months to 11 months) has declined by 1 point and 2 points respectively
- ☆ Kerala (12) and Tamil Nadu (28) have achieved the MDG target (28 by 2015)
- ☆ Delhi (33), Maharashtra (31) and West Bengal (33) are in close proximity (Registrar General, India 2011)

In India, only 35 per cent of births are registered, impacting name and nationality, out of 16 children die before they attain the age of 1, and one out of 11 die before they are 5 years old. 35 per cent of the developing world's low-birth-weight babies are born in India. The declining number of girls in the 0-6 age-group is cause for alarm. For every 1,000 boys there are only 927 females and even less in some places, 65 per cent of girls in India married by the age of 18 and become mothers soon after.

One in every three malnourished children in the world lives in India. Child malnutrition is generally caused by a combination of inadequate or inappropriate food intake, gastrointestinal parasites and other childhood diseases, and improper care during illness. Is it not ironical that in a nation with soaring GDP rates and Sensex indices, marking India's entry into the global market, children continue to die of malnutrition and starvation? The major cause is lack of public health services in remote and interior regions of the country, poor access to subsidised healthcare facilities, declining State expenditure on public health, and lack of awareness about preventive child healthcare. Great progress on tackling poor nutrition among children has been made through a number of simple, proven strategies. Vitamin A supplements have saved hundreds of thousands of children's lives. Some 82 million newborns are protected from iodine deficiency every year, thanks to campaigns to iodise salt. Exclusive breastfeeding for the first six months of infancy is one of the simplest and most effective ways to save a child's life. Keeping all these facts in view, the study entitled "Traditional Health Care Management of Common Infant Diseases through Practices" to know its impact and utility in present context.

Methodology

The study was carried out in Faizabad district of Uttar Pradesh during 2008 with three caste category groups namely, General (GN), Other Backward Classes (OBC) and Schedule Caste (SC). Faizabad district consists of 8 blocks, out of which, Masodha block was randomly identified, and under which Sirhir villages was purposively selected because of, majority of rural women adopted traditional health care practices and district hospital is 17 km. away from study location that why the peoples could not easily receive health care remedies at emergency and first aid situation. The selected village comprises of nine hundred house hold. Out of the total nine hundred house hold, 460 belonged to GN, 280 SC, and 260 in OBC caste category. A total 100 rural women were selected by proportionate random sampling technique. Information was collected personally through well structured interview schedule, and performing folk song. This was supported by the informal discussion with women. The interview schedule was pre-tested and modified based on suggestion, opinion made by the respondents and experts and finally the data was collected by personal interview method. The data were compiled and analyzed by simple statistical tools to draw the meaningful conclusion.

Results and Discussion

The understanding of prevailing Childs' health care practices in the rural area would not help only in comprehensive level of development but also in planning and taking an appropriate decision towards research and how to avail the services to the vulnerable community.

Socio-personal Profile of Rural Women

As perusal of data in Table 24.1 reveals that majority of the farmers (54.45 per cent) were middle aged. From the total selected women 46 per cent belonged to GN, 28 per cent SC and 26 per cent

Table 24.1: Socio-Personal Profile of Rural Women

N=100

Sl.No.	*Antecedent Variable*	*Frequency*	*Per cent*
1.	Age		
	Below 40	35	35
	40- 60	33	33
	above 60	32	32
2	Education		
	Illiterate	35	35
	Primary	22	22
	Junior High School	13	13
	High School	10	10
	Intermediate	06	06
	Graduate	6	6
	Post Graduate	8	8
3.	Caste category		
	GN	46	46
	OBC	26	26
	SC	28	28
	ST	Nil	Nil
4.	Family Type		
	Joint	50	50
	Nuclear	39	39
	Extended	11	11
5.	Family Size		
	Small(<5)	30	30
	Medium(5-10)	32	32
	Large(>10)	38	38
6.	No. of Women in a family		
	< 2 women	37	37
	2-4 women	54	54
	4-6 Women	7	7
	>6 Women	2	2
7	No. of Child in a family (0-5 years)		
	< 2 Child	36	36
	2-4 Child	49	49
	4-6 Child	9	9
	>6 Child	6	6

Contd...

Table 24.1–Contd...

Sl.No.	*Antecedent Variable*	*Frequency*	*Per cent*
8	House Type		
	Kaccha	39	39
	Pacca	43	43
	Hut	18	18
9	Land Holding of house hold		
	Marginal (<1 ha.)	65	65
	Small (1-2 ha.)	35	35
10	Monthly Income		
	<5000	43	43
	5000-8000	34	34
	8000-10000	14	14
	>10000	9	9
11	Material Possession		
	Low (< 2.53)	31	31
	Medium (2.53-4.19)	51	51
	High(>4.19)	18	18
12	Innovativeness		
	Low (< 15.56)	34	34
	Medium (15.56-18.78)	57	57
	High(>18.78)	9	9
13	Social Participation		
	Low (< 2.48)	26	26
	Medium (2.48-1[illegible])	49	49
	High(>11.47)	25	25
14	Transportation Facilities (multiple responses)		
	By-cycle	90	90
	Motorcycle	25	25
	Jeep/Bus	3	3
	All of above	3	3
15	Communication facilities (multiple responses)		
	Radio	42	42
	Television	28	28
	Telephone/Mobile	23	23
	Computer	2	2
	Post office	39	39
16	Information flow through community Extension Workers		
	Yes	32	32
	No	68	68

Table 24.4: Consultation and Vaccination Pattern in Selected Rural Household (N=100)

Sl.No.	*Components*	*Frequency*	*Percentage*
	Consultation pattern (Multiple response)		
1.	Recognised Doctors	43	43
2.	Mahila Savika	27	27
3.	Private unauthorised medical practitioners	62	72
4.	Advice from medical shop representative	76	86
5.	Traditional health care methods	79	89
6.	Self medication and village quack	63	63
7.	Private hospitals' Doctors	24	34
	Vaccination		
1.	Yes	63	63
2.	No	42	37

Vaccination time

S.No.	*Vaccine*	*Age*	*Per cent (multiple response) N=63*
1	BCG	Birth	23
2	Oral Polio Vaccine (OPV) and Diphtheria, Pertussis and Tetanus (DPT)	6 weeks	91
3	OPV, DPT	10 weeks	73
4	OPV, DPT	14 weeks	63
5	Measles	9 - 12 months	32
6	OPV, DPT	15 - 18 months	67
7	DT, Typhoid	4 - 5 years	43
8	Tetanus, Typhoid	10 - 16 years	21

consultation. Vaccination schedule recommended by the Government of India has fully incorporated for the study. Only 63 per cent of children are vaccinated to the selected house hold. The findings reflect that most of the rural women are aware about vaccination and she uses to cure their children from epidemic diseases. Most of the rural women are well aware to avail the OPV, DPT vaccines to their children (91 per cent) under 6 weeks followed by same vaccine at the 15-18 month. Here only 21 per cent of rural women provide the vaccination to cure against tetanus and typhoid diseases. This showed that lack of awareness among rural women about its danger and importance of vaccination.

Common Infant Diseases

Any changes that affect the normal physiology of human being are known as disease. There are various contagious/non contagious diseases that infect the child because they are very sensitive and easily grab by the diseases.

A perusal of Table 24.5 revealed that 91 per cent of the rural women agreed that vomiting and loose motion is the common problem occurred in 0-2 year age group of children followed by fever (87 per cent), common cold (84 per cent), vomiting and worm in stomach and crying (70 per cent). In case of 3-5 year age group of children vomiting of milk and intestinal worms (97 per cent) are prevailed followed by common cold (84 per cent) and fever (77 per

Table 24.5: Common Infant Diseases Occurred at Different Age Group

Sl.No.	Common Infant Diseases	Response in Percentage (multiple response)	
		0-2 years	3-5 year
1	Common cold	84	84
2	Vomiting of milk and intestinal worms	72	97
3	Diarrhoea and cholera	30	61
4	Vomiting and Loose motion	91	58
5	Whooping cough	17	56
6	Sleeping sickness	Nil	Nil
7	More crying	70	47
8	Pneumonia	42	54
9	Acidity	3	51
10	Diphtheria	63	12
11	Tetanus	57	18
12	Fever (typhoid)	87	73
13	Chicken pox	23	37
14	Others (Itching)	11	9

cent). On the basis of given response, itching is least common disease occurred in both age group category.

The data presented in Table 24.6 showed traditional methods of treatment of common infant diseases. Majority of rural women uses combination of Basil leaf extract + lemon juice + salt + Sugar (51 per cent) for curing their children against common cold followed

Table 24.6: Traditional Methods of Treatment of Common Infant Diseases

Sl.No.	*Traditional Treatment of Common Infant Diseases*	*Percentage*	*Rank*
1.	Common cold		
	☆ Extract of ginger	33	V
	☆ Boiled Ajwain	27	VI
	☆ Honey + ginger paste	46	III
	☆ Basil extract + Ginger + salt	41	IV
	☆ Basil leaf extract + lemon juice + salt + Sugar	53	I
	☆ Camphor + mustard oil/Alium + mustard oil + Ajwain	47	II
2.	Fever		
	☆ Extract of Basil + ginger	57	II
	☆ Sarpgandha	13	VI
	☆ Boiled Neem leaf extract	63	I
	☆ Bhringraj	47	III
	☆ Extract of eucalyptus leaf	12	VII
	☆ Osmium leaf extract	33	V
	☆ Flower extract of pomegranate	2	VIII
	☆ Diluted chirata	37	IV
3.	Cough		
	☆ Fenugreek paste	3	VII
	☆ Basil leaf extract	56	III
	☆ Turmeric powder + Milk + Gur	69	I
	☆ Mulethi extract	2	VIII
	☆ Coriander leaf extract	17	V

Contd...

Table 24.6–Contd...

Sl.No.	Traditional Treatment of Common Infant Diseases	Percentage	Rank
	☆ Extract of Ajwain + Lemon juice	31	IV
	☆ Roasted Aonla + Catachu + tender mango leaf	66	II
	☆ Root of Gurhal	4	VI
4.	Diarrhoea		
	☆ Bark of fig tree + milk	7	IV
	☆ Roasted cumin seed + Dahee	42	II
	☆ Sauf+ black salt + sugar	31	III
	☆ Lemon juice + salt + sugar	51	I
5.	Vomiting		
	☆ Cumin seed paste	23	V
	☆ Extract of Ajwain + Mint oil + camphor	21	VI
	☆ Roasted fenugreek seed+ curd/curd+ fenugreek seed	46	III
	☆ Lemon extract + salt	73	I
	☆ Chirata/honey/Sugar	3	X
	☆ Onion/Saunf/mint/heeng Paste	47	II
	☆ Bael juice	8	VIV
	☆ Extract of ripe mango + salt	36	IV
	☆ Bishop/Honey/Alium spp paste	18	VII
	☆ Paste of Bombyx leaf	13	VIII
6.	Pain		
	☆ Bark of Amaltas (*Casis* spp.)+water	14	III
	☆ Bishop seed+ water	12	IV
	☆ Green Aonla	32	II
	☆ *Moringa* spp.	6	V
	☆ Turmeric paste + oil + salt	71	I
7.	Cholera		
	☆ Sugar + tea leaves+ cold water	57	I
	☆ Mint + onion extract/Saunf + black salt	32	II
	☆ Jamun extract	17	IV
	☆ Lemon juice	27	III

Contd...

Table 24.6–Contd...

Sl.No.	Traditional Treatment of Common Infant Diseases	Percentage	Rank
8.	Intestinal worm		
	☆ Cowage+ black pepper	4	III
	☆ Neem oil	32	I
	☆ Leaf extract of bitter guard	21	II
9.	Tetanus		
	☆ Ash+ wild kukuraudha + neem oil	32	
10.	Loose motion		
	☆ Onion extract + fenugreek + mint extract	63	I
	☆ Bael juice	23	IV
	☆ Bishop seed + camphor	37	III
	☆ Lemon extract + salt	59	II
11.	Pox		
	☆ Neem leaf + mustard oil + turmeric + cynodon grass	13	
12.	Ricket		
	☆ Jamun (Sizium spp) extract	23	II
	☆ Massage with paste of catachu + pan leave	34	I
13.	Skin disease		
	☆ Boiled Neem leaf extract	32	II
	☆ Basil extract + neem oil	57	I
14.	Less sleeping		
	☆ Bishop seed	23	II
	☆ Chirata	27	I
15.	Injury		
	☆ Turmeric + onion paste	74	

by Camphor + mustard oil/Alium + mustard oil + Ajwain (47 per cent). Boiled Neem leaf extract (63 per cent) is very much popular in relation to controlling fever among rural women. Likewise Turmeric powder + Milk + Gur (69 per cent) for cough Lemon juice + salt + sugar (51 per cent) for diarrhoea, Lemon extract + salt (73 per cent) or Onion/Saunf/mint/heeng Paste (47 per cent) for curing against vomiting, Turmeric paste + oil + salt (71 per cent) or Green Aonla extract (32 per cent) against pain, Sugar + tea leaves+ cold water (57 per cent) uses for relief over cholera, Neem oil over intestinal worms, combination of reasonable and appropriate amount of Onion extract + fenugreek + mint extract(63 per cent) or Lemon extract + salt (59 per cent) against loose motion, Massage with paste of catachu + pan leave (34 per cent) over rickets and for curing against skin disease used by rural women is mixture of Basil extract + neem oil (57 per cent). This showed that most of the rural women initially rely on traditional health care measures for curing infant diseases.But in severe cases of ailments and disease occurrences most of the rural women prefer recognized doctors. Here one point added that women belong to high classes they consult to private doctors.

Conclusion

In India, the birth of a child is considered a blessing. The joint family system provided for many elderly people less than one roof and they helped in childbirth and rearing children. The preference for nuclear families, the lack of support or guidance in raising children, the dilemma over whether to follow home remedies or allopathic treatment is causing a lot of concern to parents. India has made some significant commitments towards ensuring the basic rights of children. There has been progress in overall indicators: infant mortality rates are down, child survival is up, literacy rates have improved and school dropout rates have fallen. But the issue of child rights and health concern India is still caught between legal and policy commitments to children on the one hand, and the fallout of the process of globalisation on the other.

Study reflected in broad sense that most of the rural women initially rely on traditional health care measures (38 percent) for curing infant diseases followed by primary health centers (20 percent), private practitioners (16 percent), and Government hospital (12 percent).Here one interesting fact is that whose standard and socio-economic status is high, they mostly approach to hospital whether it public sector or private. From the study it can be say that in the modernization era rural women still dependent on traditional health care practices.

References

"Child Rights in the Global Week of Action" concept paper prepared by HAQ: Centre for Child Rights, April 14, 2005.

Government of India 2000. National Population Policy 2000'.

Government of India 2006. Sample Registration Bulletin', 40(1).

Haines, M. 1995. Socio-economic differentials in infant and child mortality during mortality decline: England and Wales, 1890-1911', Population studies 49(2), 97{315.

http://www.who.int/medicines/areas/traditional/en/index.html.

Registrar General, India 2011. Maternal and child mortality and Total Fertility Rate. Sample registration system

Sawant, G.K., Pawar H.S., and Shinde, S.B., 1989. An analytical study of reactions of readers of Shri Sugi Periodical. *Maharashtra J. Extn. Edu.*, 8 : 73-77.

Sharada 2008. Sisuo mein hoone waali samanye beemario ka parampragat vidhion se upchaar. *MA dissertation* submitted to Department of Home Science Extension and Communication, MMV, Banaras Hindu University, Varanasi- 221005

Sharada, I. Bishnoi and R.Jyawan 2011. Management of common infant diseases through traditional health care practices. Abstract published in National seminar on *multi-sectoral innovations for rural prosperity* at NDRI Karnal.

Shashidhara, K. K. 2003. A study on socio-economic profile of drip irrigation farmers in Shimoga and Davangere district of Karnataka. *M.Sc. (Agri.) Thesis*, Univ. Agri. Sci.,Dharwad.

Singh, P. and Yadav R. J. 2000. Immunization status of children of India. Institute for Research in Medical Statistics, Indian Council of Medical Research, Ansari Nagar, New Delhi 110 029, India. *Indian Pediatr.* 2000 Nov; 37(11):1194-9.

The World Bank, 2007. India: Achieving the MDGs in India's poor states: Reducing child mortality in Orissa, Technical Report 39855-IN.

Chapter 25

Mobile SMS as Tool of Agri-Information for Hill Farmers of Uttarakhand: An Analysis

☆ *Sushrut Chauhan and Indraneel Ghosh*

There is no place in India that has been left untouched by the great Indian telecom revolution. It has changed the way India communicates, supported the socio-economic development of India and has played a significant role in bridging the rural-urban digital divide to some extent. Because of liberal government policies, over the past five years the service fees and call costs have reduced considerably enabling every person in middle class as well as lower middle class families in India to afford a cell phone.

Among 127.3 million cultivators in India, the majority are marginal farmers subsisting on smallholdings of less than 5 acres. Despite some periods of strong growth, the Indian agricultural sector is still constrained by low productivity. Serious challenges including infrastructure constraints, supply chain inefficiencies and problems in the diffusion of and access to information, exist. Low investments in rural infrastructure, adversely affects farm productivity and growth. Strengthening of agricultural infrastructure is required at all levels of the supply chain – input delivery, credit, minimizing post-harvest losses, cold storage chains, marketing etc.

Information is one of the key inputs for various stakeholders in agricultural Value chains. Traditionally information to farmers is primarily provided by the government agencies or the Public Extension System which include Indian Council of Agriculture Research (ICAR) Institutes, State Agricultural Universities, Krishi Vigyan Kendras, state agriculture departments. Increasingly private agribusiness companies and Non-Governmental Organisations (NGOs) are also getting involved. While television, Radio and other mass media have been in use for quite some time, the new technological breakthrough have brought in new channels under the broad category of ICT based agricultural information services in India.

The information needs of farmers vary from place to place depending on the geographical features of the area as well as the scale of their operations. The priority of information needs of the farmers from the plains may be entirely different from the farmers in the hills. The large scale progressive farmers may prefer information about advanced tools and machines whereas the same is not a concern of the small farmer. An International Economic Relations study classified the information needs of farmers in to 3 groups, namely,(a) Know-how, which helps a farmer with fundamental information such as what to plant and which seed varieties to use,(b) Contextual information such as weather, best practice for cultivation in the locality and (c) Market information such as prices, demand indicators, and logistical information. Similarly based on type, farmer's information needs can be classified as the information related to field acquisition, agricultural inputs, agricultural technology, agricultural credit, agricultural marketing and food technology (Vaishaki and Srivastava, 2002). Broad classification on the basis of various time periods of the farming cycle is presented in Table 25.1. Sapna A Narula (2010) reported that the information farmers need about agriculture are of four categories *i.e.* agri-inputs, market and supply chain, production and Government related, in the same orders of priority.

Table 25.1: Informational Needs of Farmers

Pre-sowing	*Pre-harvest*	*Post-harvest*	*Market Information*
☆ Information on agri- inputs such as seeds, fertilizers, pesticides etc.	☆ Good agricultural practices	☆ Post-harvest management	☆ Alternative market channels
☆ Credit	☆ Pest management	☆ Storage	☆ Commodity prices
☆ Weather	☆ Time and techniques of harvesting	☆ Grading and standardization	☆ Mandi Information
☆ Soil testing	☆ Market information	☆ Logistics	☆ Consumer behaviour
		☆ Market information	

ICT Based Agricultural Information Dissemination Services in India

Mode of operation and accessibility are differentiating factors to classify the ICT based agricultural information services for farmers in India. Broadly these are as Web based, Telephone Helpline and Mobile based. Other than these, farmers also rely on the Block level Government Offices (Agriculture) for information on Government schemes, credit assistance and input information etc. The following section discusses various players in the agriculture information dissemination in India based on the above classification.

Web Based

The web based services publish various information relevant for agri sector in their respective websites. A user can access information by visiting the website using internet. The information includes wide range of topics from current and comparative prices of commodities at various markets, to agri advisory, various schemes, promotion etc. Websites like Agricultural Marketing Information Network (AGMARKNET), National Multi Commodity Exchange of India Ltd website, National Horticultural Research and Development foundation (NHRDF), National Horticultural Board (NHB) etc. publish information of various commodities from the major Indian and international markets like daily/weekly monthly arrivals and prices, and analytical market reports and comparative charts etc. The website of Indian Council of Agricultural Research (ICAR) and the respective websites of its affiliate universities/institutes/labs/KVKs is a repository for information related to agriculture and horticulture in the country. Most of the State Agricultural Marketing Boards have their own web portals where the market information is available in the local language and english. The major among the private owned websites providing market information on various agricultural products are agriwatch.com, kisan.com, indiagriline.com, iopea.com, and echoupal.com.

Telephone Based Services like Farmer Help Lines

Kisan Call Centres established by The Department of Agriculture and Cooperation under Ministry of Agriculture, utilizes the telecommunication network in the country to provide extension services. The main objective is to respond to various enquiries of farmers instantly in their local language. In these telephone based services the farmer can call toll free number where an operator answers their queries and provides with necessary information. The help lines allow the farmers to talk to experts on various issues related to their farm practices and get advices. Famer helpline service of Vivekananda Parvatiya Krishi Anusandhan Sansthan (VPKAS), Almora, Uttarakhand, provides with expert crop advisory services for diverse agricultural and horticultural crops.

Mobile Based Agricultural Information Dissemination

Now-a-days mobile phones have coverage in almost all villages of India irrespective of the geographical conditions. TRAI (2011) data shows that there are 811 million mobile phone subscriptions and 34.73 million landline connections. This makes mobile phone as the best channel for disseminating information to the farmers. The SMS service facility in the mobile has become the key tool for the information dissemination through mobile phones. In the agriculture sector, initiatives are launched to provide the farmers with the necessary information related to agriculture activities. Brief on the mobile based agricultural information service providers are as follows;

IFFCO Kisan Sanchar Limited

Indian Farmers Fertilizer Cooperative Limited (IFFCO), in a joint venture with Bharti Airtel and Star Mobitel, has launched IFFCO Kisan Sanchar Ltd (IKSL). The farmer has to purchase an IKSL Green Sim Card which works like any other normal sim card with added features of the IKSL services under AIRTEL network.

Nokia Life Tools

Nokia Life Tools is an application that offers information services for agriculture, education and entertainment. On subscription to a service, the text messages are sent to their Nokia Life Tools inbox. The subscriber must have a Nokia handset in which programme is pre-installed. The Agriculture service sends daily information the in Nokia Life Tools inbox including, the market prices for the selected crops, weather reports and agricultural information and tips from experts. The user can retrieve any of the services on demand, or subscribe to one of 2 Agriculture packages, the Premium package of all agricultural services or the Basic package of Weather and News and Tips.

Reuters Market Light (RML)

Reuters Market Light (RML) from Thomson Reuters was launched in October 2007, provides individual farmers with "customised, localised and personalised" weather forecasts, local crop prices, agricultural news and relevant information in the form of SMS messages sent to their mobile phones in their local language. In 2008, UNDP selected RML as one of six business initiatives that have the potential to contribute to the Millennium Development Goals (MDGs). RML presently has its operation in 13 Indian States. The content of the messages is mainly sourced by RML's own sourcing network. Apart from weather and best practices information, the content is developed by RML internally. The subscription is sold in the form of prepaid scratch cards. The user can choose two crops for crop advisory and market information. Other messages like weather, news etc are provided also. A customer care provides multi lingual support to the users on various issues like personalisation, profile changes, delivery issues, etc.

Mobile Agro Advisory System (mKrishi) by TCS

The mKrishi application of TCS enable farmers to send specific queries, comprising of text, voice and pictures, to land and crop to agricultural experts, using their mobile phones. Farmers can also send pictures of their crops and pests captured with mobile phone cameras; sensors provide farm specific soil and crop data, weather stations provide microclimate details and voice based querying system local (natural) language. After analysis of the available information, the expert's advice on the farmer's query is provided on the farmer's mobile phone. The solution broadcasts best farming practices to each farmer, and provides organizations, NGOs, and the government a platform to exchange information with farmers.

Comparison of Major Mobile Based Services

All the service providers such as Reuters Market Light, IFFCO Kisan Sanchar Limited, and Nokia Life Tools attempt to provide their subscribers with the best available information through different IT-based services. Table 25.2 provides a comparison of the merits (and demerits) of different service providers.

Table 25.2: Comparison of Mobile Based Agri Information Service Providers

Sl.No.	*Specifications*	*RML*	*IKSL*	*NOKIA*
1.	Information Dissemination			
	(*a*) Market Prices	✓	✓	✓
	(*b*) Daily Weather Forecast	✓	✓	✓
	(*c*) Weekly Weather Forecasts	✓	✓	✓
	(*d*) Crop Advisory	✓	✓	✓
	(*e*) Input Info	✓	✓	✓
	(*f*) News	✓	✓	✓
	(*g*) Government Schemes Info	✓	✓	✓
2.	SMS Based Service	✓	✗	✗
3.	Voice Mail Facility	✗	✓	✗
4.	Toll free helpline	✓	✓	✓
5.	Can be operated in any handset	✓	✓	✗
6.	Can be used in any network	✓	✗	✓
7.	Options for customization	✓	✗	✓
8.	Options to choose products for market price	✓	✗	✓

The ICT tools used in these initiatives present an impressive list and include video conferencing, voice activated cell centers facility, internet enabled PC based networking, voice and text messaging via mobile phones, internet based crop specific digital video, and interactive community radio (Kokil, undated, Rajendran *et al.*, 2004; Lal, 2007; Mittal, 2010)

The lack of timely marketing information and inadequate market intelligence has limited most of the farmers from utilizing the market opportunities. Providing the right information at the right time will enable the farmers to do better planning and achieve the best benefits from it. Timely information will assist the farmers in their decision making on cultivation practices, harvesting, and also how, where and when to store/market their produce. This will contribute towards the value chain development of agricultural products at various stages.

A value chain is the full range of activities which are required to bring a product or service from conception through the different phases of production (involving a combination of physical transformation and the input of various producer services), delivery to final customers, and final disposal after use. In order to tackle the agricultural productivity, the capacity of various actors in the agriculture value chain such as farmers, middle men, wholesale, retail traders etc needs to be enhanced in terms of knowledge and information, which will enable them to operate efficiently in the knowledge economy. A strong and efficient value chain has enabling cooperation among the various actors/members, which can be ensured through transparent information exchange among the actors. Adequate information about the Input supplies (seeds, fertilizers, etc.), Market information (prices, trends, buyers), Financial services (credit, savings, or insurance institutions), Transport Services, Quality assurance etc. allows transactional transparency and efficiency among the various actors and thus strengthens the Value chain.

With an overall aim of addressing the information gaps of small and marginal farmers and thus empowering them as VC stakeholder, GIZ facilitated the implementation of the agriculture Information dissemination through SMS in Uttarakhand. This GIZ initiative was part of its Regional Economic Development (RED) Programme and was implemented in partnership with the agencies such as GRAMYA and ULIPH with technical service from the Reuters Market Light (RML). In addition, NABARD through its ICT initiative has also sponsored RML subscriptions for the farmers in the state.

Objective

This study was conducted to assess the benefits received by the agriculture producers as a result of the provision of information through mobile SMS; identification of various gaps in present mobile based information service; and recommendations for further customization of the existing service.

Methodology

The key stakeholders considered for the study included (i) Farmers subscribing to mobile phone enabled services of RML (users, subscribers), (ii) Farmers owning mobile phone but not subscribing to mobile phone enabled services (non users), (iii) GRAMYA, ULIPH, NABARD officials, (iv) HARC, CHEA and other local NGOs, and (v) Service Providers. The major tools used in the study include **Focus Group Discussions** with user groups and non user groups organized at the sampled locations, **Structured interview** of users (subscribers) and Non users o RML's services, **Semi structured interviews of** officials (from Horticulture Department, GRAMYA, ULIPH, NABARD and other partner NGOs like HARC, CHEA, etc.) The Table 25.3 lists the respondents and respective study tools used to collect data. The project was implemented in 10 districts of Uttarakhand with a growing subscriber base of 676 active users. A multistage sampling technique has been used to select the sample and understand the real impact. The 10 districts are from two regions *i.e.* Kumaon and Garhwal. The 3 districts (Bageshwar, Almora and Nainital) from Kumaon and 2 districts (Tehri and Uttarkashi) from Garhwal were considered for study. The blocks/villages have been selected according to the availability/spread of test sample across the districts. As the user population is very small, their availability was the key to selection of blocks/villages for the survey. The study covered 10 per cent of the beneficiaries (96 farmers) from 5 districts. The control group was selected in a manner to interact with farmers who despite having knowledge, is not using RML services. Snowball sampling method was adopted, wherein the user group was used as information rich- key informants and their referrals to form the control sample of 92 Non subscriber farmers.

Results and Discussion

Changes in the Information Source

The respondents have multiple sources for different type of information needs. Comparing the pattern of sourcing (Tables 25.4 and 25.5) after introduction of RML services revealed clear shift of preference to mobile SMS for all type of information with market price, weather advisory getting highest preferences of 98 per cent and 96 per cent respectively. Data clearly shows marked decline for traders as source of information for market price (from 67 per cent to 1 per cent). On average more than 60 per cent of subscribers reported sharing of information and 88 per cent reported usefulness of the service

Table 25.3: Respondents and Study Tools

Respondent Category	*Respondent Role*	*Data Technique*	*Survey Instrument*
Farmers (subscribers of RML)	Primary sample/beneficiary	Quantitative	In depth interview
Farmers (not subscribed to RML)	Control sample	Quantitative	In depth interview
Farmer groups (users)	Beneficiary group	Qualitative	FGD
Farmer groups (non users)	Control group	Qualitative	FGD
Local NGO/District program officer	Secondary sample	Quantitative	Semi Structured interview
Horticulture Department, GIZ, GRAMYA and ULIPH officials	Institutional players	Quantitative	Semi Structured interview

Table 25.4: Normal Information Sources of Users

Type of Information	*Radio*	*Television*	*Local Newspaper*	*Kiosks*	*Traders*	*Other*
Seeds	7 per cent	12 per cent	2 per cent	26 per cent	1 per cent	52 per cent
Fertilizer	8 per cent	13 per cent	1 per cent	3 per cent	22 per cent	53 per cent
Pesticides	8 per cent	9 per cent	1 per cent	3 per cent	20 per cent	58 per cent
Tools	0 per cent	29 per cent	5 per cent	0 per cent	0 per cent	67 per cent
Crop advisory	0 per cent	29 per cent	1 per cent	3 per cent	1 per cent	66 per cent
Market prices	0 per cent	1 per cent	26 per cent	1 per cent	67 per cent	5 per cent
Storage and Post-Harvest	0 per cent	14 per cent	3 per cent	3 per cent	0 per cent	79 per cent
Weather advisory	9 per cent	81 per cent	7 per cent	1 per cent	0 per cent	1 per cent
Government Schemes	11 per cent	7 per cent	40 per cent	12 per cent	0 per cent	30 per cent
News	10 per cent	49 per cent	40 per cent	0 per cent	0 per cent	1 per cent

Table 25.5: Information Source during the Period of RML Subscription

Type of Information	*Mobile SMS*	*Radio*	*Television*	*Local Newspaper*	*Kiosks*	*Traders*	*Other*
Seeds	25 per cent	7 per cent	11 per cent	2 per cent	14 per cent	0 per cent	41 per cent
Fertilizer	27 per cent	8 per cent	8 per cent	1 per cent	3 per cent	19 per cent	34 per cent
Pesticides	27 per cent	9 per cent	5 per cent	1 per cent	5 per cent	16 per cent	36 per cent
Tools	5 per cent	0 per cent	24 per cent	0 per cent	0 per cent	0 per cent	71 per cent
Crop advisory	73 per cent	0 per cent	12 per cent	0 per cent	0 per cent	0 per cent	11 per cent
Market Prices	98 per cent	0 per cent	0 per cent	0 per cent	0 per cent	1 per cent	1 per cent
Storage and Post Harvest	18 per cent	0 per cent	0 per cent	7 per cent	0 per cent	4 per cent	71 per cent
Weather advisory	96 per cent	1 per cent	2 per cent	0 per cent	1 per cent	0 per cent	0 per cent
Government Schemes	83 per cent	0 per cent	6 per cent	8 per cent	1 per cent	0 per cent	2 per cent
News	12 per cent	8 per cent	48 per cent	30 per cent	0 per cent	0 per cent	1 per cent

Timeliness and Quality of the Mobile SMS information

Timeliness is an important aspect of good communication. Overall 42 per cent of the subscribers consider timeliness of the mobile SMS service is good and 17 per cent found the timeliness is very good (Table 25.6).

Table 25.6: Timeliness of the Information

Districts	*Poor*	*Average*	*Good*	*Very Good*	*Excellent*
Almora	0 per cent	52 per cent	30 per cent	13 per cent	4 per cent
Bageshwar	0 per cent	33 per cent	43 per cent	24 per cent	0 per cent
Nainital	0 per cent	27 per cent	53 per cent	20 per cent	0 per cent
Tehri	0 per cent	0 per cent	91 per cent	9 per cent	0 per cent
Uttarkashi	4 per cent	50 per cent	23 per cent	15 per cent	8 per cent
Total	1 per cent	38 per cent	42 per cent	17 per cent	3 per cent

Farmers reported that all of them are extremely happy with the timing of weather information but the timing of market information needs to be modified. Subscribers requested early market information and also some forecast to help them to plan their marketing activities. Majority (46 per cent) of the subscribers consider the quality of the mobile SMS service is good and 20 per cent considers the quality of information is very good, though there were instances where the market price range of a product at certain markets given by the service provider varied from the actual price range at the market (Figure 25.1).

Benefits of RML's Mobile SMS Agri Information Service

Assistance of mobile based information to gain timely information from the market was evidenced from the respondents. Among the subscribers 34 per cent mentioned that the mobile SMS service helped them a lot to gain timely information from the market (Figure 25.2). When 59 per cent of the respondents reported mobile SMS service helped them slightly to gain timely information from the market, further query revealed higher relevance of local market information which if provided through mobile SMS service will allow better use of it.

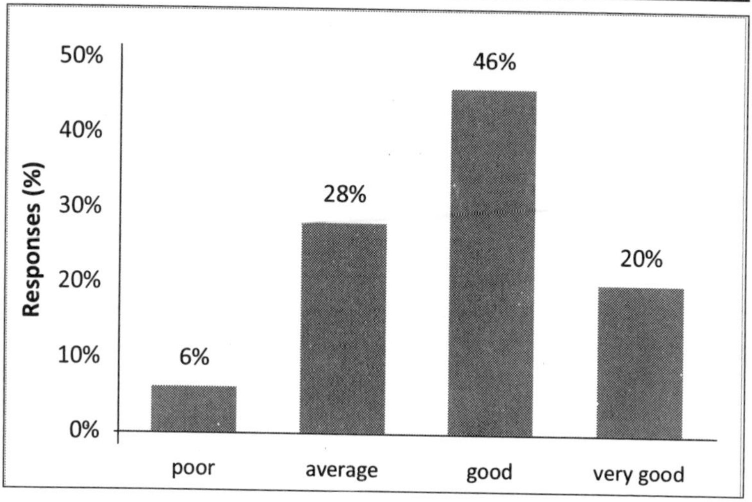

Figure 25.1: Quality of Information

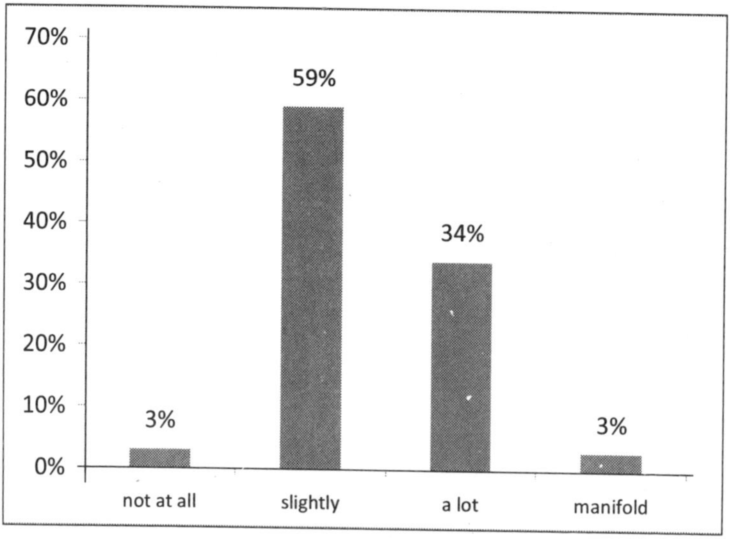

Figure 25.2: Availability of Timely Knowledge from the Market

Usefulness of Weather Advisories

Overall 85 per cent of the farmers reported the weather advisory service in the mobile SMS service as useful, for their agricultural activities. Weather forecasts for next few days help them in planning their activities. Among the subscribers 28 per cent mentioned that the weather advisory service helped them in responding to the weather changes. The respondents also mentioned that weather advisory is the best thing they like about the mobile SMS information service. Only 15 per cent subscribers reported that weather advisory service is not useful for them (Table 25.7).

Table 25.7: Usefulness of Weather Advisories

District	*Useful (per cent)*	*Not useful (per cent)*
Almora	74 per cent	26 per cent
Bageshwar	75 per cent	25 per cent
Nainital	80 per cent	20 per cent
Tehri	100 per cent	0 per cent
Uttarkashi	100 per cent	0 per cent
Total	85 per cent	15 per cent

Usefulness of Information on Good Agricultural Practices

Majority of the respondents agreed that the information from mobile SMS helped them in adopting better agricultural practices (Figure 25.3). Only 17 per cent responded that they never adopted any better agricultural practices based on the information received through mobile SMS service. One third of the respondents also agreed that the information from mobile information helped them in accessing or gaining knowledge about Government schemes for agriculture.

Usefulness of Information in Increasing the Market Value of the Product

Study shows, 36 per cent of the respondents were able to increase 1 per cent to 5 per cent of the market value for their products, 6 per cent respondents mentioned that they were able to they were able to get 5 per cent to 10 per cent increase in the market value of their product. 58 per cent of the respondents reported that the information received through mobile was not helpful to increase the market value of their product (Figure 25.4) it is too early to assess the impact of the service based on the profitability of the farmers. But it is observed

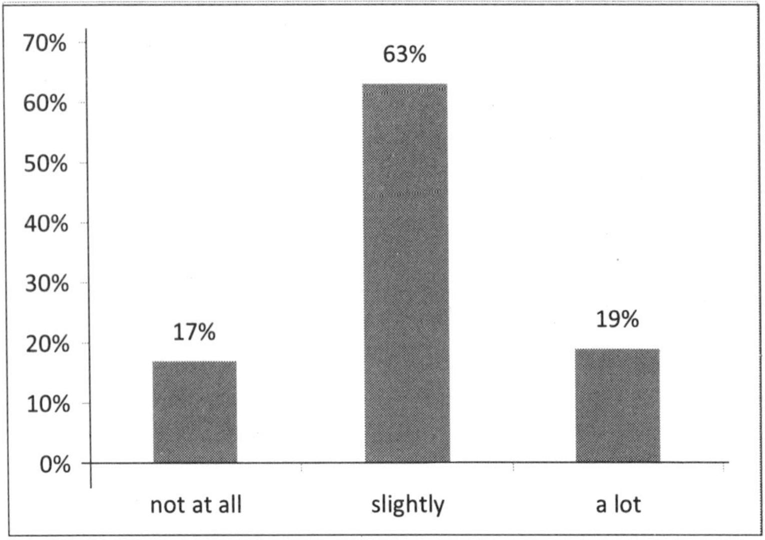

Figure 25.3: Usefulness of Information on Good Agricultural Practices

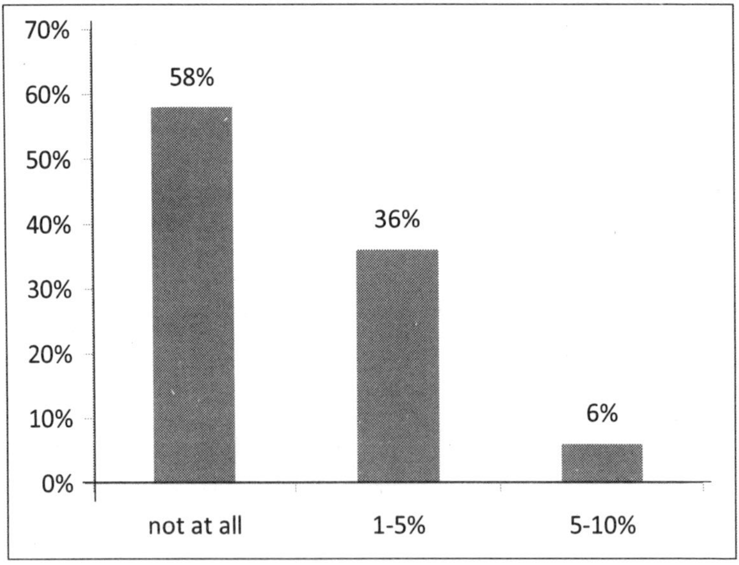

Figure 25.4: Increase in Market Value

that there were drawbacks in the selection of subscribers. As mentioned earlier, majority of the subscribers are comparatively small farmers who sell their products in the local markets. As the local market information was not being provided through the service, the increase in the market value of the product as a result of the same will not be evident. Here it is important to note that the distribution of the subscription was not done with any pre-defined criteria. Since the majority of beneficiaries were smallholders, it is evident that further customization of the content is needed to benefit them.

Key Observations and Recommendations

The launch of mobile SMS service can be perceived as an important milestone in the agricultural development of Uttarakhand. Some key issues which need further attention to improve this kind of services for the farmers are as follows:

Need for Local Information

Majority of the farmers sell their produce in local market The unavailability of agribusiness infrastructure is a major drawback in the area's agriculture marketing, even when the major markets like Haldwani, Dehradun offer higher prices the small farmers are still forced to sell in the market near to their village. The RML service currently provides only the market information of the major markets in the state. There is a greater demand for local market information. This will help them to get more value for their produce. The study clearly points out that farmers require information on market, weather, crop advisory and various inputs. Weather forecasts for the upcoming days, and soil management information were important. Hence this service should be improved by customizing necessary location specific information and made available at the right time.

Need for Improved Facilitation

Subscribing farmers need to get proper orientation in a pre-defined standard for better utilization of information. Farmers without enough marketable surpluses, apart from the weather information and crop advisory the service was of no significant use. So subscriptions should be for those farmers who have significant use of it. So it is important that facilitation is creative with proper understanding about the purpose of the service.

Need for Proper Orientation about the Service

The lack of awareness about the use of the service was very evident from the data which says that majority of the users are not aware about the customization facility available in the service. It is observed that there are subscribers who receive information about crops which they don't grow. It is also observed that in Bageshwar and Nainital, few subscribers receive the information in English which is preventing them from using the information. They are not aware about the preferred language option available in the service. These case studies point towards lack of orientation of the subscribers about the use of the service. So it is important to enhance the capacity of the users with special focus on issues like customization, communication with customer care and how to get benefited from the information received through the mobile SMS service.

Regular Sharing of Information

It is very important to note that there is no significant information sharing happened among the non-users who belong to some farmer groups/federation. Discussions revealed that the major platform for sharing of information was the farmer federation meetings on monthly or fortnightly basis. But the monthly or fortnightly sharing of information in groups is does not bring any benefit to the farmers other than in the case of crop advisory. The sharing of information like weather and market price will not bring any benefit to the farmers after the particular day of relevance. At the same time it might not be feasible for the small farmers to subscribe to the mobile SMS service where the market information is of not much relevance for them. So the partner agencies should convince the subscribers under them about the need to share the information on a regular basis and ensure the same is being taking place as expected.

Willingness to Pay

Majority of the farmers expressed their willingness to pay for the service; but the number of farmers who are willing to pay around Rs. 34 per day is very low. It was observed from the discussions that there is a lack of understanding by the farmers about the benefits the service can bring them. It won't be feasible to carry out any business activity if there is a lack of willingness by the users to pay for the service. Moreover, the farmers are more curious about the possibility of getting subsidies from the Government or other agencies towards the cost of the service. In the past the services were sponsored by the partner institutions. In an event of expansions it is very crucial that the majority of the farmers are willing to pay only Rs. 2. Hence there is a need of some cost sharing in terms of subsidy, grant etc. Hence the partner agencies may consider to bear a portion (for eg: 30 per cent) of the cost of the service in the form of subsidy. They may also use advocacy measures to bring the participation of Government in the form of subsidy or tax free benefit etc.

Collaboration with the Government

The Government officials at the state and district level needs to be oriented towards the operation and usefulness of the service. This will definitely benefit the expansion of the service in the state.

Expansion of the Service

The study shows that Uttarakhand can be a potential market for the agriculture information dissemination through mobile SMS. It is important to note that with a limited information and awareness about the service people are willing to subscribe to the service. This is the right time for the service provider to step in and take necessary actions to expand the services to other parts of the state aiming a larger group of subscribers. Therefore the study recommends that the service provider should expand the service in the state by adding more markets and more geographical information.

References

Department of Agricultural Economics (2011) Establishing and networking of agricultural market intelligence centers in India, Pantnagar, Uttarakhand.

Kaplinsky, R and Morris, M. 2000. A handbook for value chain research. IDRC, Canada.

L Shanta Meitei and Th. Purnima Devi (2009) Farmers information needs in rural Manipur: an assessment, Annals of Library of Information studies, Vol 56, March 2009, pp. 35-40.

ICRIER (2010) Socio-Economic Impact of Mobile Phones on Indian Agriculture, Working Paper No 246.

Nikhil Sharma, Sapna A Narula (2008) Implementing ICTs in Indian agribusiness, Information for development, Vol. VI No. 9.

Sapna A Narula(2010) A Study of Prioritisation of Information Related Needs of Farmers, Agriculture Corner, Available at http://www.agricorner.com/a-study-of-prioritisation-of-information-related-needs-of-farmers.

GB Pant University (2011) Establishing and networking of agricultural market intelligence centers in India.

Mr Samir Prakash and Dr Chander Velu (2010) Reuters Market Light: Business Model Innovation for Growth, Effective Executive.

Chapter 26

Trends in Agricultural Extension: A Panorama

☆ *Birendra Kumar*

Agricultural Extension is a social innovation of neo-industrial societies of the nineteenth century. The early efforts in Europe and U.S.A. by the missionaries, philanthropists, public servants and academics helped in gradual evolution of the profession. The early forms of extension service by way of traveling lecturers and agricultural societies matured with the times to give way to more organized work by the national government. Today when the idea has moved around the worldwide help support from national and international governments is matter of concern. Extension has become a sine qua non for agricultural development of developing and undeveloped nations. The chapter deals with the events and trends in agricultural extension from education to marketing extension.

Extension as Education

Extension has often been linked with education in past. Most of the definitions refer to extension as an out-of -school education. Education is one of the oldest cultural traits in the history. Extension education appeared on the scene in its full bloom in the twentieth century to address to the needs of rural people for improved production and income through use of technologies. Thus, it was not just an attempt to pass on information and advice. In fact, extension work was inspired and initiated in order to take knowledge of agriculture to its users.. Thus, the new education with emphasis on 'learning by doing' and 'helping people to help themselves' emerged. It was not merely to pass information. It is problem-oriented education for action and not for the sake of learning alone. It inspires involvement of farmers in the educational programmes. Farmers have different backgrounds as far as education, economic status or interests are concerned. Extension education must consider differential requirements of target population. Extension has been accepted as type of adult education enterprise with emphasis on technological changes. Thus, it become essential to arouse interests of farmers, provide them new technological knowledge and skill. Extension has now become part and parcel of national governments. Some of the definitions reflecting this view are as given below:

Extension as Communication Intervention

Extension as an educational endeavour uses communication as means. Education is meant to bring desirable change in behavior of people. Communication is a tool to bring voluntary change in people. The success of communication as tool depends on extent of sharing of meaning between sender and receiver of messages. How can this sharing happen voluntarily without any force or manipulation. Extension makes use of communication like many other professions *viz.* social work, public relations, marketing, advertising. Extension work is indeed planned and purposeful activity in order to bring desirable changes in rural people. Extension professionals use communication to convince people and advocate new changes. Extension presents new choices with reasons. However, the decision to accept or reject rests with people. Willing acceptance of people is supposed to be long lasting and indicative of positive change. It is indeed wrong to assume that rural people are ignorant. In fact, they have their own values, wisdom and logic to pursue a particular practice. It is thus equally essential to understand indigenous knowledge, traditional wisdom and people's logic to be able to communicate effectively. Communication with rural clientele requires informal and personal approach. Every society has peculiar means of communication like sitting near tea-shop or exchanging news and views in village market, special carriers of message in social system (like barbers in Indian villages). Besides, rural people are not always open to outsiders though they may apparently agree. Experts claim that extension workers in developing nations have to deal with largely illiterate masses having limited exposure to other sources of information. It is no wonder if such people are persuaded to accept the viewpoints of extension workers who are technically superior However, there are many other ways to persuade people to change such as use of force, coercion, change in regulations, provision of subsidy or supplies. However, the ways extension workers communicate with rural clientele have been labeled as one way top-down approach. There is simplistic assumption that all the technologies are disseminated through extension agents, people would adopt. People are assumed to be passive recipients as if they are ignorant. The technologies available with research stations are taken as desirable and superior. Most extension programmes are decided by the top executives and implemented by grass-root workers. Village level functionaries are bogged down with the pre-fixed targets.. It seems as if new technologies are the solutions of all the ills in rural areas and role of extension is one disseminating technology.

Emancipatory Extension

In socialist and Christian tradition extension is seen as an instrument of emancipation and upliftment of the poor, a 'pedagogy of the oppressed' as Paolo Freire has called it. Hence, extension is an instrument for achieving societal objectives and correcting structural problems like poverty, income distribution, etc. The extension workers should now assume the role of facilitator and development catalyst rather than mere disseminator of information. The extension worker needs to live in the community and understand and analyze socio-cultural environment along with people. Thus, he can be better equipped to communicate with the community. There are happy new trends to introduce such dialogic communication between extension workers, farmers and scientists in Farmer First Extension approach (Modi, 1990).

Freiri (1974) has criticized this notion of disseminating technology alone vehemently. Knowledge is not extended from those who consider that they know to those who consider that they do not know. Knowledge is built-up in the relations between human being and the world, relations of transformation and perfects itself in the critical problematization of these relations. According to Freiri the most important task for extension worker is to prepare himself to raise the consciousness of people to help them see their problems and participate in finding solution.).

Various Approaches of Extension Work

Extension work is conducted around the world in a variety of ways. Each approach has its own basic assumption, structure and set of activities, as discussed below:

- ☆ *Technology/Research Centered Extension* : In most cases extension work is viewed as vehicle for distributing pre-decided research findings to the clientele. It has its emphasis on findings available at the research centre. The unique circumstances or constraints at the farmers' end are often ignored or not considered.
- ☆ *Commodity Focussed Approach* : This approach is quite popular in Western Africa where set of activities are geared to accelerate production of a single crop. Technical, administrative and input requirements for such crops are managed by board or private company. Technical messages are systematically conveyed to the farmers. There is provision for inputs, marketing of outputs, prompt payment for output etc.
- ☆ *Community Development Approach* : This was the approach launched in India in 1952. This approach covers all aspects of rural life *viz.* agriculture, family planning, health, education, illiteracy, etc. This broadens the responsibilities of extension workers. The wide-ranging set of duties results in low performance, lack of mobility and confused supervision. The knowledge and ability of farmers to contribute towards the generation or improvisation of technology is never appreciated.
- ☆ *Extension as merely Advisory Function* : Under such approach, it is assumed that the role of extension worker is toadvise clientele what to do or what not to do. Extension worker does not have any other involvement.

- *Service or Supply Approach* : The extension organization provides information on crops and livestock. Besides, it also arranges for supply of inputs such as fertilizers and seeds. Many Asian countries follow such approach. Extension workers are overburdened with supply function. Due to lack of well developed infrastructure such provisions work as incentive.
- *Training and Visit System* : This is an organized effort overcoming the lacunae of weak management. The approach mobilizes the entire extension apparatus and research system for systematic and effective extension work. It promotes regularity of training, systematic visits by extension workers, effective supervision and technical recommendations. There are enhanced research-extension linkages.

Extension as a Tool for Human Resource Development

Extension education is now recognized as important non-formal adult education enterprise with technological base. The central emphasis of extension work is on developing manpower in the rural areas so that they can absorb scientific knowledge and skills in solving their day-to-day problems. There has been variety of approaches to extension work emphasizing on different components, *viz.* technology, commodity, community, advisory role or service/ supply or a combination of these. However, development of human resource is central to extension. work. Rao (1992) explained that HRD is a process in which employees of an organization are continuously helped in planned manner to acquire and sharpen capabilities required to perform various functions. They develop their general capabilities as individuals and discover and exploit their potential for their own and organizational development purposes, develop an organizational culture in which supervisor-sub-ordinate relationships, team work and collaboration among sub-units are strong and contribute to professional well-being, motivation and pride of employees. Thus, it can be said that HRD is an approach to facilitate both developments of competencies and creation of environment conducive to stimulate and nurture continuous growth of individuals and organizations. Rural development is complex process of catalyzing social, economic and cultural factors. Thus, Human Resource Development 'lays stress on development of individual, the family and the village community. HRD in rural areas must be understood in the socio-cultural context of the rural communities. It should focus on the development of inner resources of the individual and community. This calls for organization of groups and creation of structure which would enable involvement of one and all in planning and implementation of programmes of development. Such group or organization calls for motivated leadership. Rolling (1988) has elaborated HRD approach to extension work in terms of five function *viz.* mobilization organization, technical support and systems management.

Extension as Agricultural Knowledge and Information Systems (AKIS)

Extension is sub-system of a larger system in which research and utilizers also form sub-systems. In fact, it seems unfruitful now a day to look at extension in isolation from these other sub-systems. AKIS: is a set of agricultural organizations and/or persons, and the links and interaction between them engaged in such processes as the generation, transformation, transmission storage, retrieval, integration, diffusion and utilization of knowledge and information, with the purpose of working synergically to support decision making, problem solving and innovation in a given country's agriculture or a domain there of.

Agricultural information system is a system in which agricultural information is generated, transformed, transferred, consolidated, received and feedback in such a manner that these processes function synergistically to underpin knowledge utilization by agricultural producers. In this concept the institutions generating, transferring, transforming and receiving information are emphasized as well as the information flows and linkage mechanisms between them. Agricultural knowledge system is a system of beliefs, cognitions, models, theories, concepts, and other products of the mind in which the (vicarious) experience of a person or group with respect to agricultural production is accumulated. In the concept of a knowledge system, the cognitive system, its structure and the order it imposes up on the environment is emphasized. Different groups of people have different knowledge systems; *e.g.* 'Indigenous knowledge system', official knowledge system etc.

AKIS can be defined in three different ways:

1. As sets of organization and people engaged in knowledge and information processes.
2. As sets of coherent cognition that have evolved among members of an organization, communities or societies.
3. As computer-based 'intelligent' software.

The institutional approach looks at sets of interconnected actors, each engaged in different activities such as research technology transfer, production or consumption and hence enhance functioning synergically. The institutional approach leads to theory building about the way people and organization receive, transform and transmit information about the interfaces between them and about complementary roles institution play in relation to each other. The purpose of the approach is to improve the management or the design of the AKIS so as to make it function in the ways deemed desirable by policy makers, farmers and other participants in the system. The total impact of AKIS should be more than the sum of the impacts of its constituent parts. An important goal of the analysis, design and management of an AKIS is to increase the synergy of its components. Research results that remain unused, farmers without access to technology transfer services, extension that has no links with research all show signs of an AKIS that is not operating synergic ally. And all provide good reasons for taking the AKIS as a whole rather than its individual parts. Recent approaches to improving agricultural technology systems. Such as FSR and T and V are attempts to improve AKIS basic.

Privatization of Extension

Extension work, which began as voluntary work and public service in the nascent stage, is at the verge of being privatized in India. In fact, many European countries took lead in past one decade. Experiments are being done with help and support from the World Bank to make extension more efficient and effective service through involvement of private sector. Extension service is indeed a daunting task to reach villages with appropriate messages for the diverse audiences. Provision of extension service in the country has so far been the role of the government. India owes a lot of its scientists and exlensionists in making the country self-sufficient in case of food grain production taking the benefits of green revolution. Policy makers are planning to double the food production by 2010. Keeping this in view, the planners and administrators have started questioning the public extension system on economic and efficiency grounds. Privatization of Agricultural extension seems to be the answer to achieve the tall dream of achieving exportable surplus.Thus, there is growing tendency in developed nations towards making agricultural extension in to a profitable enterprise. It is believed that clients should pay partially to fully for self financing of extension work. With resource crunch and financial crisis being encountered by many national governments, there is probably need to generate funds. Many large scale farmers and agribusiness organizations can willingly pay for the advice and assistance received from extension organizations.Of late, Government of Rajasthan state of India has decided to involve private sector voluntary agency to undertake extension at the grass root level and gradually minimise governments role in extension work. Such private sectors are known to be private extension service provides.Private extension service provider is an individual or organisation other than government who is providing singly service or integrated services to the farmers. In the Indian context, following service provides are identified:

1. Un employed Agricultural Graduates
2. Agricultural Consultants/Firms.
3. Para techniques
4. Progressive farmers.
5. Farmers organisations/Co-operative
6. Non Governmental Organisations (NGO's)
7. Krishi Vigyan Kendras (KVK's)
8. Agribusiness companies
9. Input dealers
10. News papers
11. Agricultural Magazines
12. Private Television Channels
13. Private sector banks
14. Internet
15. Donor Agencies

Farmer Participatory Extension

The earlier extension efforts have been criticized severely because of the manner in which they were implemented in the developing and under-developed countries of the world. Extension organizations are mostly part of the government ministries/ departments of Agriculture and/or Rural Development. Thus they follow similar rules, regulations, organizational hierarchies that promote government's plans and programmes. Agricultural technologies have been input intensive and expensive. Appropriateness of technologies for farmer of different socio-economics background is also being questioned. Methods of extension have been attacked by various experts. Of late, extension has been serving general farmers only indirectly through contact farmers. A very high proportion of women farmers are women but even higher proportion of extension staff are men. Moreover, there are cultural barriers in many countries to approach women through male extension workers. Keeping in view the high expenditure required to make extension service viable through trained staff, motivated with huge infrastructure *viz.* a *viz.* shrinking funds, it is becoming difficult for public sector to contrive with the investments. There are pressures on most governments to seek alternative ways of doing agricultural extension to minimize pressure on public budgets . The challenges of participation are many. Extension workers have large area of cover. It is often very difficult to interact with farmers. Above all, professionals who are outsiders and educated have additional barriers in communication understanding view points perception and preferences of farmers call for participation. However nature and extent of participating will vary farm place to place culture to culture. There is no single formula. Extension work, in past, had mostly be befitted the rich and resourceful specific problems of the rural poor living in complex diverse and risk- prone areas with several socio-economic worldwide to provide appropriate technical support to the rural poor some institutionally ways . The problems of the poor are many.

Farmer Participatory Extension is a new concept that indicates community ownership and involvement in extension process. It refers to the leadership and control of farmers over the process of extension. Farmers have say in design and delivery of extension service.

This new approach is farmer oriented and non-prescriptive. It gives equal importance to farmers along with other professionals. While the approach values formal research and development activities, it motivates farmers to try out their own experiments as well. Farmer to farmer extension is also encouraged. Problem solving must begin at the farmers' level. Outsiders have facilitative role. Participatory Agricultural Extension Approach is still in the making. Many efforts are being made to establish such an approach to educate and empower farmers to define and solve their problems and help them take same responsibility. Putting responsibility in the hands of farmers to initiate, implement and evaluate extension programme with support from outside so that

Marketing Extension

The profile of Indian farmer in 1950s was one of subsistence farmer dependent on agriculture for livelihood. He was seen as fatalist, conservative using localized source of information with little or no motivation for commercialization. Generally use of inputs was on lower to moderate extent. He was not keen to seek information. The image changed offer 60s and 70s. Having tasted the fruits of green revolution educated, better than average farmer with access to information and resources is ready to invest for better agricultural production. More than that, though few enlightened farmers have undertaken enterprises due to their economic motivation risk taking opportunities growing market and

The profile of Indian farmer in 1950s was one

- ☆ Subsistence farmer dependent on agriculture for livelihood.
- ☆ Fatalist, conservative using localized source of information with little or
- ☆ No motivation for commercialization.
- ☆ Generally use of inputs was on lower to moderate extent.
- ☆ He was not keen to seek information.
- ☆ The image changed offer 60s and 70s.

However, Indian farmer today is a

- ☆ Shy information collector and
- ☆ Needs support of the peer group.

- He weights information in view of his resources and capabilities,
- Even tries on a small scale before adopting. He likes to see things working at the farm of other farmers.
- He is sensitive to the social influence.

There are several factors coming in the way of exploiting higher potential of agriculture.

- In efficiencies of pro-current and storage of agricultural produces
- Wastage of fruits and vegetables on farm, in procurement and in storage due to lack of suitable infrastructure.
- Low value addition due to past-harvest loses and lack of processing and packaging facilities.

Some of the important issues facing Indian agricultural export are:

- Consumer orientation
- Development of verities suitable for market
- Value addition to products
- Research and development of new users of products
- Promotion of consumption of high quality commodities
- Improvement of marketing, transport, quality infrastructure
- Importance of medicinal plants, organic farming, floriculture, export has to be appreciated.
- Bringing farmers under an umbrella of agriculture to take came of production and other needs for export related activity minimization of farmer risk and incurring productivity is the need.

Thus extension has important role to play in making farmers aware about the export opportunities and facilitate in making the process smooth. Knowledge of technologies of product on processing and packaging as well as contract facing has been tried by some companies.

However, Indian farmer today is a shy information collector and needs support of the peer group. He weights information in view of his resources and capabilities, even tries on a small scale before adopting. He likes to see things working at the farm of other farmers. He is sensitive to the social influence.

Growing economic liberalization new international treaty regime under WTO has created opportunities for agricultural export. Thus information has become most important input for which electronic media, Private agencies and information technologies have to be put to use production need to be dictated by market requirement. Agricultural produce marketing require connectivity between the market and exporters/growers/traders industry consumers, etc through networks. Day to day information regarding commodity arrivals, preventing rates to provide link on-line under national market information. Farmers will heed information regarding marketing package and storage.

Chapter 27

Participatory Rural Appraisal for Sustainable Rural Development

☆ *B.B. Singh*

Application of high inputs in Agriculture, in terms of chemical fertilizers and pesticides has endangered the sustainability of production system. Indigenous knowledge of agriculture is the, result of farmer's thousands years of experience with nature. Indigenous practices are known to the farmers and are helpful in maintaining and enhancing the quality of environment. With the dissemination of modern practices the indigenous practices have started to loose their ground and have been eroded to a large extent. It is, therefore, absolutely necessary to stop any further erosion in the traditional practices and also to try to find out those practices, which have been dropped in the erosion process. The efforts in this direction will not only help in identifying the practices/technology which have been extinguished but to revive, assess, validate and to put use to the farmers. Today when we are introducing location specific technologies and practices as a part of strategic research and extension plan, it becomes necessary to identify such indigenous knowledge which is close to our farmers and they have all emotions about them for use. To achieve this Participatory Rural Appraisal when introduced in eighties where people's environment/ participation in both research and extension of technologies were sought.

People's participation has become a standard rhetoric in India today. Different people interpret in different ways. One view is that participation means getting people to agree to and go along with a project, which has already been designed for them, or to get support of a few leaders. "I manage, you participate" was dominant underlying principles behind such projects. These tended to try to make people aware of their responsibilities without giving them any authority to spend funds or to manage assets. The important question is, participation for whose benefit, and on what terms?

Participation should include the notion of contributing, influencing, sharing, or redistributing power and of control, resources, benefits, knowledge, and skills to be gained through beneficiary involvement in decision making. Participation is a voluntary process by which people, including the disadvantages (in income, gender, caste, or education), influence or control the decision that affect them. The essence of participation is exercising voice and choice, and developing the human, organization, and management capacity to solve problems as they arise in order to sustain the improvements. There have been shifts in the past decade in approaches of agriculture and rural development. These shifts include the now familiar reversals from top-down to bottom-up from centralized standardization to local diversity and from blue print to learning process.

In the mid 1980's, the word participation and participatory entered in the RRA vocabulary. Rapid Rural Appraisal (RRA) is still essentially extractive and 'elicitive' in nature. Analysis and utilization of the results remain largely in the hands of outside experts. Participatory Rural Appraisal (PRA) is a way of thinking and behaving that demands a reversal of roles. It stresses that those actually affected should assume an active role in conducting and analyzing their own living conditions and evaluating the results. The outsider's role is that of a catalyzer, a facilitator and convener of processes within a community.

Participatory Rural Appraisal can be defined as an intensive and systematic learning experience carried out in a community by a multidisciplinary team, which includes community members. It is a way of learning from and with community members to investigate, analyze and evaluate constraints and opportunities; need assessment and development of such plans but modalities for implementation of such action plan may also be developed and executed. Thus, for preparing strategic research and extension action plan at the village level (location specific) different approaches and techniques of PRA can be used. These may pave the way for highlighting the core issues concerning to the people of the rural areas and farmers in particular. These approaches/methods are Timeline. Venn diagram, Seasonality analysis, Matrix ranking, Mapping (social and resource mapping), Transacts, Sorting, Wealth ranking, Case Studies, Semi-structured interviewing, Direct observation, and Focused group discussions, etc.

Timeline

It is a chronology or sequence of events that have taken place in a particular village or area. These may pertain to the general history of the village or the specific subjects or sectors such as health, education, agriculture animal husbandry etc. Timeline is also an entry point exercise in PRA, while it may take time to pull the people around for more serious or larger exercise like making and transact timeline. The timeline exercise can be applied to find out the background of a village or the evolution of activities or programmes such as health, education, and other social amenities, animal husbandry and agricultural programme, other programmes and other economic activities. The timeline for agriculture for example would indicate bottlenecks in the adoption of new crops and varieties, fertilizer uses. Similarly the timeline in animal husbandry would indicate the trend in animal husbandry practices, shifts in the population of small and large animals, major diseases, epidemics and so on.

Venn Diagram

These show relationship of various institutions, organizations, programmes or individuals with each other and with the village as perceived by the villagers. The exercise is carried out with the use of circles or paper contents, which indicate the relative priorities in the areas of agriculture, small-scale rural enterprises, and any other social and economic development programmes addressed to village development.

PRA has several strong points. By transferring the initiation to rural people, it generate rapport, and forces outsiders to learn. It elicits, presents and cross-checks much information in little time. Increasingly in India, NGOs are adopting the PRA approach and methods as part of the process of identifying development actions by and with villagers.

In domains which includes watershed management, social forestry, rural credit, horticulture, and marketing cooperative development. The PRA approach and methods appear versatile and other application can be expected. PRA also enhances capabilities. It can entail not just shared knowledge, but also shared analysis, creativity and commitment.

Participatory Rural Appraisal (PRA) includes a wide range of techniques that are useful ways of initiating the process of participation. The participatory process includes

1. Information generation.
2. Analysis of information generated.
3. Planning (including budgeting and information sharing).
4. Implementation of the action plan.
5. Management of the initiated activities on an ongoing basis.

These are comprised of a range of semi-structured tools that can be used to learn quickly, with the rural people at least their situation, problems, and opportunities. PRA approaches and techniques are nowadays being used in a variety of situations to highlight the issues in rural areas, which can be further, worked and solutions offered to the concerned groups/communities. These are preparations of Strategic Research and Extension Plan; conducing field studies for determining background information and institutional analysis; Agro-Eco System Analyses (Village studies) for ascertaining productivity trends, technological gap analysis, SWOT analysis etc. Development of strategic Research and Extension Action Plan for bringing out extension strategies, research strategies and action plan is also successfully done. Not only importance or importance of a particular institution, individual to that particular village. The placement of circle with reference to the village/community by its distance will also indicate the intensity of relationship/interaction or performance of the institution.

In general terms this method may be used to establish the total picture in terms of the villages relationship with different institutions. Specifically, the exercise may be done by asking the villagers to indicate, for example, their position and ranking of various constituents of veterinary infrastructures such as artificial insemination, hospitals, milk societies, cattle, markets etc.

Seasonality Analysis

It is an extremely important and useful exercise, which is used to determine 'seasonal pattern in rural areas as related to rainfall, farming practices, employment and so on. In seasonality analysis an attempt is made to determine the seasonal calendars as understood and practiced by villagers. Seasonality exercise has a wide range of applications. It can be used to indicate rainfall, agricultural operations, employment, credits, and fodder availability, grazing pattern, milk yield etc. These indicators will helping identifying appropriate interventions and measures for the appropriate time.

Matrix Ranking

This exercise is done when required to compare and study the merits and demerits of variety of items such as different types of crops or varieties of crops, animal breeds, trees, technologies, approaches, methods etc. The exercises done by means of preparing a visual chart with the items on one side and the criteria of comparing other items on other side. These criteria are to be listed by the villagers themselves: for example in case of crops the criteria could be grain yield, straw yield and disease resistance etc. Once the chart is established scoring is done by giving points by placing seeds or stones.

It can be used to study the range of subjects like trees, fodders, crops and varieties, soil type etc. Pair wise ranking is another method, which will help to identify specified preferences of people among giving options.

Mapping

Social Mapping

This is the construction of map of village living areas using Rangoli powders or coloured chalks on the ground or on cemented floor. Through this exercise an understanding of the village layout showing the main features such as housing, temples, stores, and other infrastructures is done. Once the base map is established, it is possible to build other infrastructures like human census, education, health status, land holding, economic status etc. Social mapping is essentially a preplanning exercise. It helps to identify availability and access to basic amenities based on development priorities. Location can also be identified. Social maps can be used to identify different caste groups, crossbred owners, small animals, land holding, past and future IRDP beneficiaries, household educational status etc.

Resource Mapping

This method is used to locate the resources of an area such as village, forest, watershed etc. This helps to establish the extent and location of these resources and understand them better. Rangoli powder and colored chalks can be used for resource mapping. This method can be used to prepare treatment plans for soil and water conservation etc. Both social and resource mapping can also be used as monitoring tool and for carrying out pre and post project situations, to identify the changes that are taking place.

Transacts

It is a cross-country walk with the farmers preferably from "Ridge to Valley". It will give a clear idea of the topography and terrain. It is also called, as farm walk by multidisciplinary team, discussion with farmer's enroute will indicate how and why resources are being managed. The transact farm walk is to explore and study main land use zones. It is useful method for knowing rural ecological conditions, it enables to conserve different aspects of rural ecology, example soil condition, land use pattern, crops, live stocks, forestry, horticulture, Agro-Eco-System of a village etc.

Sorting

It is a method by which household in a village could be grouped in to certain categories, for example poor, very poor, non-poor etc.

Usually names of all the households are written on a slop of paper and kept. Three or four baskets as may be required to denote each category is kept. Someone usually a child is asked to take out the name from the basket. The name is read out and the group is asked to determine. The process is continued till the names are cleared.

This is very useful technique to identify the target group for any programme.

'Through this method the group is selected by the community by consensus and also in shortest possible time. It is quite useful in target group identification based on participatory approach and helps identifying the most needy for whom succour is most immediate.

Wealth Ranking

It is an analytical exercise carried out by local key informants based on their own criteria such as income, assets, employment status and other local measures of well-being. This helps to explore the village people's local wisdom and their criteria used in classifying the entire households of a village.

Wealth ranking helps to identify whom among them is more or less well off, poor or below poverty line. This help to investigate the perception of wealth differences and inequalities in community. For example list of all houses in the village as pakka, katcha huts, lowest strata of poverty, agricultural labour, poorest of the poor, relatively better etc. Apart from this, methods like case studies/success stories, semi structured interviewing for getting more information through interaction, focused group discussion and observations both participant and non participant are the other methods to study the problems and issues at the village level involving people at all levels of identification, prioritization, solution finding, action plan building and action plan implementation.

To conclude top -down planning and actions have suffered because of lack of people's participation in the governmental programmes. PRA offers the opportunity to involve the people at all levels from initiation of discussion, for identifying problems to the development of action plan and its implementation. The wide range of PRA techniques involves people both physically and emotionally which turns the event from government programmes for the people to the people's programme run by the government and the people.

The Philosophical reversal in the approach is the gift of PRA. Thus PRA techniques not only help us to identify the among other thing ITK also but also its further planning for implementing action plan.

References

Action Aid, (1991) Jacked: Participatory Rural Appraisal in Identifying Major Illness Health Care Providers and Costs, Action Aid, Ban galore.

Bebbingoton, A. J. *et al.* (1994) Farmer's and Community Organization in Agricultural Research and Extension, Proceedings of International Symposium on System Oriented Research in Agriculture and Rural Development, 1994.

Chambers, Robert, Arnold Pacey, and Lori Ann Thrupp (1989) farmer first London: Intermediate Technology Publications.

Jaiswal, N. K., A.P. Purandare and A. K. Jaiswal (1984): People's Participation in Watershed Management. A Case Study of DVC journal of Rural Development. 3: 409440.

Mukherjee, Neela (1992), Villagers' Perception of Rural Poverty through the Mapping Methods of PRA, RRA Notes, 15 pp 21-26.

Singh, R.P. (2000) perceived Cohesiveness of Group Members and Participation in Development Activities: unpublished Ph. D. theses submitted in the Deptt. of Agril. Communication, GBPUA and T, Pantnagar.

Chapter 28

Community Radio Pantnagar: An Experiment of Development Support Communication

☆ *S.K. Kashyap and Gaurav Papnai*

Background

Reaching millions of farmers one to one through interpersonal channels is impossible and touching them through mass media has proved to be less effective if our concern is sustainable and inclusive development. Various reports on media (by Islam, 2002; Global Forum for Media Development, 2006; Norris and Zinnbauer, 2002; UNESCO-CPHS, 2006 etc) puts the role of development media in following way :

"Media outlets are crucial to the exercise of freedom of expression because they provide the public platform through which the right is effectively exercised. The idea of media as a platform for democratic debate embraces a variety of overlapping functions. Media, in this context, refers to all those channels that carry news and public information. The media may be seen as:

- A channel of information and education through which citizens can communicate with each other
- A disseminator of stories, ideas and information
- A corrective to the "natural asymmetry of information" (Islam 2002:1) between governors and governed and between competing private agents
- A facilitator of informed debate between diverse social actors, encouraging the resolution of disputes by democratic means
- A means by which a society learns about itself and builds a sense of community, and which shapes the understanding of values, customs and tradition
- A vehicle for cultural expression and cultural cohesion within and between nations
- A watchdog of government in all its forms, promoting transparency in public life and public scrutiny of those with power through exposing corruption, mal-administration and corporate wrongdoing
- A tool to enhance economic efficiency
- An essential facilitator of the democratic process and one of the guarantors of free and fair elections
- An advocate and social actor in its own right while respecting pluralistic values

(*Source*: Media Development Indicators: A framework for assessing media development, UNESCO, 2008)

Media which ensures people's participation in design and development of programmes with sole intention of people's empowerment may emerge as an answer to the above needs. Participatory medium of communication which links to masses with a touch of location-specific and need-based information dissemination as a potential to create an environment of participatory development as exemplified in hundreds of cases of development support communication throughout the world. Several such success cases have been compiled in book *Making Waves*, written by Alfonso Gumucio Dagron. (www.communicationforsocial change.org/pdf/making_waves.pdf).

The concept of community radio has emerged in this respect where a low power transmitter covers a location of 15-20 kilometers to provide a medium to the people to share their voices in their community effectively. Community radio is also called as third model of radio broadcasting after commercial and public broadcasting. Community radio stations are meant to serve specific geographic communities having similar agro-ecological conditions, uniform cropping patterns and common needs and interest. The content that is selected for broadcast through these stations is more relevant and linking to the audience. It is expected that these Community radio stations be governed and guided by the communities they serve.

Pantnagar Janvani: A Model of Development Support Communication

Pantnagar Janvani, the community radio service of G.B. Pant University of Agriculture and Technology, Pantnagar, initiated its broadcasts on 15th August, 2011. The duration of broadcast initially was three hours which has been extended to six hours broadcast each day now.

Concept of Pantnagar Janvani

Community radio of Pantnagar University has been initiated to evolve two-way linkage with farmers of 15-20 kilometres around University campus. The mantra of Pantnagar Janvani is community collaboration, community contribution and community co-creation. It is a peoples' participatory communication intervention of a state agricultural university to bring people nearer to the university framework of research and extension. The model works on principle of Pantnagar Janvani Clubs, the farmers clubs formed at village level. These clubs have been initiated to synergise the rural participation right from situation analysis, need assessment, content development, content treatment, decision of format, programme designing, programme recording, broadcast, evaluation, impact assessment and reconsideration. The experts and facilitators intervene in between at several junctures as per the community need to empower the community through free-flowing information accessible by the community as per their pace and requirement.

Sources of Information for Pantnagar Janvani

Pantnagar Janvani, the community radio service of Pantnagar works with the support of Directorate of Extension and different

Colleges for technological information and solution to problems of the community. Directorate of Extension has been working for dissemination of farm information through out the state and the community radio service facilitates their efforts at local level. The CRS also works with District Rural Development Authority to gather information of Government Schemes and plans to be communicated to community. The indigenous knowledge available at farmers' level is also an important source of information for Pantnagar Janvani. Similarly, community skills of folk lores, stories, songs etc also form an important inventory of information for Pantnagar Janvani.

Transmitter and Transmission

The 50 Watt Transmitter was supplied and installed by Bharat Electronics Limited, Bangalore. We have not faced any transmission downtime.

Management of Institution/Radio Station

1. Sri Subhash Kumar, Vice-Chancellor, Chairman
2. Dr Vir Singh, Director, Communication
3. Dr Y P S Dabas, Director, Extension Education
4. Dr J P Singh, Director, Research
5. Dr J Kumar, Dean, College of Agriculture
6. Dr R S Raghuvanshi, Dean, College of Home Science
7. Dr G K Singh, Dean, College of Veterinary and Animal Husbandry
8. Dr Uma Melkania, Dean, College of Basic Science and Humanities
9. Dr H C Sharma, Dean, College of Technology
10. Dr Devendra Kumar, Dean, College of Agribusiness Management
11. Dr I J Singh, Dean, College of Fishery
12. Dr D.S. Murti, Dean, Student Welfare
13. Shri J C Bhatt, Comptroller
14. Dr Neelam Bhardwaj, Head, Agricultural Communication
15. By Designation District Magistrate
16. By Designation Chief Development Officer

17. By Designation Chairman UASTDC
18. Dr S K Kashyap Associate Director Communication, CRS

Programme Content

The five key programmes of Janvani Pantnagar are *Krishi sandesh, Os ki Boonden, Gaon ki baat, Laghu Natika* and *Lok Paramparaon ke geet*.

1. *Krishi Sandesh* (Empowering Farmers) is a need based daily programme of first line technology dissemination in which the research scientists talk to farmers about the latest technological innovations in farm sector. It is in interview mode. The duration is ten minutes daily. It is our Signature Programme.

   We try to design this programme according to the need of the farmers, season, priority of scientists and recent technological developments. Agricultural scientists who are directly working on related research projects address this programme. This programme has been extended as *Gaon Ki Baat* in which farmers directly ask questions related to their agricultural problems and concerned scientists provide solutions. This programme has emerged as a single window solution provider for farmers.
2. *Os Ki Boonden* (Life Skill Building) is a feature on life skills and community living based on stories, folktales, motivational cases, etc. The duration is 5 minutes daily. *Lok Paramparaon ke Geet* (Folk Songs) is a community programme in which community dwellers get a chance to present their singing talents for the community radio. We involve different segments of linguistic groups of our locality and develop interesting programmes with musical support. The duration is 5-7 minutes daily.
3. *Gaon Ki Baat* (University Village Linkage) is a programme developed to directly involve community people with the scientists and experts of Pantnagar University in favour of the community. Villagers get an opportunity to talk with scientists and directly ask the solutions of their problems related to agriculture and allied fields. The duration is 8-10 minutes on weekly basis.

4. *Laghu Natika* (Social Drama) is a social awakening programme which addresses the social evils and attitudinal challenges of the community. It has addressed dowry, caste system, educating girl child, female foeticide, environmental issues, superstitions, etc. It is in drama format. The duration is 10-12 Minutes weekly.

Community Participation

Community radio clubs have been established in our local villages. The clubs have one coordinator and five active members from the village who voluntarily participate in the village development process through radio programmes. The club members regularly organise meetings to discuss about the problems of the village regarding agriculture, veterinary, fishery, health and other issues with the Janvani Pantnagar team and initiate the process of development intervention through community radio.

The club members are invited to the Pantnagar University by our community radio for training and workshops related to village survey, problem identification, problem prioritisation, message designing and orientation of latest developments in agriculture and allied fields. Thus a two way linkage has been established with the villages of our locale. We broadcast programmes in Hindi, Kumaoni, Garhwali, Bhojpuri, Bengali and Punjabi to encourage participation.

Key Challenges Faced

The prime challenge of Janvani Pantnagar is sufficient human resource for content development and programme production. The other challenge is that of funds for content development. Without any funds, we are running our community radio with the help of University experts, scientists and the community on honorary basis. We earnestly need funds for human resource recruitment for content development, programme production, research and field work. We need to have funds for content development and programme production to sustain in the long run.

References

Banisar, David (2006), *Freedom of Information Around the World 2006: a global survey of access to government records laws*, Freedominfo.org (http://www.freedominfo.org/documents/global_survey 2006.pdf)

Commonwealth Broadcasting Association (CBA) with support from UNESCO, *CBA Editorial Guidelines*, 2005. (http://unesdoc.unesco.org/images/0013/001356/135672e.pdf)

Davis, Alan (2006), 'A Road Map for Monitoring and Evaluation in the *Media Development Sector', in Media Matters: Perspectives on Advancing Media and Development from the Global Forum for Media Development*, Internews Europe and the Global Forum for Media Development, pp.89–93

Holtz-Bacher, Christina (2004), *What is "good" press freedom? The difficulty of measuring freedom of the press worldwide*. Paper presented at the International Association for Media and Communication Research, Porto Alegre, Brazil

Islam, Roumeen (2002), 'Into the Looking Glass: what the media tell and why' in *The Right to Tell: The Role of Mass Media in Economic Development*, Washington, DC: The World Bank Institute (http://64.233.183.104/search?q=cache:XUOfPOiFZvUJ:www.worldbank.org/wbi/Ri ghttoTell/righttotellOverview.pdf+right+to+tell and hl=en and gl=uk and ct=clnk and cd=1)

Norris, Pippa and Dieter Zinnbauer (2002), *Giving Voice to the Voiceless: Good Governance, Human Development and Mass Communications*, UNDP Human Development Report Office. (http://hdr.undp.org/docs/publications/background_papers/2002/Norris-Zinnbauer_2002.pdf)

UNDP (2006), *Communication for Empowerment: developing media strategies in support of vulnerable groups*, United Nations Development Programme, Bureau for Development Policy, Democratic Governance Group. (http://www.undp.org/oslocentre/docs06/Communicationforempowermentfinal.pdf)

UNESCO, *Public Service Broadcasting. A Best Practices Source Book*, 2005. (http://portal.unesco.org/ci/en/ev.phpURL_ID=20394 and URL_DO=DO_TOPIC and URL_SECTION=201.html)

Chapter 29

Communication Centre of Pantnagar University: A Unique Model of Communication Intervention for Education and Development

☆ *Vir Singh and Neelam Bhardwaj*

Communication Centre at G. B. Pant University of Agriculture and Technology serves the university education and extension efforts through need-based communication and media support in form of radio, video, photography, audio-visual and multi-media support. The University has the privilege of having the first centre of communication within any State Agriculture University in India. Although the Communication Centre was created in 1970, its roots can be traced back to the first decade of establishment when communication functions were carried out by several different units scattered throughout the University. The journey towards communication centre was started with realization of need for communication for fulfillment of teaching, research and education mission of the first agricultural university. The generous grant from

Ford Foundation helped in procurement of equipments, getting overseas training and consultant services. University remodeled one wing of the College of Agriculture for the Communication Centre and administratively reorganized some of its personnel to provide the initial staff. Subsequently, new positions were added and people were recruited to fill them. Some land marks in the journey towards communication centre are as below :

- ☆ 1961 : Appointment of two artists signaled beginning of audiovisual service
- ☆ 1965 : Appointment of oilman and procurement of utility printer represented beginning of university press
- ☆ 1967 : Information and publication section was started in Extension Directorate
- ☆ 1968: The first magazine for Farmers and Extension personnel "Kisan Bharti" was launched
- ☆ 1969: Plan to bring the communication activities of the University together under one umbrella was conceptualized in collaboration with Ford Foundation
- ☆ 1970: The beginning of historic unit called Communication Centre, first of its kind in the country

Communication was recognized as an important input for development to disseminate and create dialogue among different stakeholders about the technologies and issues of agriculture, environment and sustainable development. G.B. Pant University of Agriculture and Technology, Pantnagar, established a Communication Centre with the help and support from ICAR and UNDP. A humble beginning was made with establishment of radio studio and procurement of television equipments. Over the years the Centre has flowered into a full-fledged Directorate. The Directorate now has well developed infrastructure of radio programme production, video production, photography and audio visual media. It operates in close collaboration with well trained faculty members and technical personnel of the Department of Agricultural Communication. In past it was supported by UNDP/FAO/ICAR funds for international training of faculty in communication, visit of international experts to develop curriculum and initiation of Masters and doctoral programmes in Agricultural Communication at the College of Agriculture.

Our Mandate

1. *To disseminate information for the farmers through different mass media* : The major emphasis of the existing information service of the Centre is to disseminate information through radio, television and publications. The advances made in the field of information and communication technologies call for our attention toward their application to reach the unreached
2. *To provide distance learning opportunities* : Open and Distance learning provide immense scope a education in far flung areas. The premier agricultural university can not restrict itself within the campus.
3. *To organize training in communication* : A vast machinery of field functionaries is engaged in development work today. This includes workers directly involved in agricultural information and communication work. These field functionaries have not fully succeeded in producing the desired results because of their out-dated approach and technique.
4. *To conduct researches on communication for development* : The sooner this is done, the greater would be the benefit as it would server as a model for other centres.
5. *To provide audiovisual services for teaching and research* : This is needed to support the academic mission of the university.

Our Communication Support Infrastructure

1. *Video Production Unit* is well equipped with necessary facilities for production of video programmes. The unit has one editing and one recording room equipped with latest cameras and non-linear editing system for production. It produces video programmes for teaching, training and telecasting from Doordarshan Kendra, Delhi, Lucknow and Bareilly. About 8-10 educational programmes are produced every year by this unit. Besides, regular news capsules are fed to the media on topical themes. This unit also serves as a laboratory for teaching purpose for the students of M.Sc. (Agricultural Extension and Communication). The unit has involved interested

students under „Earn While You Learn scheme for assistance in anchoring, sound recording and editing. A monthly documentary on news and events of the campus is prepared and shown regularly on cable network. This also serves as audiovisual documentation of the University activities.

2. *Radio Production Unit* produces radio programmes relevant for farmers and extension personnel. The centre has well-equipped radio studio in which about 200 radio programmes are produced in a year for the benefit of the farmers. These programmes are being broadcast through different All India Radio Stations.
3. *Farm School on Air* Realizing the importance of radio in rural communication a programme on „Farm School on Air has been launched since 2001 to provide systematic radio lessons to interested farmers on different important topics of current interest in agriculture and allied subjects. So far Farm School on AIR has been broadcast on themes likely Rice Production, Sugarcane, Organic Farming, Litchi Production, Importance of Agriculture Implements, Floriculture, Integrated Insect and Pest Management and Fisheries Production, etc.
4. *Community Radio System (FM Radio)* Community Radio is a powerful medium to reach the un-reached in far flung, rural areas in the hills of Uttarakhand. An innovation in development communication, community radio aims to fulfill the needs and aspirations of the local community through information, dialogue and education. Keeping in view the Directorate approached the Ministry of Information and Broadcasting, Government of India to establish a Community Radio System (F.M. Radio) at Pantnagar in order to broadcast knowledge based programmes as per the demand of the local people. After the completion of all formalities, the Community Radio Station was inaugurated on 8 August, 2011 by Vice-Chancellor Dr. B.S. Bisht. Pantnagar Janvani, the programmes of community radio are being broadcast regularly since 15 August, 2011.

5. *Publication Unit* disseminates useful information through print media. Two monthly magazines, Kisan Bharti and Indian Farmers' Digest are brought out every month for the farmers and extension workers both the magazines have been immensely popular only with farmers in the Country but also in neighboring countries. A quarterly magazine Pantnagar news also being published to disseminate information to different stoke holders regarding progress and achievements of the University. Besides, a variety of other print materials like leaflet, folders and technical bulletins are also published by this unit.
6. *Media Centre* was started on December 30, 2004 to facilitate the media persons and improving communication about the university activities to general public and other stakeholders. This centre sends press releases related to university functions/programmes, activities/achievements to various Hindi and English newspapers through fax and e-mail for publication in regional and national newspapers. The Section maintains contacts with representative the mass media and assists them in coverage of university news. It also maintains up-to-date information about the University news and events.
7. *Photography Unit* produces photographs, exhibits and display materials for teaching, training, extension and other activities like kisan melas, state, national and international exhibitions and for information centers of the colleges. About 2500-3000 photographs and slides are prepared every year.
8. *Audio-visual and Projection Unit* provides support for screening of video films for training and teaching purpose. Besides audio services, slides and overhead projection facilities are also made available by this unit for teaching, training, seminars, symposia, conferences, workshops, etc.
9. *Distance Learning Programme*: The open learning system is unique and challenging mode of education offered at the university level. This system provides ample opportunities for those who desire to have university education at their place of work or residence. The university in collaboration with IGNOU has established centre at Pantnagar. Presently

the Centre is running 11 UG/PG level programmes on different degree/diploma programmes since January 2008. In addition to above the University is also contemplating to start its own Open Distance Learning for the benefit of the youths, women and adults.

10. *Facilities Available*: The audio and video cassettes produced by us for educational purposes are available for the interested clients. Two monthly farm magazines *viz.* Kisan Bharti in Hindi and Indian Farmers Digest in English are also available for subscription. We have the expertise to provide consultancy to the public sector, private sector and NGOs in planning, implementation and evaluation. We also possess all the important milestones and events of our University since inception in audio, video and news form

Conclusion

Communication Centre is a unique intervention which has immensely contributed in the growth and development of Pantnagar University since inception. It is an eminent organ of Pantnagar structure which plays an indispensable role through providing central facility of communication support and media coverage to help in realizing the mandates of teaching, rearch and extension in an effective manner.

Chapter 30

Impact of Community Radios in Rural Development: An Overview

☆ *Pankaj Kumar Ojha and Kalyan Ghadei*

Community Radio

Community radio is a radio service providing a third model of radio broadcasting in addition to commercial and public broadcasting. Community stations serve geographic communities and communities of interest. They broadcast content that is popular and relevant to a local, specific audience but is often overlooked by commercial or mass-media broadcasters. Community radio stations are operated, owned, and influenced by the communities they serve. They are generally nonprofit and provide a mechanism for enabling individuals, groups, and communities to tell their own stories, to share experiences and, in a media-rich world, to become creators and contributors of media.

A community radio station is one that is operated in the community, for the community, about the community and by the community. The community can be territorial or geographical - a township, village, district or island. It can also be a group of people with common interests, who are not necessarily living in one defined territory. Consequently, community radio can be managed or controlled by one group, by combined groups, or of people such as women, children, farmers, and fisher folk. What distinguishes community radio from other media is the high level of people's participation, both in management and program production aspects. Furthermore, individual community members and local institutions are the principal sources of support for its operation (Dunaway, 2002).

Role of Rural Radio in Dissemination of Scientific/ Agricultural Research

There exists a gap between the scientific/agricultural researchers and the farm users. A lot of findings from the research institutions and laboratories are not used by farmers. Research information on improved seed varieties, better farming techniques, post-harvest handling and marketing are not used by farmers either because the information not reach to them, either because the implementation of the received information is not clear. The gap between the researcher and the farmer is even wider in the rural areas; large distances separate researcher from rural farmer. Other barriers like language and diversity of cultures also come into play making it even more difficult for the research information to reach the intended farmers.

Rural Radio can be Used to Disseminate Agricultural Researches

There are some following ways:

1. Research findings can be distributed through radio to
   - ☆ Non-governmental organizations (NGOs) dealing in agriculture
   - ☆ Extension workers
   - ☆ Farmers themselves
   - ☆ Academic institutions
2. Rural radio can make the link between researchers and extension workers by offering information on
   - ☆ Where research can be obtained and used
   - ☆ How to pass it on to users
   - ☆ Farmer's feedback regarding research.

3. Rural radio can be used to collect feedback from the farmers
   - ☆ Through rural or through extension programmes, farmers give their responses to the further research regarding agricultural problems.
   - ☆ Farmers share experiences on the use of researches
   - ☆ Rural radios capture the farmers' views/ recommendations on how to improve the conditions of the rural areas which are undeveloped.
   - ☆ Rural communities provide alternatives depending on their experiences.
4. Rural radios also be used to announce processes of the research and extension work
   - ☆ Give venues for meetings with extension workers/ rural development officers to know more about rural development programmes and recent developmental schemes.
   - ☆ Advise on where to get inputs/services
   - ☆ Advise on where to get technical support.

Some Constraints for Rural Radios

- ☆ Rural radio is expensive to manage. One must have enough finances to run this kind of community-based broadcasting because it involves dealing with rural people who may not have communication skills.
- ☆ Translating messages into various languages is not an easy task. One needs to have people who are well versed in the language.
- ☆ Lack of collaboration between researchers, extension staff and rural people may hinder the smooth operation of rural radios.
- ☆ The scientific jargon is sometimes very difficult to interpret.

Relation between Community/Rural Radio and Rural Development

It is evident that development implies change, and the first change takes place is the attitude of the people who will be directly affected by the development in this case, the farmers and rural communities. In order to achieve this goal, there must be a fundamental change in the way farmers approach agriculture and the rate at which they adopt new technologies, husbandry and farming practices.

In order to achieve this change farmers and rural communities need to be informed on the importance of adopting these new practices.

Attempts by extension workers through demonstration farms and working with rural communities have not been sufficient to bring about change in attitudes. Radio has often been used to complements the efforts of the extension workers. However the use of the radio as a mass media has its limitations such as poor signals, limited reach in certain areas, top-down approach, and limited airtime and in appropriate programming. This calls for a shift in the use of radio from mass media to community centered as already illustrated in the paper.

Taking on any of the already mentioned forms:

- ☆ Rural radio encourages villagers to take an active part in the development process or even or even better to take their own initiative to improve the living conditions in their communities.
- ☆ Since most farmers have not been to school, rural radio acts as a substitute for formal education.
- ☆ A rural radio enables communities to articulate their experiences and critically examine issues and policies affecting their lives for example a community can use the radio to highlight new agricultural and rural policies. The policies can be debated upon and discussed using the radio and immediate feedback can be given for relevant authorities to take action.
- ☆ In cases where extension workers may not be able to reach, rural radio/community radio takes on that role. Here a community can be given a recording on cassette to substitute the extension worker who has not been able to reach that community.
- ☆ Vital information for rural and agricultural development can be passed on through the use of radio, for example information on better farming methods, improved seeds,

timely planting, agroforestry, better harvesting methods, soil conservation, marketing, post harvesting handling and diversification and new schemes for the rural people for their overall development which leads rural development.

- ☆ Since rural/community radio targets a specific community, geographical area or interest, then the language of choice can be used to ensure that the message is clearly understood. Therefore rural radio gives us the option of using the prevalent language.
- ☆ The community radio gives farmers an opportunity to interact with each other and other relevant authorities, eg. Extension workers, crop and animal experts through like live talk shows, phoning programmes and location broadcasts.
- ☆ Since the community radio is community based, it can be used to mobilize people towards community or rural development work. Eg. Construction of valley dams, protected wells and immunization of animals.

All the above can be arranged at the convenience of the recipient (rural people) because they are involved in the planning an implementation of the radio programmes.

The reality today is that communication technologies exist and are advancing rapidly in terms of availability and lower costs, especially the telecommunication technologies. The challenge is to use the information technologies and communication media effectively for sustainable agriculture and rural development, which often means utilization of a range of media- traditional, folk media (story tellers, songs, dance, village theatres), training videos, audio cassettes, community radio as well as new information technologies (e-mail, world-wide-web).

Traits of Community Radio

Community participation is a fundamental characteristic/trait of community radio- live public shows, village's debates and participation in the actual management of the radio station are just a few examples. This approach empowers rural people to participate in the dialogue and decision making processes essential from them to control their own economic, social and cultural environment and play an active part in development activities.

Special Report on Community Radios

The incisive letter that the National Advisory Council (NAC) member Aruna Roy wrote to the Congress president Sonia Gandhi on 6 July has had desired effect. Roy had opposed the five-fold increase in license fee for community radios, as per sources. The sources have told 'Millennium Post' that the communications minister KapilSibal has decided to scrap the fee for community radio stations altogether.

Highly placed sources in the Ministry of Communications and Information Technology have said that Sibal has issued instructions to R Chandrashekhar, a secretary in the Department of Telecommunications, to waive off all license fees for community radio stations. It will come as a huge relief to such radio stations.

In a letter addressed to Gandhi, Roy had highlighted the issue 'regarding the exorbitant fivefold license fee hike from Rs 19,700 to Rs 91,000 by the Ministry of Communications and Information Technology.'

In her petition to Gandhi, Roy pointed out the following: 'The Information and Broadcasting Ministry has been largely supportive of Community Radio and I and B Secretary Uday Kumar Verma has written a letter to the Secretary DoT, R Chandrashekhar to reconsider the hiking of the fees in May 2012.'

Roy's petition also had support of many community radio organizations, like the Digital Empowerment Forum, Barefoot College and the gram panchayat of Dandasli. Roy reminded Gandhi in the letter that earlier a similar petition was sent to her by the community radio activist Stalin K.

Conclusion

As we know the radio is a very strong and convenient medium of communication.We can transfer any news to the rural people because in rural areas radio is frequently used mean.Community radio is an effective tool for the poor, NPOs meant to serve society. They have more benefits as an information and communication tool and are being used to great effect over all the country. So, community radio signifies a two-way process, which entails the exchange of views from various sources and the adaptation of media for use by the rural people/rural communities. It allows members of a community to gain access to information, education and entertainment and offers an opportunity for the community to participate actively in the media as planners, producers and performers. It is the mean of expression of the community rather than for the community. It is different from urban radio in that it is directly specifically to rural people and to their information needs. So, at last we can say that community radio is a "effective package" of rural development.

References

http://www.memoireonline.com/11/11/4928/m_Contribution-of-community-radios-in-rural-areas-development-case-study-of-Habwa-Ijambo-program-aire6.html retrieved on 4.9.2012 at 10.56 pm

http://www.communityradioindia.org/retrieved on 4.9.2012 at 11.01 pm

Chapter 31

An Initiative in Private Public Partnership by Indo-Dutch Horticulture Technologies Pvt. Ltd.: A Study of Constraints and Opportunities

☆ *Aakansha Melkani, Mamta Rautela, Goldi Tiwari and S.K. Kashyap*

Introduction

The state of Uttarakhand, nestled within the lap of the Himalayas, being a newly found state holds immense potential as well as challenges for development of its agricultural industry on an organized basis. Cultivation in the hilly state is practiced on 766,360 ha of land. Agriculture maybe divided broadly under two categories:

1. *Agriculture followed in the foothills of Himalayas* consisting of narrow strips of fertile plains of the Tarai and Bhabhar. These areas follow commercial farming on large scale with

considerable use of modern techniques, management and marketing strategies.

2. *Agriculture being followed in the hilly tracts* which covers major portion of the state but suffers various constraints, both environmental and economic.

Constraints and opportunities are inseparable from each other. Some of these facing the state are elucidated below:

Constraints	*Opportunities*
Adverse environmental conditions like low temperature and rugged terrain not suitable for growing conventional crops.	Diversification of agriculture to non conventional areas like seed production, floriculture, orchard management etc.
Poor resource base because of lack of capital.	Provision of adequate capital and guidance for proper utilization.
Lack of information regarding latest developments in agriculture, prices and costs, future prospects of various crop markets	Development of effective communication systems.

There is need for both private as well as state intervention to create the adequate infrastructure and services so that the development in this direction is spurred. This paper explores one such initiative by renowned agriculturist Mr. Sudhir Chaddha, in the remote hills of Chaffi village near Nainital. The Indo Dutch Horticulture Technologies Private Limited was founded by him in collaboration with Mr. Jan Neele of Netherlands. The findings of the paper are based on a 15 day training programme which was undertaken under the above mentioned organization.

About Indo Dutch Horticulture Technologies Pvt. Ltd. (IDHT)

IDHT was established on 28th February, 2009 as a joint venture supported by the Dutch government, with cooperation from the Government of Uttarakhand to produce and process the planting material of flowers like lilium, gladioli, zantedesia and chrysanthemum in India to cater to demands of both domestic and international markets.

All the machinery and technology have been imported from the Netherlands. The facility of tissue culture laboratory enables production of around 2 million flower bulbs per year.

The company is a single window to supplement and provide the infrastructure for greenhouses/planting material/training/and support in marketing as well. It provides access to Government schemes and subsidies thus acting as a suitable upcoming model of Private Public Partnership. It is located in Chafi village of Nainital district of Uttarakhand.

The corporation is a joint effort by Mr. Sudhir Chaddha, renowned progressive farmer of India,recipient of "National Most Innovative Farmer Award", 1991 by Former Prime Minister of India organized and selected by ISEE a body of ICAR, poularly known as the "Papaya Man of India" . The partner of the project is Mr. Jan Neele of Netherlands, Director of Neele Exports, a company specialized for several generations in production, preparation and export of flower bulbs world-wide and President Director of Neele Consultancy and Expertise.

The thrust areas of the company include :

1. Provision of high quality planting material of horticultural and particularly floricultural products.
   - ☆ Lillium
   - ☆ Gladioli
   - ☆ Chrysanthemum

- ☆ Zantedesia
- ☆ Apple and strawberry

2. Infrastructural facilities relating to greenhouse establishment, irrigation facilities, etc.
3. Easy access to loans from banks and Government schemes and subsidies.
4. Technical expertise and training
5. Storage and marketing facilities (in some cases)

Infrastructure of the Unit

1. *Main office and training rooms*: It includes the offices of the General Manager and other permanent staff. There is provision of well furnished rooms for training of farmers students and others along with computer facility and LCD projectors for audio visual aid. It also includes boarding and logding accomodation for visiting farmers, students etc.

2. *Tissue culture lab*: The tissue culture lab consists of facilities for production of 2 million flower bulbs per year. It employs local women and youth for propagation of material on a large scale. It has facilities to maintain high levels of aseptic conditions and to provide proper temperature and humidity for further development.

3. *Cold storage and processing and packing centre* : The centre has rare facility for storage of delicate planting material at sub zero temperatures and controlled humidity. Also it has machinery for sorting, processing, grading of the palnting materials.

   There is ample space for storage of crop for short terms before it is marketed.

4. *Greenhouses and Shadenets* : The planting material produced within tissue culture labs is palced for hardening under these structures. Further trials are conducted to test the performance of new planting material and demonstrations held for farmers, students and visitors.

Mechanism of work of IDHT

Five major tasks performed by the IDHT:

1. Planting material
2. Training
3. Greenhouse establishment

(1–3: primary focus areas)

4. Technical expertise
5. Marketing

Impact of the Company

1. *Increased incomes of farm families* (Showing in Table 31.1 and Figure 31.1).
2. *Employment generation* : The company hires a number of local women and youth for various services thus developing human resource and providing employment
3. *Awareness generation*: Information dissemination, generation of awareness towards latest developments in the field of agribusiness and agricultural technology.

Constraints and Prospective Solutions

Despite the immense potential of such an ambitious project, the growth has been slow. Various constraints are faced by the company stakeholders, staff members and the associated farmers. Some of the outcomes of the survey of the company and adjoining areas have been compiled as follows:

1. *Poor resourse base of farmers* : Most farmers of the areas adjoining IDHT own land not exceeding 1 Nali (approximately 200m^2) in area. Due to lack of access to subsidies on projects smaller than 1000 m^2, the farmers are unable to adopt the technology.

   Moreover even the smallest projects under greenhouses cost atleast Rs. 3 lakhs. This is a huge investment for small

Table 31.1: Economic Analysis of Lillium Crop (for 100 m^2)

Costs					Returns	
Fixed Costs	Production		3200 spikes			
	1	Green House Structure	Rs.625/sqmt	62500		
	2	Irrigation Structures		150000	Asiatic	Rs. 40 per spike
	3	Power Tiller		100000	Total return	**Rs.96000**
Total fixed costs				**312500**		
Working Costs					Oriental	Rs. 50 per spike
	1	Planting material			Total return	**Rs.128000**
		Asiatic (smaller with no fragrance)	Rs. 15 *3500	52500		
		Oriental (larger with fragrance)	Rs. 20*3500	70000		
	2	Fertilizer	Rs.13 *25kg	325		
	3	Labour Costs				
		Sowing	Rs. 150 *2	300		
		Irrigation(12 times)	Rs. 150 * 12	1800		
		Weeding(2 times)	Rs. 150 * 2	300		
		Harvest and packing	Rs. 150 *4	600		
	4	Corrugated boxes(packing)	Rs. 50 * 160	8000		
	5	Transport(approx.)	500			
	6	Commission agent	10% of returns	10000		
Total working costs		Asiatic		**74325**		
		Lillium		**91825**		

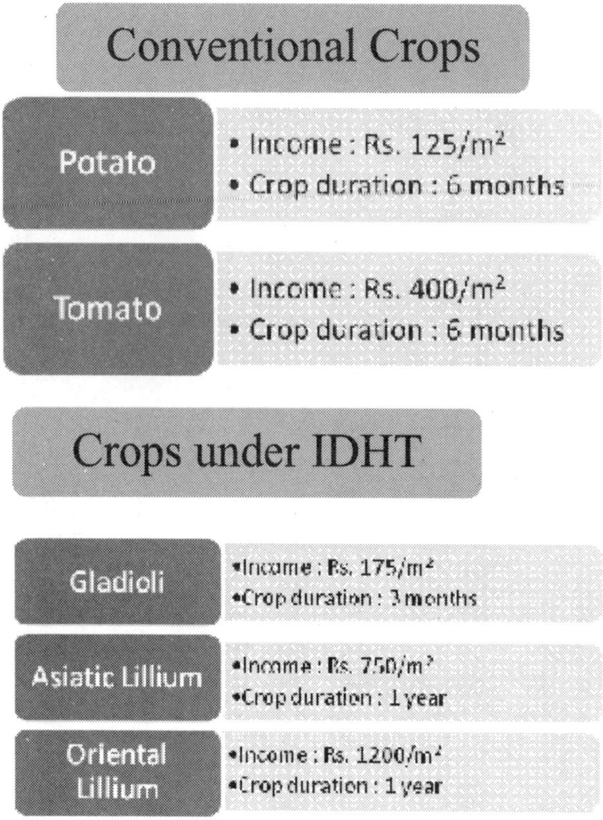

Figure 31.1: Comparative Analysis of Income Generated Under Various Crops for a Period of 1 Year (Based on survey conducted with farmers residing in adjoining areas)

farmers with little capital backing. In a few cases farmers adopted the scheme without proper capital backing and ended up with losses instead of profit.

Prospective solution: Instead of subsidy on small enterprises which tend to make the farmer too dependent on Government support, easy access to similar projects with smaller capital investment can be introduced.

2. *Risk prone nature of floriculture industry*: The floricultural market is considerably more elastic than markets for traditional agricultural crops. The prices of the various products may vary widely from year to year and from market to market. Infact demand of certain flowers may go down considerably in international markets while the farmers, ignorant of such developments may continue to grow the same. This has been the case with some growers of Gerbera who could not dispose of their produce due to glut in the Gerbera market.

   Prospective solution: Intervention can be made in two directions. Firstly, facility for reliable information for the farmers. Until and unless the farmer is not well informed about the market conditions he cannot take wise decisions. The present and future prospects of various floricultural products, national and international conditions influencing trade, latest interventions and developments in floriculture – these are only some of the aspects where intervention can be made by state or private sector or by both. Also the information needs to be provided in a manner that is easily comprehendable by the farmer and is accessible in remote areas. Initiatives in Information Technology which also generate employment for local youth can act as a viable option.

   Secondly, insurance of agricultural enterprises remains an area where much needs to be done. The awareness and acceptance on part of farmers is also very much needed with regards the introduction of crop insurance.

3. *Complicated procedures* : The obtaining of loans and subsidies is a complex process with formalities and paperwork. Farmers are skeptical of obtaining these facilities through the company as the procedure is not understood by them. Moreover, opacity in these procedures may result in farmers ending up investing unintelligebly without prior scrutiny and analysis. In case of any disrepancy farmers may end up blaming the company.

   For example, the subsidy on the greenhouse establishment is paid 36 months after the loan is approved to the farmer. The subsidy is directly transferred to the bank which first clears the dues of the company. The farmers on receiving less than the promised amount of subsidy and that too with a delay of 3 years end up feeling cheated.

Prospective solution: The procedures may be simplified and be addressed under a single window system of a bank instead of approaching multiple Government offices. Further information regarding the procedures may be made available to the farmer in an easy and local language.

4. *Inadequate marketing facilities* : It is a major drawback related to the entire agricultural scenario of most hilly regions. Very few farmers own personal vehicles to tranport their produce to regional and national markets where major transactions of high value commodities occur. Public transport is unreliable because of remote location and long hours of journey. The delicate produce generally undergoes 30 per cent loss in produce during transport and storage. Public transport only aggravates the problem.

   Moreover, farmers have little or no contact with commission agents without which they may not be able to dispose of high quality material in international markets at high rates. Such approaches are unimaginable for farmers at ground level and an agency is very essential for this purpose.

   Provision of marketing by the company has been sporadic due to various problems:

   (*a*) Scattered locations of farms make marketing unprofitable

   (*b*) Many farmers may not conform to timely harvest and standardized packaging procedures which are a must for export quality material, in which the company cannot accept the produce.

   (*c*) Many farmers are skeptical of the company's motives in marketing the produce as they do not understand the complexitties of the procedure.

   Prospective solution: Development of a system of marketing preferably with intervention of Grameen Banks or Cooperatives. Farmer associations can be developed with help of grassroot organizations and NGOs.

Conclusion

Reforms in the agricultural input and services sector will not only lead to better farm familiy incomes and develop efficient agricultural practices but in the long run it can expand the premises of the entire agricultural sector to include transport, marketing, finance, information technology, retail, research and development, consultancy etc. Thus, generating employment for the large mass of disguised unemployed within our nation and attracting the large rural youth mass which is evading the agricultural field and can trasform it into a valuable asset for the nation.

Index